prais… CHRONICBABE

"*ChronicBabe* is just what patients with chronic illness need: a savvy voice of wisdom, insight, and encouragement from someone who's been there!"

— Laurie Edwards, author, *In the Kingdom of the Sick: A Social History of Chronic Illness in America*

"*ChronicBabe* is a needed safe place for people with pain to become empowered. Jenni is an inspiration and a role model to me and many others."

— Paul Gileno, founder/president, U.S. Pain Foundation

"I remember a past before *ChronicBabe*, and it was a bleak, lonely one. Now women with chronic illness everywhere know where to go to get support and even cheer each other on. It teaches you, even on your worst days, how to live your best life possible—to minimize isolation and maximize fabulousness."

— Paula Kamen, author, *All in My Head: An Epic Quest to Cure an Unrelenting, Totally Unreasonable, and Only Slightly Enlightening Headache*

"Jenni Grover is a witty, insightful, and passionate writer and advocate. *ChronicBabe 101* offers readers much needed healthy strategies for managing chronic disease."

— Peter Abaci, M.D., author, *Conquer Your Chronic Pain*

"*ChronicBabe* is empowerment and compassion in action. It's like having a wise, rocking (and stylish!) best friend by your side. With *ChronicBabe* in your corner, an incredible life with illness is accessible and achievable."

— Grace Quantock, award-winning international wellness provocateur, writer, founder of Trailblazing Wellness and Healing Boxes CIC

"Many physicians don't know what it's like to live with the diseases they treat. It's tremendously instructive reading from the perspective of a patient, and *ChronicBabe* provides an important window for providers to appreciate the journey patients take in our health system."

— Kevin Pho, M.D., founder of *KevinMD.com*

"*ChronicBabe* has become a go-to source for many babes (like myself!) living with chronic illnesses to find the support, empowerment, and humor needed to navigate life with pain."

— Nicole Hemmenway, vice president, U.S. Pain Foundation

"At *ChronicBabe*, we women in pain find uplifting self-care tools to realize our fantastic selves. It's a nurturing space that enables our inner Babe to THRIVE!"

— Cynthia Toussaint, founder and spokesperson, For Grace: Women In Pain

"I have been inspired by the tireless efforts of *ChronicBabe* to help and advocate for others."

— Regina Holliday, founder of the Walking Gallery of Healthcare

"*ChronicBabe* is the ultimate resource for people dealing with chronic illness—it's filled with practical advice and peppered with Jenni's sense of humor! An uplifting read for anyone battling chronic illness."

— Jessica Gimeno, chronic and mental illness writer and TEDx speaker; founder of the *Fashionably Ill* blog

"What *ChronicBabe* does is so important that I started my TED Talk by noting how empowered patients say THEY will define the terms of their lives, the terms of their success. Nobody's a more perfect example than Jenni. You go, girl! Preach!"

— Dave deBronkart, a.k.a. *e-Patient Dave*, international keynote speaker, author, and health policy advisor

ChronicBabe 101

ChronicBabe 101

How to Craft an Incredible Life Beyond Illness

Jenni Grover

orange grove media

Special discounts are available on quantity purchases by corporations, associations, and other entities. For details, contact the publisher at chronicbabe@gmail.com.

Graphic design and lettering by Alyse Ruriani: AlyseRuriani.com
Author photography by Alix Kramer: AlixKramer.com and Elizabeth McQuern: ElizabethMcQuern.com
Editing by Elizabeth Bagby: BagbyCopy.com
E-book conversion by Erika Nygaard: ErikaNygaard.com

First published 2017
Published by Orange Grove Media

Printed in the United States of America

ISBN-10: 1534677887
ISBN-13: 978-1534677883

Library of Congress Control Number: 2016909884

CreateSpace Independent Publishing Platform, North Charleston, SC

my dearest ones

Without Natalie, this work would never have come to be. You've cheered me on from the start. Thanks for being my bonus sister.

Without Joe, this book would not exist. You are my favorite, forever. ILYSDM!

Without my family—and my family of choice—I would fall. The safety net you've woven for me keeps me calm, and that is everything.

Without Team ChronicBabe, this work would be impossible. There are too many to name...y'all know who you are.

Without my awesome Kickstarter backers—almost six hundred of you!—this book would still be languishing. Thank you. Thank you.

Without my second family at U.S. Pain Foundation, this book wouldn't be nearly as awesome. Y'all inspire me every day to be the loudest, wackiest, and most passionate activist possible.

...And to all the people who strive to craft incredible lives every day, despite being dealt the world's crappiest hand of cards: You are my heroes. Your courage, resilience, and humor make this work powerfully fulfilling. Who knew something so painful could also be so beautiful? Thank you.

"People have a hard time letting go of their suffering. Out of a fear of the unknown, they prefer suffering that is familiar."

— Thich Nhat Hanh

"Find a place inside where there's joy, and the joy will burn out the pain."

— Joseph Campbell

"The most beautiful people we have known are those who have known defeat, known suffering, known struggle, known loss, and have found their way out of those depths."

— Elizabeth Kübler-Ross

SYLLABUS

Welcome to *ChronicBabe 101*! Your syllabus includes all the topics covered in this course-in-a-book. You can read *ChronicBabe 101* from page 1 to page 289, or you can jump around from lesson to lesson. I think there's something in each lesson for every reader, but who am I to dictate your learning process?

Take things at your pace, mark up the book, fill it with sticky notes and bookmarks—you're here to learn, and I encourage you to embrace the methods that work best for you.

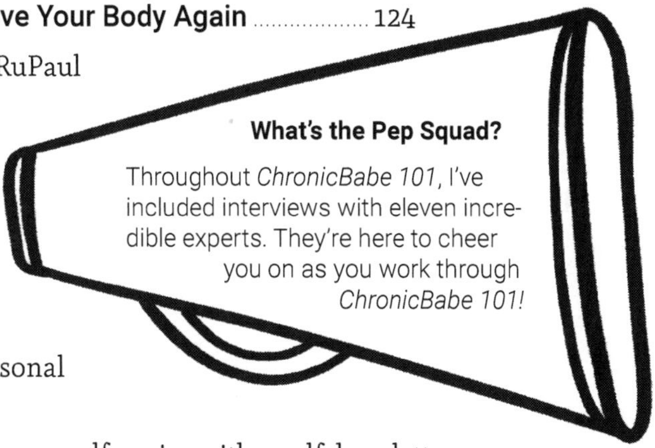
What's the Pep Squad?
Throughout *ChronicBabe 101*, I've included interviews with eleven incredible experts. They're here to cheer you on as you work through *ChronicBabe 101!*

By—and for—caregivers
Throughout ChronicBabe 101, you'll find first-person perspectives from caregivers. They're part of our team, and it's essential to understand them—their voices matter.

INTRODUCTION:
AWAP, authenticity, and some vocab

"I hope you're well!"

This is how I used to start every email: Wishing the person well. It's a fine sentiment, and I *almost* always feel that way when I reach out to people.

But to say that to someone who has chronic illness is thoughtless. That person is definitely *not* well. And I email *a lot* of sick chicks! So...what to say instead?

AWAP

AWAP = As Well As Possible. To wish someone is AWAP is to send them love and care, to let them know you see them and respect that they might not be as well as they wish—and to hope they can still rise above it.

There's a lot of feeling packed into AWAP.

In addition to being a handy greeting or email sign-off, AWAP is a perfect example of what it means to be a ChronicBabe: To love yourself even if you're in pain, to accept it but to never give up, to get creative when things get bad.

Millions of us need to learn how to live well in spite of chronic pain and illness, and that's why I created ChronicBabe.com more than twelve years ago—to make a fun, creative, helpful space where women with chronic illness could learn from each other.

The project has grown exponentially, and my lifelong dream to publish a book has come true! *ChronicBabe 101* is a crash course in being kickass in the face of chronic illness.

Before you dive in, some essential advice for you:

Girl, do NOT let your chronic condition become THE ONE THING that defines you. Don't do it. I've met too many people over the years who've been swallowed up by their illness; they never give themselves a day's rest from talking or thinking about it. When every Facebook post, every email, every point of contact you make is related to illness, you're going to fall down a hole of depression. TRUST ME on this. I've done it.

I'm not recommending you live in denial. Like me, you probably have daily symptoms that make it impossible to truly forget you're sick.

But I AM saying *don't give it so much space*. If what you've got is *stickin' wichoo* for good, you've gotta learn ways to enjoy life in spite of it. And that starts with giving yourself space to be YOU again.

This book includes numerous exercises, meditations, and instructions on how to reclaim your identity—your life!—even if you're super-sick. This is your chance to stop being "that woman who's sick" and start being "that intriguing, delightful woman who happens to be sick." See the difference?

There will be days you just can't get your game face on, and that's okay. But whenever possible, focus your attention back to something you love, that brings you joy, that's unique about you. The thing that is authentically *you*—not your illness.

One last word...

Throughout this book, I use *disease*, *illness*, and *condition* almost interchangeably. That's because our community of ChronicBabes uses these terms that way.

> **What's a bit.ly?**
> I've included hundreds of links to resources, and I use a link shortener. When you see a bit.ly link, go explore!

If you have a different preference, feel free to cross out words or scribble in the margins—*you* get to choose the vocabulary that describes your life. That's the whole point of this: for you to learn new options, create even more, and do what works best for *you*.

Have fun, doodle as you go, and let me know what you think at ChronicBabe101.com.

So much love,

Lesson 1

IT ALL STARTS WITH LEARNING TO PRACTICE acceptance

This might be the hardest place to start. Acceptance is the concept about which I get the most pushback. But acceptance practice is *essential* for living the ChronicBabe life.

Acceptance is about learning to love yourself as you are, which can be tough. After all, women are bombarded by constant messages to be thinner, prettier, smarter, more fashionable...

Acceptance can provide true freedom from those pressures, help you stop fighting your body—and help you learn to work with what you've got.

Acceptance: Jenni's story

When I was diagnosed with fibromyalgia—at the age of twenty-five—my first doctor handed me a pamphlet about fibro and told me to get ready for a life of pain. I fired her on the spot—bedside manner much?

My second doc told me the best thing I could do for myself was exercise every day.

I was extremely athletic back then. I had been a competitive swimmer throughout childhood, played Ultimate Frisbee, loved skiing and running track—so I tackled the task of exercise like a champion.

I was in the YMCA pool every day during my lunch break, swimming so hard and fast there were days I thought my arms would fall off. I had always been competitive, and I thought: *I'm going to swim this illness away.*

There were days I swam so much I could barely walk afterward. But I kept going. I thought if I fought hard enough, that I would make the pain and fatigue go away. I would defeat fibromyalgia through *sheer will.*

You know where I'm going with this. Fibro didn't go away. In fact, I made myself much sicker, for a long time, by exercising so hard. Then I spent months recovering from that fight. I just wasn't ready, yet, to accept new limitations.

Eventually, I *did* get there. I accepted I couldn't defeat fibro. But it took many years, help from many people, and tons of therapy and spiritual pursuit before I could accept my situation. I'm stubborn; I bet it won't take you as long!

What does acceptance mean, exactly?

For many people, it's essential to mourn before we can reach acceptance. Have you heard of Elizabeth Kübler-Ross's five stages of grief? At the risk of oversimplifying, they are denial, anger, bargaining, depression, and acceptance.

The stages are complex and not usually so linear; depression often shows up right at the beginning, amirite? But these are the essential five stages we deal with when mourning a loss. Chronic illness is just that: a loss. We lose our "old" selves, and many qualities of our "old" life.

There are some who believe acceptance is a form of giving up, tantamount to surrender. That it means planting ourselves on the couch in our rattiest pajamas and saying "Aw, the hell with it" and wallowing.

They view acceptance as a loss in itself—a defeat. The problem with this view of acceptance is that it requires us to view our experience with illness as a war. In this paradigm, we are fighting: our body, the illnesses we live with, the medical system, and everyone who doesn't understand us.

When we live in this mentality, our illness experience becomes a war to be won. We view our body as the enemy. We start to live in the fight-or-flight space, which wreaks havoc on our already-compromised bodies, minds, and hearts. We feel like every doctor appointment, new medication, and conversation about our symptoms is a battle that's part of a bigger war, a war that puts us right in the middle of the direst of circumstances.

The problem is, we can't win. When we view acceptance as defeat, and our experience with illness as a war, we can only lose.

I take a different view: "Yes, and..."

For me, acceptance is about getting quiet, touching base with what's real and true for me. It requires me to look deep, to not shy away from hard truths.

I like to think of acceptance as a "Yes, and" kind of thing.

"Yes, and" has a rich tradition in improvisational comedy. Have you ever done any improv? The "Yes, and" concept is one many of our finest comedians use today.

In a commencement address, Stephen Colbert once said "Well, you are about to start the greatest improvisation of all. With no script. No idea what's going to happen, often with people and places you have never seen before. And you are not in control. So say yes. And if you're lucky, you'll find people who will say yes back."

Tina Fey once told Oprah:

> "When I meet someone whose first instinct is 'No, how can we do that? That doesn't seem possible,' I'm always kind of taken aback. Almost anyone would say, 'It's Friday at two in the morning. We don't have an opening political sketch. We can't do it.' Yeah, of course you can. There's no choice. And even if you abandon one idea for another one, saying yes allows you to move forward. Life is improvisation."

"Yes, and" is a cornerstone of improvisation. It accepts the premise that certain things exist, and you can add to them—manipulate them to fit your needs. Tina is SO right: Life is improvisation.

Like: "*Yes*, I have fibromyalgia, *and* I can still be a successful businesswoman."

Or "*Yes*, I haven't been to the gym in months, *and* I'm going to try to go for ten minutes today."

Or "*Yes*, I spent the day on the couch feeling sorry for myself, *and* it's okay—tomorrow's a new day."

Or "*Yes*, I have a serious medical condition, *and* I can still have a smokin' hot sex life." Acceptance is all about "Yes, and."

A field guide to spotting acceptance

Because acceptance is about getting real, we need a guide to spotting the difference between acceptance and denial, acceptance and resignation, acceptance and defeat:

- Acceptance is peace. Denial is fight.
- Acceptance is saying, "I know I'll have pain today, so I'll modify my schedule to accommodate more rest breaks." Giving up is saying, "I know I'll have pain today, so I guess I won't plan anything and lie on the couch instead."
- Acceptance is knowing that because you need to eat gluten-free, you learn to read labels and find local sources for baked goods for an occasional treat—embracing what you *can* eat. Resignation is deciding that being gluten-free means never eating baked goods again. Harrumph.
- Acceptance is recognizing your back hurts too much to sit in a movie theater seat for two hours, and inviting friends over instead so you can stream a movie together and take rest breaks. Denial is saying, "My back hurts, but I'll show my body! I'll watch a movie and I'll be fine!"...and hurting *more* after sitting in a theater for two hours.
- Acceptance is buying cute, cheap undies one size too big so you can enjoy nonbinding undies on pain days. Giving up is wearing granny panties with worn-out elastic.
- Acceptance is pacing yourself at the gym, adding one minute to your workout every three days so you can gently build up your exercise practice. Giving up is deciding you can never work out like before, so you'll never work out again.
- Acceptance is telling someone you have a limit, and asking them to help you develop workarounds. Resignation is telling someone you have a limit and ending the conversation.
- Acceptance is seeking solutions. Denial is seeking a "fix."
- Acceptance is blinging out your cane, wheelchair, boot, or brace—because you're stuck with it, so it might as well be cute. Resignation is leaving it plain, and grumping about its ugliness.

Does any of this seem familiar to you? Spend a little time writing out some of your acceptance challenges—practice spotting more opportunities to shift your mindset.

ChronicBabe stages of grief

As I've spent more time thinking about acceptance, I've developed ChronicBabe stages of grief. Babe, don't take me too seriously on this... but I think they're pretty right on:

- *Stage 1: Denial.* What the frack?! No more Saturday night dancing on tables? Hell no! My friends can just spot me in case I fall off. They're cushy...they'll be fine!
- *Stage 2: Apologies.* My friends did not appreciate the whole table-dancing thing. I'll have to come up with a good "I'm sorry" gift for their bruises.
- *Stage 3: Sobbing.* My "I'm sorry" gift of a friends' group massage made me flare up (guess I should have listened to my physiotherapist when she said no massages until we get my pain back to baseline), and now I'm too mortified to explain I can't get off this massage table without help. I'll just sob here quietly for a bit.
- *Stage 4: Realism.* I think my friends just held an intervention. It started as a small dinner party at home, but turned into passionate conversation about how I need to start thinking long-term. *But I don't wanna!* I have to admit, though: they may be right.
- *Stage 5: Denial.* I can't dance on tables or get massages, but I can water-ski, right? I used to be so good at it.
- *Stage 6: Circling back, in anger.* Oh no! I'm back at stage 1. How did that happen? Sigh. I guess I'll just watch the others from shore. Jerky-jerks who get to have fun.
- *Stage 7: Apologies, again.* I should not have said "jerky-jerks" out loud to my friends, who are currently not speaking to me. It's starting to sink in: I need to do something different.
- *Stage 8: Depression and therapy.* Why did I put this off? Did you know there are ways to cope with this? I have some reading to do. And crying, apparently—on the bus, on breaks at work, on the phone to my BFF. I'm lucky she's so supportive.

- *Stage 9: Resignation.* I don't think I'm resigned to a crappy life, but I get the sense I'm settling for less. It doesn't feel like I have a choice. But also: I feel calmer.
- *Stage 10: Realization.* I did not anticipate this. I read a couple of blog posts by amazing sick chicks, and suddenly I know people who really "get" me! I forwarded them to my friends and we've had some great conversations. I understand their frustration better, and they understand why I keep pushing myself—and I've given them permission to (gently) push back.
- *Stage 11: Is this acceptance?* I made a dinner date and called ahead to make sure they had a menu I could enjoy, and comfy chairs, and asked to be seated away from any large parties. It worked! I think this is acceptance, but I'm not sure. I'll keep practicing.

This tongue-in-cheek version of the stages of grief feels more true to my experience. It's messy, nonlinear, and still a work in progress. (Like we all are.)

And that's a key component to acceptance: You don't just wake up one day and fully accept. It's a daily practice. Some days, you'll be surprised at anger over a limitation; other days, you'll relish a feeling of peace you've not experienced before. Stay open to the many ways acceptance practice can develop.

What does acceptance give you?

When you practice acceptance—and I do mean *practice*, because it's an ongoing pursuit—you regain a few things, and gain some new ones, too:

- *Energy.* You have more of it because you're not wasting it fighting against your new limitations. You can use that energy to develop workarounds and think creatively about new approaches.
- *Responses to fear.* That inner voice who sometimes freaks out about the changes in your life? You can now respond: *Babe, we don't need to freak. We have options, and we have answers. The more we focus on developing strategies to handle this, the less fear we'll have.*
- *Confidence.* Because you stop questioning and fighting, you stop feeling off-balance all the time. You know what's up, and you've

got your to-do list ready. And because you're not in full-time questioning mode, your self-esteem gets a nice boost, too.

- *Resilience.* Acceptance gives you the space to take note of what's permanent and what's not. What's workable, and what's not. This is part of resilience: the ability to distinguish between these things so you know where to focus your energy. You may also find you have a fresh perspective, some clarity—so you don't get caught up in sadness about inconsequential things.
- *Humility.* Because you're accepting your situation, you're getting real about what you need so you're able to identify areas where you need help. Asking for help can be humbling, but it can also be a beautiful moment of connection with another person.
- *Futurecasting.* When we feel less freaked out and more grounded, we're able to plan for the future with less fear and more confidence.
- *Peace.* When I was fighting my disease, I was angry all the time, scared, and lacking confidence—I was a frazzled mess. Now, I'm able to find more peace throughout my day. We *all* need more peace, babe.

Can you reach acceptance even if you don't have a diagnosis?

Yes! If you still don't have a diagnosis, or you have something dianosed but still have a few symptoms docs can't explain, it is still possible to reach a state of acceptance.

To accept does not require you to name a thing. It is just as powerful to say, "I accept that I live with unexplained pain and fatigue" as it is to say, "I accept that I live with rheumatoid arthritis."

Accepting some things about your situation does not preclude you from continuing to seek diagnoses or answers to issues you face. You can accept that you live with lupus and still get a second opinion on that relentless foot pain you've been having.

Acceptance is an ongoing practice, and it's fluid. It will serve you well to think of it as an evolving state of mind.

POP QUIZ

A plan to come back to acceptance

Here's the first "Pop Quiz" of the book, one of many designed to give you a brief moment of challenge. Ready?

We all drift away and need help coming back—no one's acceptance practice is perfect—so if you work on acceptance but find yourself drifting away, what's your plan? What tools, resources, and visual reminders will you use?

For this Pop Quiz, take a few minutes to think about things that inspire you to feel a state of acceptance, and make a list to keep handy (perhaps on your phone). Maybe a paragraph about how acceptance helps you; maybe a locket with a favorite inspirational saying. Collect these items and keep them close. Consider sharing them with a confidante. Together, they are your plan for coming back to acceptance.

Two ways you can start building an acceptance practice today

Embracing acceptance as a way of life includes intentional practice. At first glance, this might sound like a drag—*can't I just accept and get on with it?*

Daily practice is an important part of learning to live in a state of acceptance. This is critical for several reasons, including:

- We know from experience that daily practice and routines help us turn a *desire* into a *habit.*
- We will enjoy more success if we approach this pursuit with intention.
- We live in bodies that give us daily opportunities for practice, whether we like it or not!
- We are surrounded by people and influences that might try to dissuade us from pursuing an acceptance practice.

Here are two exercises relying on meditation and writing to help you practice acceptance:

Daily writing exercise

A powerful way to work on acceptance is through writing. I'm a big fan of this process—I'm biased, of course, being a lifelong writer—but I'm not alone. Writing exercises for acceptance are recommended by many experts.

Grab your journal (or start a new one) and a favorite pen or marker, and get ready to write!

Find a time and space where you can write uninterrupted for at least ten minutes. I like to set a timer if I'm feeling crunched for time, or if I'm having physical symptoms that won't like it if I write for longer.

Take a few minutes to write down the things you're really angry about—the challenges that are frustrating you—that you can't change. These could include things like "difficulty breathing without my inhaler because it's hot and humid today" or "pain because of fibromyalgia is limiting my ability to work out." Write down as many as you want.

Review the list. You might get emotional, and that's okay—part of acceptance is looking at difficult things head-on and dealing with the ramifications, including big emotions.

Now, begin to write out "acceptance answers" to these challenges. For example: "I accept that I have asthma—today and many other days—and I have tools to manage it." Or: "I accept that I feel pain today, and I will use the skills I have to minimize it." The key here is *not* to write out thoughts about *fixing* it or *eliminating* it; the key is to accept it and acknowledge that you'll be okay anyway.

As you write out your "acceptance answers," add phrases about being okay. For example: "It's okay," or "I'm okay," or "It is really okay."

Try not to judge your writing or thoughts. You might feel inclined to doubt everything you just wrote down—that's understandable. At first, you might feel like a fake. This is the practice. We take small steps each day.

Daily meditation

You can practice acceptance by meditating on the concept daily. If you already meditate, it's easy to incorporate acceptance into your practice—but I'll spell out a simple meditation here in case you're a newbie:

Create a mantra for the day. This might be something like "I accept I have asthma, and I have tools to manage it," or "I accept I feel pain today, and I will use the skills I have to minimize it."

Find a comfortable place to sit or lie down undisturbed for ten minutes. (I like to set a timer.) Close your eyes. Breathe deep and release. Breathe deep again and release. Allow your breathing to slow to a natural pace, and focus on the breaths in and out, in and out.

Silently repeat your mantra along with your breath. If you feel yourself judging or doubting, that's okay—just notice it and come back to the mantra. You can't do this wrong. Seriously. As your mind wanders, gently return your attention to the mantra.

After a few minutes, wind down with a simple "It's okay" mantra. Silently repeat "It's okay," or "I'm okay," or "And everything is okay. " Take a few deep breaths and open your eyes.

Congratulations! You're meditating on acceptance. You can't screw this up, so don't worry if your mind wandered or you had an emotional reaction. Sometimes when I tell myself I'm okay, I burst into tears...because it's such a relief to accept and stop fighting. *And that's okay.*

✱ The secret to good caregiver communication: non-blame

Andrew and Cat have been married for nearly forty years. When they met, Cat already had early manifestations of fibromyalgia. Over the years, she's also been diagnosed with diabetes, arthritis, and a few other conditions. I talked with Andrew about his experience as a caregiver, and the tradeoffs he and his wife make to manage their life.

This is something I just have to accept, and not try to resist or pretend it isn't. It is.

I do think the secret to good communication is to be non-blaming. I can easily imagine relationships where the person who doesn't have the illness blames the other person. But I'm very non-blaming about this.

This is something Cat cannot help, so it makes no sense to blame her for any of this. Nevertheless, this is something we both struggle with. I'm thankful I don't have to struggle with it in the same way she does, but there is a sense in which this has happened to me too, because this is something I have to cope with, too.

A third person in the mix here is our son, Liberty. He has disabilities, too, so that complicates things somewhat. But Cat is super-organized. I find it very helpful to use Cat's calendar keeping and that kind of thing. It reduces the kinds of conflicts people have when they don't realize somebody needs to be picked up at a certain time or whatever—those kinds of things give rise to significant conflicts. It's because of Cat's organization that we're able to avoid a lot of that conflict.

For the past few years, I've had a lot of work to do, so Cat has spent a lot of time homeschooling and taking care of Liberty. But one of the recent developments in our lives is Cat has had a certain amount of withdrawal from taking care of Liberty, and is doing things on her own that make her happy. There's a certain tradeoff here between my responsibilities to Liberty and her responsibilities to Liberty. I recognize that if Cat is going to be happy, she needs time and space to do the tremendously creative things she does in her painting and blogging.

Hugs help. I have a sense of humor—a black sense of humor helps.

Mindfulness and acceptance go hand in hand

You may have heard people talking about mindfulness lately; as it gains more mainstream exposure, more people are also *commercializing* it. I prefer a noncommercialized approach. I don't need an app or a weekend workshop to learn it, and I don't think you do, either.

Mindfulness is about staying present in the moment. Sounds simple, right? But our culture does not encourage mindfulness. Smartphones buzz, TV commercials get loud, Facebook is designed to keep us clicking.

All those distractions can take us out of the moment and dampen our enjoyment of what we have that works—which can dampen our *acceptance*.

For example, I love to garden. I have a small plot at a community garden a few blocks from my condo, and I walk over each day to tend to my Tiny Farm, as I call it. While I'm there, I could get distracted by text messages, phone calls, and alerts from apps—but I usually turn off my ringer and focus on the plants.

Why? Those distractions keep me from being with my little green friends. When I focus on them, I gain much: A sense of being grounded. A feeling of self-confidence and ability. The joy of seeing something develop naturally. All the sensory experiences, like the sun on my shoulders, the sounds of other gardeners chatting, the smell of my herbs.

That brief moment of peace in my day is *medicinal.* Looking at my phone the whole time would ruin it.

How does this help maintain my acceptance practice? On days when my body doesn't work properly or I've blown a few hours on the phone with insurance bureaucracy instead of writing, a trip to the garden reminds me there are things that I *can* rely on, that I *can* accomplish, even with all the other B.S. Yes!

If you want some mindfulness instruction, I recommend Thich Nhat Hanh's book *Peace Is Every Step*, a phrase I love so much it's tattooed on my arm. Pema Chödrön also offers many free online talks, as does Tara Brach. While these are Buddhism-based, they are applicable to people of any spiritual leaning.

Love the one you're with

We'll talk more about body image in lesson 5, but I want to address it briefly here as well, because acceptance gives us so much opportunity to love ourselves again, no matter how "flawed" or "broken" we are.

Have you, at times, hated your body? I have. Sometimes when all my systems are short-circuiting, I'll say something to myself like "I hate you, body." As I type that, I'm feeling a desire to comfort myself; that hatred is awful.

If you've experienced that bruising feeling, acceptance offers a salve. As you begin to accept the truth of your condition, it's easier to be kind to yourself. And really, we *must* be kind to ourselves. The world can sometimes be an unkind place, so we need to cultivate a strong sense of self-love and kindness.

POP QUIZ **Ten-minute pity party**

You get to throw yourself a pity party. For ten minutes. Set a timer, put on some depressing music, break out the tissues, and lie down on the floor.

Now, pity yourself! Wallow in it. Say all the saddest things you can think of. Whine about the unfairness of it all.

When the timer goes off, that's it: Pity party over.

I recommend you throw yourself a pity party every once in a while, and then *that's all you get*. Got it?

How acceptance helps us set goals and make plans

Goals: many with illness don't want to make them because there is so much uncertainty in our lives.

But avoiding goal-setting perpetuates the feeling that nothing good is happening, that you don't have anything to look forward to. When you have no goals, you're set adrift, and then you're just floating in a sea of uncertainty. We already live with so much uncertainty; avoiding planning or goal-setting makes you feel that even more.

Some uncertainty we must accept. But we don't have to walk around every day feeling like we don't know what's happening next, that we have no plan. Goal-setting, even if it is just small things, can really help.

Avoiding goal-setting does something else, too: it keeps you from self-motivating. You have an innate ability to move yourself forward. But you must be proactive. If you're not setting goals, you're missing out on a natural tool for feeling more like a ChronicBabe.

I can't help but think about my experience yesterday at the gym. After a long hiatus, I've been working out daily; I had to start back small, with just five minutes each of treadmill, elliptical, and stationary bike. The first few days, I left feeling kind of wimpy. A fifteen-minute workout? Really?

Every few days, I added one minute to the workout. Just one minute. Again, I felt kind of wimpy! But yesterday, I realized I had accomplished my goal: I did a thirty-minute workout. Sure, it took me weeks to work up to it—but I did it!

I really needed that win. Part of being a ChronicBabe is committing to taking little steps each day, about being patient but persistent. This kind of behavior, when reinforced daily, helps you feel a tiny sense of control in the face of uncertainty. It may not *solve* everything but it offers a feeling of confidence and accomplishment.

Acceptance (and patience) are key for caregivers, too

Annee is mother to a woman with lupus. Her daughter was diagnosed at nineteen; now forty-three, she's married with two children. Annee has watched her daughter go through a lot. We talked about her experience, and the role of acceptance in her life as a caregiver:

When she was married and had children, her disease seemed to progress a little bit more, and it made it hard for her to care for the children. I got very much involved, being that we live close together and her husband had to work. I was working a full-time job myself.

Some of the challenge is trying to let her be an independent mother but seeing her unable to do things. I would have to take the children to give her a break to rest. It was challenging to work my full-time job, still be a wife to my husband, and watch her go through pain.

I have a very deep Catholic faith, which gets me through the really tough times. I do have friends I can talk to, but I'm more of a listener than a talker, so it isn't easy for me to talk to people about things. It's really frustrating for the person with the chronic illness to deal with it every day, and then it's very frustrating for a caregiver. I don't feel the pain, so I feel for her—yet I don't feel her pain.

It's happened where emotionally I would break down, but my breakdowns would be in private, in silence. I would go to my faith and try to find strength there, and it always brought me back up, knowing that everything is temporary—I know chronic disease is forever, but when [it was] really low, I would tell my daughter, "Give it another day or two and you're gonna feel better," trying to give the positive outlook. It's really hard when you're not well to think of positive things.

I would advise [other caregivers] to be patient, be a good listener, advise in every way that you can. But to realize that the patient isn't always going to be receptive to what you're going to say, so you have to have a thick skin in some ways—your patient may get annoyed

> *and lash out at you, and you have to not take it as something personal toward you. They're just going through something really tough at that moment.*

HOMEWORK assignments

Each lesson has a few homework assignments. I won't be grading them...but I encourage you to try one or more of them, anyway!

1) Your ten best qualities

Write down ten qualities about yourself that you love and accept. Examples: your smile, your sense of humor, that fabulous booty. Spend a week reading the list every day and adding to it; extra credit if you double it.

2) A quick conversation with a friend

When we're sick, we become blind to the good things about ourselves. As an exercise, grab your best friend, your sister, or someone else who will be honest and kind. Ask *them* to name five qualities they admire about you. Do the same for them. This is a terrific bonding opportunity!

3) Pick one small thing to accept

Pick one small thing to accept and practice that for a week. (Spell out what that looks like.)

PEP SQUAD

An interview with Toni Bernhard

Acceptance opens possibilities for peace, even for us sick chicks

Toni Bernhard is an author, a blogger for *Psychology Today*, and a chronic pain and illness advocate. She is the author of three incredible books, two of which focus on living with grace and joy despite chronic illness (which includes chronic pain), and one which focuses on the Buddha's path to awakening to a life of peace and wellbeing. They are: *How to Live Well with Chronic Pain and Illness: A Mindful Guide* (2015), *How to Wake Up: A Buddhist-Inspired Guide for Navigating Joy and Sorrow* (2013), and *How to Be Sick: A Buddhist-Inspired Guide for the Chronically Ill and their Caregivers* (2010).

Toni has been a practicing Buddhist for over twenty years. She was also a law professor at the University of California, Davis for twenty-two years, serving six years as the dean of students. She writes in a conversational style, with the intention of helping everyone, regardless of circumstances, learn to live with compassion, joy, and purpose. She lives in Davis, California with her husband and their endearing, if goofy, gray lab named Scout.

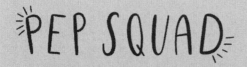

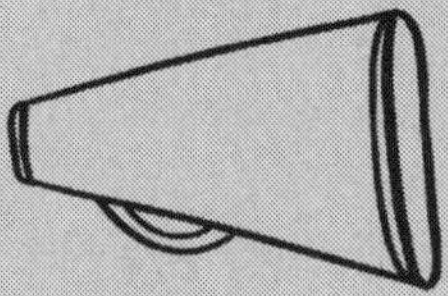

Connect with Toni:
Facebook: facebook.com/tonibernhard
Twitter: @toni_bernhard
Pinterest: pinterest.com/tonibernhard

Jenni: Today we're talking about acceptance, which is really a fundamental aspect of being a ChronicBabe, of living well in spite of chronic illness. Toni, you've really had to accept an entirely different way of life since you became ill. When you first got sick, did you even think about acceptance? Did you think acceptance was a possibility for you?

Toni: I have to be honest and say no. And I had ten years of Buddhist practice behind me, and yet when I first got sick, I was in a state of denial for years. I don't think that's unusual. I think it just illustrates how hard it is to accept that the life you were living and your plans for the future sometimes just have to drastically change.

So the first few years of being ill, when I didn't recover from what we thought was this acute illness, I would go to bed at night and try to will myself to wake up feeling healthy again. It was like hitting my head against the wall, because there are some things about life we just can't control.

And it took me, I don't know, somewhere around four years—a long time—to realize this was a losing strategy, that all I was doing was adding mental suffering to the physical suffering of the illness. I think when I saw this, that's when I began this process of accepting my new life.

Jenni: I spent many years after my diagnosis with fibromyalgia fighting it, and fighting really hard, because I'm tough, and I did not want to feel like I was giving up. I felt like acceptance was kind of giving up or giving in to the illness.

Toni: I don't think it's about giving up either. The right words to describe giving up would be *resignation* or *indifference*, and that attitude and state of mind carry aversion with them, which is a turning away from our life as it is.

In contrast, *acceptance* means opening to our life as it is. When we say to ourselves, "I just give up," that kind of negative attitude makes it difficult to make constructive changes to our life, because we're refusing to look at our life as it is right now. So I feel strongly that we can be accepting of the state of our health *and* be proactive in continuing to look for treatments, find new doctors if we need to, and also be proactive about figuring out what new things we can do with our life as it is now.

And if you come from a place of acceptance, there's a certain calmness to it, and that makes it easier to make wise decisions and to take constructive action.

Jenni: That's the experience I've had. When I fight it, when I'm angry about it, I tend to be more irrational and I tend to leap at things, or feel and act out of fear and frustration, and make choices that are not the healthiest.

Toni: It's just not a linear process where one day you wake up and say, "Okay! I accept." You know, I have my ups and downs, I have my bad days, but at least I know what to work on. I understand that resignation, that kind of negative attitude, doesn't do me any good. And so at least I know to try to cultivate acceptance in the face of that. But I still have my ups and downs.

> *"**The first thing to do is to start by treating yourself kindly** about what's happened with your health—it's not your fault. That, to me, is the first step toward acceptance."*
>
> —Toni

Jenni: Well, we're all human. For myself, though, the moment of time in my life when I really came to accept that I wasn't going to get better and I was just going to learn to work with it and still live a great life, it was very powerful; it really changed me in a very profound way.

I'm wondering why, you think, this happens to us, because I know it happens to a lot of people. Why is acceptance such a powerful concept for those of us with chronic conditions?

Toni: I think it's so powerful because, bottom line, we have the life we've been given. This is our life as it is. We're in bodies, and bodies are subject to illness and injury; it can happen to anyone, and it can happen to anyone at any age. And so, for me, the only peace to be found is to start where I am. It's a wonderful expression; it's the name of a book by Pema Chödrön, *Start Where You Are: A Guide to Compassionate Living*.

Well, where am I? I'm in a body that's not in good health, and I've found that when I spent all my time fighting that, my whole life was subsumed with thinking about my health. It becomes this total identity; if you spend all your time fighting what is, refusing to accept your life as it is, you kind of become what you're fighting. I was this sick person; that was my total identity: "sick person."

Jenni: I know that you know, you're so much more than that.

Toni: Right, but we don't see it when all we're doing is fighting it. And if we also have a chronic pain condition, it's the same kind of thing. We feel as if we're nothing *but* the pain, because we're spending all our time fighting it.

When we accept it as part of our life, then we begin to see that we're much more than that. I mean, look what you've done, Jenni! I find it hard to believe that you could have done everything you've done with this big community and all the things you do, if you weren't coming from some level of acceptance of your health difficulties. Otherwise you'd just be spending your days as "person in pain," consumed by that.

Jenni: Yes. Unfortunately, there are so many people who get stuck there. And the thing is, I understand that because I've been there before myself. It took me quite a while to really get to that place and be able to speak openly and try to help people.

So what do you think is one of the first steps people can take toward acceptance? Especially people for whom acceptance may be a really new concept?

Toni: It's a great question because, you know, we're talking about acceptance opening up possibilities. But the question is "Well, how do you get there?"

When I don't know what to do about the stressful thoughts running through my mind or what to do to help myself, the first thing I do is to treat myself with compassion. Even if it's just compassion for the fact that I can't get to acceptance, it's amazing how directing compassion at ourselves can soften everything, and out of that can flow the beginning of acceptance.

I'm going to share something, which is that I do a lot of talking to myself. I don't talk out loud, but I do talk to myself. And I talk to myself with compassion, because it's not my body's fault that I'm sick—this just happened to me.

So I might say something like, "It's so hard to have to miss this wedding that you really want to go to when all your friends and family are going." I'm using this example because it's something I'm working with right now. This coming weekend, I can't go to a wedding because, even though it's nearby, it's in the evening. Sometimes I can go somewhere during the day for an hour or two, but by the evening, I'm sick in bed.

And so, when I speak to myself that way, it's like I'm acknowledging the sadness, the unhappiness, and that's the first step toward acceptance.

To me, if you're turning away from that, and trying to pound it out of your life—"I'm not sad, I'm not!"—then you don't get to acceptance. You have to see it and treat it with compassion, which means treating yourself kindly, over all the things that are troublesome for you, and that are making you unhappy and making you sad. And when you do that, that's when the crack of light of acceptance starts to shine through. That's how it works for me.

So I would tell people the first thing to do is to start by treating yourself kindly about what's happened with your health. It's not your fault. Treat yourself kindly and with compassion. That, to me, is the first step toward acceptance.

> *"We're in bodies, and bodies can get sick and injured at any time during our life, and* ***it's not our fault.****"*
>
> —Toni

Jenni: That's something that I think a lot of us, in moments of intense pain or struggle or sadness, can use. It can be really hard.

It sounds like what you're talking about is, there's a difference between acknowledging the sadness of something you can't do and wallowing in it. You're not talking about wallowing.

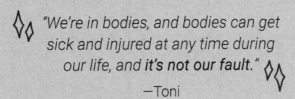

Toni: Right, I'm talking about acknowledging that the sadness is present. Sadness and unhappiness are among the myriad arising and passing thoughts and emotions that flow through the mind. We don't have to think of them as a permanent part of who we are, because they're not.

One of the universal laws that all religions and all scientists recognize is impermanence, this ever-changing nature of what arises in the mind and passes in the mind. But we sometimes tend to grab onto something and think, *I'm always gonna be sad, I'm always gonna be this way*. And so, simply try to recognize the sadness and, then, having recognized it, try not to grasp onto it, but see that it's only temporarily there and treat yourself kindly about it: "My dear, sweet body. It's so hard to be sick."

I know this is easier for some people to do than for others. A lot of people find it easier to be compassionate about others than they can be about themselves. But it helps to recognize that the inability to be self-compassionate is just conditioning, maybe from something your parents told you, such as "Don't ever complain about pain." You may have internalized that conditioning, but you can change.

We change our conditioning every time we treat ourselves kindly. It's as if we're laying down a new and fresh track in our minds. And each time we treat ourselves kindly, it's easier to do the next time.

You have to just dive in and start doing it, even if it feels fake at first. Do it. Because you're changing yourself into someone who is able to be kind and loving to themselves. And that opens the door to acceptance.

Jenni: Do you have favorite suggestions for people when they're kind of exploring the idea of acceptance, books or podcasts or even strategies for practicing it that you like?

Toni: Well, I can share some strategies. I know there are wonderful books but I don't have any to recommend offhand, because it's difficult for me to read, so I mostly listen to audiobooks and fiction, that kind of thing.

But I do feel very strongly that if someone is starting to explore this idea of "How can I accept what I don't want?" it's really important to be patient with yourself. It kind of goes back to what I was saying about how, for some people, it's hard to be compassionate towards themselves. Well, because acceptance flows from that, for some people, acceptance may be long in coming.

But that's okay. Be patient with yourself, treat yourself kindly, the way you would if you were trying to teach something to a child. Recognize that it takes time because you're developing new skills, and then relish each little victory. Be content with baby steps.

If there's just one moment during the day when, maybe you're lying on the bed, and you're just having this moment of feeling, *I'm okay with my life as it is right now. Even though I'm in pain.* Relish that little victory. And know that, as I said before, that this is setting the stage for the next moment when you're going to feel that way. Be patient, take your time, and be content with baby steps.

Jenni: You and I both share a pursuit of Buddhist learning, and for me, acceptance is a big part of that, and my spiritual practice has really helped me come to a state of acceptance.

I'm wondering if you could talk about how your faith or your spirituality [impacts] your work on acceptance. And also, I'd like to think about people of other faiths, and how they may find resources too.

Toni: You know, people talk about Buddhism, and there really is not a thing that is "Buddhism." There are dozens of different schools of Buddhism, and I don't actually consider it to be a religion. To me, it's a practical life path. It was only given the label "religion" when it was discovered by Westerners.

The Buddha himself avoided metaphysical questions. He refused to answer them, and that's why his teachings are compatible with any other faith. He was interested in our day-to-day life, and what we could do to ease our suffering. To ease our difficulties.

And I've said this before, but to me the number one thing we can to do ease our suffering is to start where we are. In other words, accept our life as it is, rather than spending our days bemoaning what might have been and what we thought was going to happen.

I had other plans, I was going to be a law professor for another twenty years, but it didn't happen that way.

What makes us unhappy, according to the Buddhist teachings, is when we are continually dissatisfied with our life as it is. The thing is, we're never going to get everything lined up exactly how we want it. Even if I woke up tomorrow with my health restored, I'd have other difficulties to face.

So the key to happiness is not trying to get everything fixed so it's just the way we want it. It's acceptance—acceptance of both the joys and the sorrows in our life, of both the pleasant and the unpleasant experiences.

To me, the essential teaching of the Buddha really is about acceptance. We have to look at the hard facts and realize that acceptance is going to include some of the things we don't like. Whether it's personal or more global—like who's president of the United States.

We can spend all of our days in what I call "like/don't like" mode, but it's just not fruitful, because we're never going to get the world or our life to be exactly how we like it. So change what you can change, but accept what you can't.

"If there's just one moment during the day when, maybe you're lying on the bed, and you're feeling, **I'm okay with my life as it is right now. Even though I'm in pain.** *Relish that little victory."*

—Toni

Jenni: In my life experience, I've said the serenity prayer many, many times. And at different times I've said *god* or *goddess* or *universe*, grant me the serenity to accept the things I cannot change, courage to change the things I can, and wisdom to know the difference.

Toni: That's what I was referencing there. It's so helpful. I'm really glad you quoted it.

Jenni: And I do believe people of any faith can say that, and they can call it a prayer or a meditation or a quote or whatever they want to call it, but the basic idea is so solid and foundational.

I'm wondering if you have any final tips or a piece of advice that you would offer someone who is maybe struggling with the idea of acceptance?

Toni: It's important to remember that suffering from chronic pain or illness is not a personal failing on your part. We live in a culture where we're subject all the time to advertising claims and to people around us who think that all we have to do is take this pill and we'll be fine—or that only people who are older develop health problems. It simply isn't true.

As I said before, we're in bodies, and bodies can get sick and injured at any time during our life, and it's not our fault. And when I finally got that it wasn't my fault, that my body was working as hard as it could to try and be better, it opened a new world to me, and allowed me to live gracefully with the hand I've been dealt.

"Acceptance is a kind of middle path, this acceptance of the fact that ***everybody's life, including our own, has its share of joys and sorrows."***

—Toni

Jenni: Such an awesome idea, such an awesome concept. It seems that it's easy for us to *say*, it's not the easiest thing to *do*, but like you said earlier, baby steps, practicing it every day.

Toni: And always let compassion for yourself be that fallback position. So if you feel like, *I just can't accept that I can't go to this wedding!* Always go to compassion: "It's so hard to not be able to go to the wedding." It softens everything. It just softens your mind. And opens the door to acceptance.

This interview has been shortened and edited to fit this book. To read the full transcript or listen to the full recordings of this and all the Pep Squad interviews, head to ChronicBabe101.com.

Lesson 2

learn to kick those BAD HABITS to the curb

We learn them, and they hold us back. Now is *not* the time to judge yourself for having bad habits—we all do! Instead, this lesson is about recognizing them, owning up to them, and changing them into good habits that support you.

How (and why) we form bad habits

There are many reasons why we form bad habits. Your upbringing shapes much of the way you approach habits, for starters. My childhood was full of donuts and smoking and beers and staying up all night. I also lived with a lot of anxiety-inducing situations. But my early years were also full of athletics and outdoor activities and hard work and creativity.

As a young adult, I still ate a lot of donuts and wondered why, when I started working out, I gained weight; only now do I have a daily game plan for avoiding donuts. I smoked for ten years, and I used it to cope with stressful situations. For a long time, I drank too much beer, and I had to find other ways to chill out. I bit my nails when I was nervous, but getting involved in nail art as a hobby stopped that. I'm not nearly as athletic as I was as a child, and it's a continual effort, but I stay active. I grew up with some *terrible* habits, but I've mostly trained myself to pursue positive alternatives.

We often form bad habits as a response to negative stimuli. If we're stressed and don't have an outlet, we may pick at our skin, snack too much, or soothe ourselves with junk TV. If as kids we had to go without healthy food, we may develop a junk food habit—which doesn't serve us well and is hard to break—in adulthood.

Bad habits aren't impossible to break. And I'm not saying you should *never* smoke a cigarette or drink a beer or eat a donut. But we must seek balance. To do so requires us to look at ourselves with fierce honesty.

What are the benefits of forming good habits?

A daily good habit means routine. And routine feels good to most of us, especially when we're sick. I don't know about you, but I feel like I'm constantly thrown for loops; my illnesses always show up in weird ways and challenge me with new issues. Every day, I feel like much of my life is up in the air.

Having good habits gives me a routine I can count on. So no matter how cruddy I feel, whether it's blizzard or bathing-suit weather, whether I've slept eight hours or two, I know when I get out of bed, I'm doing my morning routine. It includes heating up my bad back, doing twenty minutes of yoga and stretching, drinking tea, making a healthy protein-packed breakfast, and meditating.

A good habit helps reinforce your sense of accomplishment. Chronic illness can rob us of our sense of accomplishment. Developing (and keeping) good habits helps us feel like we really *can* do something.

If I'm having a rough day and can't work, can't sew, can't even get a brush through my hair, I still relish the accomplishment of doing my twenty minutes of stretching and yoga. On my worst days, if it takes me thirty or forty minutes to do it because I take breaks, that's cool, too—the point is, I do it. Daily, without fail. It helps me feel like I accomplished *something* that day. (This also highlights the beauty of having a good habit in the morning; it starts your day off right.)

A good habit helps us feel grounded. The surprises that chronic illness or pain offer can make us feel unsteady. Sometimes that means we feel adrift, being tossed about on the wind. That feels awful!

Feeling grounded is an amazing thing. It helps us get in touch—and stay in touch—with who we truly are, deep inside. I do a lot of things to help myself stay grounded. One of those things is maintaining daily good habits.

The daily good habit that helps me feel most grounded is meditation. It's a quiet, thoughtful (or, on my best days, *thoughtless*) practice. It quiets my mind, and I get in touch with who I am deep inside. It helps me disconnect from the rush of influences outside, like social media, friends and family, street noises, or client demands. When I'm meditating daily, I feel grounded. When I don't do it regularly? I feel anxious, scattered, and just plain weird.

A good habit reminds us we love ourselves. We love ourselves enough to take good care of ourselves. We love ourselves just as we are, and we do positive things for ourselves no matter how we feel each day. We love ourselves.

That's a big challenge for us ChronicBabes, because our bodies are always playing tricks on us—and we live in a society that values *work* over all else, while many of us are not able to work. We can feel less valued, less important.

I call bullshit! We are valuable, essential, amazing. We deserve love. We deserve to feel good. So even if the rest of our day feels like crap, doing one small good thing for ourselves—flossing, eating an apple, taking a shower, listening to our favorite song—making that good habit stick is a show of *love.*

Checklist: You're a Good Habit Goddess!

Sometimes, we simply need a small way of tracking our progress to lock in a good habit. I created a quick checklist for you to try. Make copies of the next page of the book, or print them out at ChronicBabe101.com.

Pick a handful of things to work on this week. Each day, check off the ones you accomplish. Watch your progress. For people who like to earn a gold star, this technique can be very motivating.

YOU'RE A GOOD HABIT *goddess!*

habit:	SUN	MON	TUES	WED	THURS	FRI	SAT

What's a "bad habit" versus "making occasional unhealthy choices"?

Let's clarify the difference between doing something habitually naughty, and occasionally making an unhealthy choice. Some examples:

Bad habit: Slacking off until your house is filthy and you haven't moved from your bed/couch in a week or more
Occasional unhealthy choice: Procrastinating on doing the dishes for one day

Bad habit: Having non-nutritious meals every day
Occasional unhealthy choice: Letting yourself enjoy a sweet snack on Wednesdays

Bad habit: Continually buying things outside your price range and adding to your debt
Occasional unhealthy choice: Splurging on a cute top as a pick-me-up when you need a confidence boost

Bad habit: Drinking until you fall asleep
Occasional unhealthy choice: Having a couple of drinks for stress relief or celebration

Everyone needs to indulge sometimes. Leaving dishes in the sink overnight on a flare-up day is no biggie, as long as it doesn't become a daily occurrence.

A word of caution: If you've identified something that you're not sure is a bad habit, but that you know is keeping you from accomplishing things you care about, it's time to talk to a professional. There's no shame in seeking help—sometimes, we need an extra assist to shed a destructive habit.

One of the most common bad habits: Isolation

Over the years, I've seen a lot of unhealthy stuff in the ChronicBabe community. Spend enough time with people and they'll reveal the nasty habits they usually keep private. The thing is, these habits are self-destructive—and we don't have to keep doing them on the daily.

One of the most common bad habits I hear about is isolation. People will tell me, "I'm lonely!"—but those same people will also say that they don't like to initiate plans with friends, that they don't believe online relationships are as real as in-person, or that it's too much effort to figure out how to plan an outing that's healthy for them.

Illness isolates us, that's a fact. Research also shows us that isolation brings increased health risks comparable to obesity and smoking. Yikes! *(Read about it: bit.ly/DontBeLonely.)*

But we can choose to push back against that isolation. If we're forgetful, we can create weekly calendar reminders that alert us when it's time to text a friend to plan a lunch date. If we're nervous about eating out because we have food allergies, we can plan something that's not food-focused. If we live in a rural area where it's hard to meet people, we can use Skype, FaceTime or other apps to chat live with friends around the world.

You don't have to live in isolation, babe. It may take more effort than you would prefer, but making connections habitual is worth it. #isolationsucks

Pace yourself!
Changing bad habits and making new ones is robust work, babe. Take it easy. Don't beat yourself up if you're imperfect—we all are!

What do our bad habits teach us?

Bad habits aren't entirely useless. We can examine them and discover their origins, or the things they give us, before we banish them.

A bad habit of procrastinating on answering work emails might indicate dissatisfaction with your career, poor time management, an imbalanced workload—or the need to devise a new approach to email altogether. Maybe you need to switch to a project that excites you, or you need a manager's help to lighten your workload. Maybe you need to reevaluate how you spend your mornings; could you devote an extra half hour to email?

A bad habit of eating junk food when you're tired might indicate that you've never learned a self-soothing habit that's healthy, or that your tiredness could be related to a hormonal imbalance that also causes food cravings. Maybe you need to talk to a therapist about strategies for self-soothing when things are tough. Maybe you need to research healthy snacks to stock your fridge. Maybe your primary care doc needs to run a thyroid panel.

In both cases, we could benefit from changing our habit to something healthier. By evaluating the potential causes of the unhealthy habit, we're better equipped to devise a good habit to replace it—and more likely to adopt it successfully.

Baby-step a new habit

Creating a new habit is not easy. I've tried and tried to get into a daily workout routine, only to falter over and over. But I keep getting back up again and trying, because that's what I do, babe. Same thing for cutting back on sweets; I'll go a couple of weeks just fine and BAM some chocolate crosses my path. Then I feel like I'm back at square one.

But that's not right. One piece of chocolate does not equal a habit destroyed! Keep that in mind, because you *will* make mistakes; you *will* falter. Don't beat yourself up for being imperfect.

I've developed a short series of steps to help you baby-step a new habit:

1. Write down the habit you want to create.
2. Write down the roadblocks you've experienced. Can you eliminate any? Or is mindful awareness of them enough, so that when they show up, you can bypass them and stay on track?
3. Baby-step it. Write down all the tiny, incremental steps you need to build the new habit. Do you need to buy anything? Schedule something? Enlist help?
4. Grab your calendar and pencil in the baby steps.

Example: Going back to swimming at your gym's pool

This is one I recently did myself. Here are the steps I took:

- Day 1: Order a new bathing suit.
- Day 2: Find my goggles and swim cap.
- Day 3: Download the pool schedule.
- Day 4: Pack my pool bag to ensure I have all the things I need for the locker room.
- Day 5: Head to the pool. Swim for ten minutes. Use the hot tub or sauna after my workout.
- Day 6: Assess how I feel. Did I overdo it? Do I need new goggles?
- Day 7: Back to the pool. Add one minute to my workout. Reward myself for hard work with a green smoothie.
- Day 8: Rest and reassess.
- Day 9: Back to the pool. Add one minute again.

Can you see how I've broken down the process into lots of little pieces? This is how we methodically build a new habit. When we hit a bump in the road, we pause, reassess, and get back at it the next day, ChronicBabe-style.

✱ Making tradeoffs is a big part of the caregiver experience

Bruce's wife has lived with chronic fatigue for a handful of years, and he says she sometimes pushes herself past her limits in her desire to feel better. They don't plan much because her condition shifts daily, but they do try to organize the occasional social outing.

We had suspicions from our own research that she had chronic fatigue, and there was just no information around. I'm not the most patient man in the world; that's part of the battle. Once we understood what she was going through, it made it a little bit easier to help her.

I've had to learn to stop being the slob bloke. The dogs need to be fed, we need to be fed...I've had to pick up more of the household chores. We didn't put anything formally in place. It all boils down to how she is that day.

Now there's not much of a social life, so to speak, where we go out somewhere together. She just can't handle the noise and the people. I tend to go to a lot of events on my own. Most of the people we socialize with are aware of her illness and understand it. Usually the first thing I get when I walk through the door is "How's Erica?" Oh, okay. What about me? They all ask after her, and no one asks, "Are you all right?"

I've just got to go, "Well, okay, I'll go pick up some extra chores in the household so she can get some extra rest, so she can come out and socialize," because that takes so much out of her. Just sitting talking to somebody can actually have a big impact on her. We do plan for that sort of thing, but mostly just take each day as it comes.

Caregiver resources
For a list of caregiver-focused resources, head to the Extra Credit section at the back of the book.

Sometimes you feel really resentful. "I'm over this, make it go away." But I think it's just the emotions you go through every now and then. It's a huge change in our lives. Most of the time, it's, "Well, there's nothing I can do about it; let's just get on with it."

I think the biggest problem I have here is meeting other partners [of people with chronic illness]. It's getting to be an online support thing; I've certainly started to look into that a little bit more.

How do we turn a good habit into a default?

Repetition, babe. I didn't become a daily yogi overnight. It took months of doing the practice daily, and figuring out workarounds. I had to get the right equipment, like a thicker-than-standard yoga mat to care for my joints. I had to ask my physical therapist (and the Internet) for workarounds when I injured myself but didn't want to get sidelined. I bought an ultrathin travel mat for road trips.

Then I did it every day. That repetition pushed the habit into my brain and body, like a sweet memory I recall every morning.

I've heard a few estimates for how many days it takes to create a good habit. Twenty-one, twenty-eight, sixty...the truth is, it will vary for everyone. To make a habit into your default, you'll have to repeat it perhaps hundreds of times.

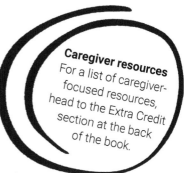

Having a yoga practice that's now my default means that on the rare day I skip it, I *feel* the difference. In fact, on those days, I feel like crud. And that's a reminder of why it's so essential in my life—why it's now my default.

"Start where you are, use what you have, do what you can."

I love this quote: "Start where you are, use what you have, do what you can." Tennis great Arthur Ashe made it famous, and when I get in a pickle, it pops into my head. Let's break it down as it applies to creating habits—specifically, becoming better organized.

Start where you are

If you're feeling disorganized, you might not know where to start. Maybe it's more than your cluttered coffee table; maybe you also have a crazy email backlog, or your car's backseat is covered with bags of stuff you keep meaning to take to the thrift shop. It can feel overwhelming.

The first trick to moving past that overwhelm is to stop and breathe. Just breathe. Now look around you. Is there something within reach you can tackle today? Can you start with making your bed, or emptying the overflowing trash can? Can you delete a bunch of old emails you're never going to answer? Can you spend ten minutes cleaning out your junk drawer? Can you empty your crisper drawer of wilted veggies?

Start where you are. You don't have to go far to find a task that will help you feel more on top of things. Even ten minutes of work is enough to break the spell of overwhelm and get you onto a fresh path of personal organization.

Use what you have

You don't have to buy a bunch of stuff to get organized. You may want to, and it might even be fun and motivational—but it's not *required*. You can use what you have right in front of you.

If you already have a filing cabinet but it's overflowing, you're in luck: You have the essential equipment. If you've been using file folders, no need to buy new ones; just grab some blank label stickers and relabel your folders (or flip them inside out). If you're looking for ways to beautify your existing pill organizer, look no further than your nail polish collection, some glue and glitter, or your sticker stash.

Sometimes it helps to get new stuff (including digital stuff, like apps) when you're starting a new habit. But sometimes, it distracts you from the real work. The work is not in learning a complicated new app to manage your email; the work is in unsubscribing from dozens of newsletters you never read. The work is in sorting that overflowing file cabinet and getting real about trashing the stuff you don't need. The work is in tackling one dresser drawer each day and filling small bags of stuff light enough to carry to the thrift store.

Do what you can

This is the biggie, babe. Do what you can. What you *can*. What YOU can.

Not what you *should*. Or what others think you should. Or what others wish you would. Or what you used to be able to do.

Do what you can, today. From where you are, and with what you have.

I used to be able to pull all-nighters and catch up on hundreds of emails in one night, and wake up pumped the next day. But my body doesn't accommodate that kind of activity now. Instead, whenever I fall behind, I aim to add an extra twenty minutes per day of email until I'm back to Inbox Zero.

I used to have a huge office that was all mine, with tons of bookshelves, a table, and three filing cabinets. I saved every scrap of paper for "posterity." But my living situation doesn't accommodate that kind of work arrangement now, so I've downsized. *Significantly*. Turns out, I like it more!

You must first acknowledge what you are able to do right now, and look it in the eye. Do you see it clearly? Not what you wish for, or what used to be, but what you can do *today*.

Second, you must do it. Own up to it. No one else will do the work for you—and you don't want them to, anyway, do you? That's not how you learn and grow.

You can do this if you put your mind to it.

✳ Caregivers need to care for themselves, too

Kieron's wife has Ehlers-Danlos syndrome (EDS), a connective tissue disorder. They've been together for a little over twenty years.

This condition is genetic; she's been having symptoms her entire life but never had any idea what they were until only a few years ago. She has a lot of dislocations, many times a day, and there are some blood pres-

sure issues. It's pretty tough for her—there's a lot of pain involved. She often needs help to relocate joints, many times a day.

It's a little distressing when you hear a mild sort of clack that's obviously bone hitting other bone as the joint realigns itself. It can take a certain amount of physical strength. But mostly it's just sort of about patience, really. I feel bad complaining about it because it's obviously a lot more painful for her. It does take a certain amount of perseverance.

I suffer from depression. I'm not immune to feelings of frustration. I have a therapist I see about that, although that's not just related to the caregiver thing. But I have discussed being a caregiver with my therapist as well, which I think is probably important.

I try to concentrate on the things we can do, even if it's on a day she's not able to get out of bed or something—okay, then I bring the laptop in and call up Netflix and we can binge-watch some old TV shows or something together, and that's a thing we can do together.

If it's changed me as a person, it's probably for the better, as it's made me a bit more empathetic than I might otherwise have been. It's been a long time; I was eighteen when we got together, so it's a bit hard to really relate to the way I was back then as a teenager. So I think I probably would be quite a different person. But I don't think I would have been a better person if it weren't for being a caregiver.

The best advice I could probably give is to be patient, be caring, but don't forget to care for yourself as well, because that's important too. And just try to find the joy in life wherever you can.

What happens when our best intentions fail and we go back to bad habits?

Wow—the list of things that could trigger us to slip up, even when we have the best intentions, is long.

Family members might not be supportive, or might make weird demands. Friends might expect us to be perfect, or expect us to fall into old habits and patterns...and act weird when we don't. Colleagues might not be understanding. We might get hormonal and have intense cravings. We might have a flare-up. There might be a sale at the store. It might be a full moon. We might get sad after watching an old movie. We might stub our toe.

These myriad triggers are life's way of putting up an obstacle course for us, and everyone's triggers differ.

What happens when one of these triggers trips us up? What if we have a great week, and then fall short for a couple of days? What if we start to feel ashamed, as though we failed? What if we're embarrassed to own up to our slip-ups? What if we feel we're disappointing others by not improving or changing in ways they wish we would?

What happens? You choose:

- Option 1: You get sucked down into a shame spiral, justifying behavior that's all about beating yourself up. You feel like a loser, a has-been, like you're going to be stuck forever and nothing will ever be good again because you messed up. Yuck! Or:
- Option 2: You take a deep breath, and remind yourself that tomorrow is another day. You apologize to anyone you've hurt by your behavior, but you don't apologize for being imperfect. You own up to falling short but remind yourself progress is not linear—ups and downs are normal. You breathe in the confidence and clarity that you are doing your best. You remind yourself that you love yourself, just as you are.

You choose. I hope you choose option 2, because that's what I would say if you called to tell me you fell back into a bad habit, babe.

POP QUIZ

Stop swimming and learn to surf

Quick! To the Internet! Listen to the Superchunk song "Learned to Surf."

This is one of my favorite songs when I need a reminder to roll with the waves. Life hands us big waves that can feel like a high, but when the waves crash there is a dip that feels so low. Instead of paddling madly to stay on top, imagine you're on a boogie board and you're surfing those waves. Calm waters will return.

Special announcement: Progress is not linear

We tend to believe if we do everything "right" we will be rewarded with success, happiness, wealth, and health. Even after twenty years of life with chronic illness, I still fall into this trap. I'll wake up in intense pain and think:

"Why? I ate healthy yesterday, minimized alcohol and sweets, exercised, did my yoga, went to bed on time, and slept eight hours. Why the hell do I feel so crummy? This is so unfair!"

Yes, it is unfair. Even when we do everything right, things still go wrong. Outside factors may exist; the causes may be total mysteries.

As a girl who's always been a "why?" person, this is especially tricky territory for me. What's the cause? What should I have done differently? Tell me, dangit!

Sometimes we just don't know why. And when we're striving to make progress, this can be maddening.

This lesson has been hard-won for me—but worth it: *Progress is not linear.*

No matter how "right" you do everything—no matter how "perfect" your self-care routine—you may slide backwards. You may never know why.

The trick is to pick yourself back up again, reminding yourself that life is like a roller coaster, packed with twists and turns, ups and downs, that you may or may not see coming. A dip in your progress is not a personal failing; it's nature in action, and the sooner you learn to ride it out, the less of a bummer these dips will be.

The next time you have a dip—an off day, an unexpected bad test result, or a flare-up—remember to ride the roller coaster. It's headed back up again, I swear. Bonus points for going hands-free!

What are your "nuts and bolts"?

Years ago, my coach, Jackie Sloane, taught me how to identify my "sacred practices"—and it was powerful. (You can read her interview in lesson 9.) Riffing on that idea, I developed the "nuts and bolts" exercise to help us ChronicBabes learn how to prioritize healthy habits—the basics we need to make the most of each day.

Step 1: Go somewhere quiet; plan to spend twenty to thirty minutes. Bring pen and paper, your digital device, or whatever means of recording you prefer.

Step 2: Imagine your ideal day. How do you feel? What are you able to do? This might be difficult—your mind may not want you to think outside of what you're currently able to do—but give it a try.

Step 3: Think about the actions you personally took that made this ideal day possible. What steps did you take? What personal practices? What self-care did you do that was important in making this happen, or to you feeling this way?

Step 4: Write down all the things you did on your ideal day to make it great, dropping them into these four categories: physical, mental, spiritual, and spatial.

- *Physical* regards your body and its needs.
- *Mental* regards your mind and its needs.
- *Spiritual* is about your connections to the earth and to others, and to a higher power if that applies.
- *Spatial* is all about your surroundings.

Did you get wonderful sleep? Enjoy healthy meals? Make time for exercise? Put on makeup? Call a friend? Pray? Meditate?

Get creative here—write freely, without judgment if you can. You can have as many items as you like, and they don't have to be evenly spread across the four categories—but include at least one item in each category.

Step 5: Pause. Take a breath. Walk around your house for a minute. Drink some water.

Step 6: Review your notes. Identify which actions you took that played a big role in making your day ideal; would you consider doing these more often, even daily? This is the moment when you get to choose how to best help yourself.

Circle or put a star next to the items that seem most essential for you to feel good. In this step, we're narrowing things down.

Step 7: Take the essential items and write them out as short phrases. Imagine what it will be like to take these actions daily, consistently. They can make every day a little closer to your ideal.

For example, if you wrote "I ate a lunch with protein, lots of flavor, and variety, and I felt satiated without feeling overfull," condense that to something like "eat a variety of healthy, protein-packed meals."

If you wrote "I had fun doing a dance routine to favorite songs and then I felt so pumped I even had the energy to take a walk to the lake," condense that to "exercise in a fun way."

The resulting list comprises your "nuts and bolts"—the essential things you need to prioritize to have your best day.

- *Physical* items ensure your body is as supported as possible, and may include food, drink, medications, and exercise.
- *Mental* items ensure your mindset is productive and positive, and may include meditation, creativity, and free time.
- *Spiritual* items keep you grounded and guided, like prayer or connecting with others.
- *Spatial* items ensure your surroundings promote your success, like good sleep hygiene or using a lumbar support.

What makes for a great day for you is not the same as what makes a great day for me, so don't try to fit your needs into someone else's standards. This is *your* list.

Your goal: to come up with *your* list of the most essential daily self-care nuts and bolts. You won't always be able to do them all each day, but by creating a list, you're acknowledging your needs, and prioritizing self-care. By taking these actions daily, you're increasing your odds of having an ideal day—or, at least, the best day possible.

Once you've narrowed down your list to simple phrases, I recommend making it cute. I keep mine in a text document on my laptop, and I modify it periodically. I print it out, decorate it, and display it in my bathroom, on my nightstand, and over the kitchen sink. It's in my phone, too.

This list will help you learn essential habits, babe. Have fun with it—and don't forget to update it as your needs change.

HOMEWORK assignments

1) You've been a bad, bad girl!

List your bad habits, which may include things your mother or grandmother wouldn't be proud of. Don't worry yet about trying to change them—this is simply your moment to get honest with yourself.

2) Make one tiny change

Step one: Think of one tiny thing you can do to improve your health—the tiniest of things. Drink a glass of water with each meal. Walk up one flight of stairs at work. Park five parking spots farther away than usual. A *tiny* thing.

Step two: Do it. Every day. If it helps, mark your calendar with gold stars each day you complete the task.

Step three: If you miss a day, do *not* beat yourself up. Simply start again.

Rinse and repeat! It may seem simple, but this consistent repetition makes for a new habit.

PEP SQUAD

Pep Squad: An Interview with Kerri Morrone Sparling

Accountability and thoughtful rewards reinforce positive behavior

Kerri Morrone Sparling has been living with type 1 diabetes for over thirty years. She manages her diabetes and lives her life by the mantra "Diabetes doesn't define me, but it helps explain me."

Kerri is a passionate advocate for all things diabetes. She is the creator and author of *Six Until Me*, one of the first and most widely read diabetes patient blogs, reaching a global audience of patients, caregivers, and industry. Kerri speaks regularly at conferences and works full-time as a writer and consultant.

Kerri's first book, *Balancing Diabetes* (Spry Publishing), was released in 2014. She and her husband, Chris, live in Rhode Island with their two children.

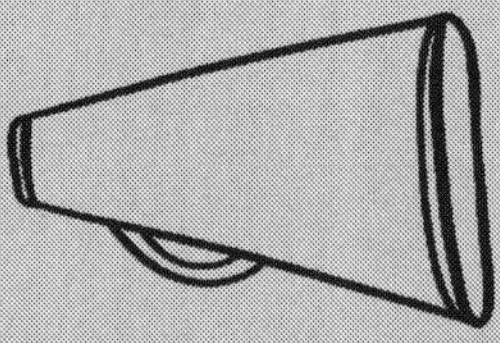

Connect with Kerri:
Website: SixUntilMe.com
Email: kerri@sixuntilme.com
Facebook: Facebook.com/sixuntilme
Twitter: @sixuntilme
Instagram: @sixuntilme

Jenni: It's always a pleasure to talk to you. You have been online since about the same time I started ChronicBabe.com.

Kerri: Yes, I started in May 2005, I think we started just a couple weeks away from each other.

Jenni: Yes, because I started in June, so we are like online health advocate sisters.

Kerri: I thought you were going to say dinosaurs, because in Internet years, that's like forever!

Jenni: It's true! Today we're going to talk about building good habits. It's one of the things I think is really challenging; I work on it all the time, and I'm always trying to relearn good habits.

Bad habits can really derail me even when I have the best of intentions. We already face negative situations all the time, and we try to do what we need to do to stay healthy, but sometimes bad habits really get in the way. What kind of bad habits have you tried to kick to the curb over the years?

Kerri: With type 1 diabetes, it's one of those chronic illnesses where every single day comes with a laundry list of things you need to do to keep tabs on your health. So an average day for me includes testing my blood sugar somewhere between seven to ten times, doing either insulin injections or using my pump treatments for insulin, calculating food, keeping note of what my blood sugar is on my continuous glucose monitor.

There's always something to worry about, something to look at. It's not like I think about it in the morning and again when I go to bed; this is an all-day party. So, super fun and you've seen it in action! We're at conferences together and you're like, "Again? We're doing this again?"

Jenni: Yup! "What's that beeping sound? Oh, it's Kerri!"

Kerri: And it's always me!

Jenni: She's a robot!

Kerri: And when you're trying to keep tabs on a million different things every single day, burnout is almost inevitable, and you have to kind of allow yourself to have a little burnout and gosh—I've gone days without testing my blood sugar throughout the day and I'll just test in the morning or maybe test at night and just try to keep tabs. I'll go use my insulin without calculating the carbs, or I think one of the worst things I do is that I'll put off doctors' appointments because I don't want to go—talk about negative reinforcement—sometimes I don't want the doctor to tell me, "Hey, your A1C has gone up" or, "Oh I see you're only testing four times a day," so I'll avoid them.

Jenni: I'm a stress eater, and I've been working on losing weight, and it's so challenging. Every time I go to the doctor, I know when he weighs me, I know what he is going to say and it just kills me.

Kerri: You're right, though, you know what you weigh, you don't need the doctor to tell you. It's like you go into that appointment knowing, *Oh, boy.* I do the same thing with the diabetes stuff: *Told you.*

> *"**I bounce out of [burnout] faster knowing I'm not alone,** seeing proof of that in these blogs and communities online and having that community reinforcement of, 'Okay, pick yourself up, keep on going.'"*
>
> —Kerri

Jenni: Burnout is so hard—I don't have to do the testing and tracking you do, but I have a lot of things to do throughout the day to maintain a good baseline of health: flexibility by stretching a lot, drinking a lot of water, making sure I exercise every day, meditating—all that stuff.

You know, I will totally fall out of that habit. I love to meditate but I am not the best about doing that every day because I often feel strapped for time and it seems like the kind of thing, "Do I really need to?" which is so silly, but: "Do I really have ten minutes to devote to this?" and I'll be like, "Yeah, you do."

Kerri: Right, because later on in the day you find yourself devoting twenty minutes to checking some ex-boyfriend's Facebook profile, and it's like "wait a minute, what are you doing?"

Jenni: Exactly!

Kerri: Not that I've ever done that...

Jenni: No, no, we've never done that. Well, it's good to know I'm not alone. I think all of us have bad habits we have to work on continually.

What kind of good habits have you have developed over the years to manage your health issues?

Kerri: I've been diabetic since just before I started second grade—basically, I can't remember life without it. It's been forever.

Since I've started immersing myself in online health communities, I feel like connecting with other people who have diabetes, instead of trying to be an isolationist about it, has been the best habit I've formed for myself. We were talking about those moments of burnout. I bounce out of them faster knowing I'm not alone, seeing proof of that in these blogs and communities online and having that community reinforcement of "Okay, pick yourself up, keep on going." So, this has to be good habit number one for me.

Jenni: Yeah, that sounds like a great one.

Kerri: And I think it's something a lot of ChronicBabes can tap into. You can't do this by yourself, and there's this huge emotional component to living with a physical chronic illness, and you have to do what you need to survive.

That leads into good habit number two. I think being a part of these communities and putting my health information out there, and letting other people see what I'm doing, keeps me accountable. I can admit the bad stuff, we're talking about bad habits right now, but something about putting it out there almost makes me examine myself emotionally and physically and make a change. I've already said that this is my problem, admitting it is the first step, but doing something about it—I'm hoping—is the second.

Jenni: That makes a lot of sense. Accountability is so huge; the weight-loss thing is a big goal for me. My [husband] and I have been texting each other every morning with our weigh-ins, which sometimes I am mortified to tell him, except that it's great because we have accountability to each other and we're both aware of it.

We're not freaking out about each other if we don't reach our goal each week, but I know he is going to keep me in check. Even just the simple task of texting him "I gained a pound" reminds me that somebody is keeping an eye on me, not in a judgmental way, but in a supportive way.

Kerri: But I'm also sure when you text him and say, "I lost two pounds," the celebratory moment is even more sweet because you have somebody to share it with.

Jenni: There is a lot of overtexting on those days. It's great, and I know he feels the same way. I have the same kind of thing with a lot of ChronicBabes online too and other friends of mine. Checking in, being honest about what's going on. I think it's hard to be honest sometimes.

Kerri: It's amazing that you and I are living with different chronic illnesses and we're not even talking about the pills you take or the pills I take—we're talking about emotional support, we're talking about a really emotional side to a physical thing. It's crazy how that really spans across all different health conditions.

Jenni: Do you have any other habits that are not strictly related to diabetes, but [that] kind of keep you healthy in general, or keep your sense of humor going, or keep you from getting bored?

Kerri: Well, diabetes being a disease that so revolves around food and lifestyle and—well, you've seen it, hardware—it's kind of like an all-day thing. Everyone says, if you want to be healthy, you have to eat right, exercise, and take good care of yourself. That is really the core of what living with type 1 diabetes is all about, aside from taking insulin.

My husband is very tuned into his own physical fitness and is dedicated to a workout, so being with someone like that, it is very easy to make exercise a part of my life. You almost get swept up in it, like, "Okay, fine, I'll go be healthy too, you jerk."

Then on the eating front, diabetes fuels me to be a healthier eater because if I eat crap, then my blood sugars reflect that and my weight reflects that, so I try to eat as healthy as I can. We have a daughter and there is something about wanting to be a good example for her.

So, we don't sit down in the morning and have chocolate cake for breakfast. We want her to see her parents taking care of their bodies, and I want her to pick up on that. Even though she's so young, I know that she does. She's the only kid I know who eats avocado.

Jenni: You're right—that ingrains a good habit right from the beginning. Some of us didn't have that, and then it takes so long to build that new habit into place, if you've had that long history of not doing it.

*"I try not to constantly reward myself because—this is going to sound super cheesy—**the reward of this work is to have good health in the first place.** It's hard to quantify if nothing's changed."*

—Kerri

Kerri: The kid's had more than her fair share of donuts, but she understands the difference: that's a treat, and now here's the regular food.

Jenni: I do think about that when I'm around my nieces—or my best friend has sons, and I really consider them like my nephews—when I'm around them, I do watch everything I do, because they're just like little sponges; they absorb every nuance.

Kerri: Every donut!

Jenni: Every donut, exactly! So I want to be a really good role model to them. And again, a lot of what we are talking about is accountability.

Kerri: And support. Because not all accountability, in my opinion, should be negative. Like, "Oh you didn't lose the weight." Or, "No, you didn't check your blood sugar." It's more like, "Hey, you did!" And that—even if it's a virtual pat on the back—makes it easier to do it again.

I hate to sound like I'm using social media as a total crutch, but I think one of the biggest things for me is using my website and Twitter tools and that sort of thing—to say that I have a goal and to hold me to keeping that goal. Again, it comes back to that accountability, and it's documented.

Before I wanted to have a baby, it was a two-year planning process—to get my diabetes under control, to get my life under control in a non-health-related sort of way. But part of preparing my body for pregnancy was logging blood sugars. We talked before about how many things I do in the course of a day to keep track of my diabetes. Writing down my blood sugar in a book and keeping track of it was like, the *last* thing I gave a shit about. But I had to make it a priority, right?

I used a spreadsheet, but then I would put that spreadsheet on my blog or on some kind of public place where someone would see it and say, "Oh girl, you did not fill that out. You don't even use it!" I wasn't talking about my own health, but working toward my future child's health, so there was a goal at stake. And having a goal like that, and having people watching me try to achieve that goal, inspired me to really do it.

"You might be really focused on your health, and thinking about 'Oh, my diabetes is making me do this or that,' but it's not who you are. ***You are way more than your disease."***

—Kerri

Jenni: Wow. That's pretty brave. I think a lot of people would be pretty shy about putting themselves out so publicly, in that way. You do it a lot, which I have a lot of respect for.

Kerri: But I mean, if you're looking at blood sugars, those are quick snapshots of a moment. So I don't feel defined by those, you know?

Jenni: Yeah, that makes sense. So what do you think is the equivalent, then, for people who maybe don't have a big online audience? I'm trying to think about how I might do something like that in a more private way. I guess maybe if I were keeping track of good habits—like, in this chapter, a worksheet I have is a "You're a Good Habit Goddess," a checklist that people can print out.

I'm really excited about these, and I've been using mine a lot, very consistently. Publicly, everyone can hold me accountable. I keep a list of the good habits I want to maintain every day, and I keep that thing in my pocket, and every time I achieve one I check it off. It feels really good to do that, even if it's just for myself.

Kerri: There's a power in doing it for yourself, too. It's not like everything has to be public and this big, like, social media mess. Sometimes it's as simple as—honestly, buying a pack of those stickers teachers have, and sticking one on the calendar every time you exercise. Which I definitely did after I had the kid, when I was like, *Holy moly, I definitely need to get to the gym*. You know what I mean? And no one saw that calendar.

Jenni: What did your stickers look like?

Kerri: They were the little gold stars that you would get on a spelling test. I wanted to keep it as second-grade as possible, because when I looked at the calendar, and it looked like a constellation, I felt like I was empowered, just by that visual. Something about that was the positive reinforcement.

I'm so motivated by hope, not by negativity and fear, so when someone's like, "Oh well, once you have a baby, it changes your body forever," it's like, "Oh hell no, we're gonna go back!" You know what I mean?

Jenni: Right.

Kerri: And my gold stars prove I'm doing that. The same goes for my diabetes. If people say, "You can't do this, you can't do that," it's like, "Oh yeah, well, I can. Watch me. See those stars?"

Jenni: I think it's a good idea for [anybody] to think about: *What do I need to do every day to maintain my health?* And that's why I have the worksheet, so people can go through and make that list for themselves, and think really carefully about all the things they want to achieve throughout the day.

It can sometimes feel overwhelming. Except when you start looking at [the tasks] and checking them off, it's like, *Oh, well, that was a small thing; I was able to do that.* I have really simple stuff on my list like "wash my face before I go to bed." It sounds so junior high, but I can be really lazy about it—I'm tired at the end of the day, and I fall into bed and I don't do it. Honestly, how long does it take to wash my face? A minute. So it's like, *Let's get that going again.* Especially because I'm not twenty-five anymore, I gotta take good care of my face.

Kerri: And you have a good face, so you don't want to wake up in the morning and be all, "Hey, that's yesterday's face! I want today's face."

You're talking about putting simple things on there. My husband and I do that all the time because we both work for ourselves, so the to-do list for an average day can be pretty significant; I always find myself sneaking in to find his paper to-do list and adding things like "hug your wife." You know? Because that's something that takes two seconds to do, it's really simple, you can cross it off afterwards, and it makes you feel good. It's a nice thing on your list instead of a daunting item.

Jenni: Totally. Instead of this huge, monumental goal that you have every day. Breaking it up and having nice little chunks and stuff that's not even health-related. You want those positive habits. One of the things I have on my list is "put on a cute outfit." Because, like you, I work for myself, and because I'm often working from home, it's really easy to just sit around in old pajamas.

Kerri: They're never new pajamas, either. They're always old. What is that?

Jenni: I need some kind of service where people deliver new, cute pajamas to me on a weekly basis.

When you're building those good habits, do you have ways to reward yourself, besides the gold stars or the positive reinforcement? Like verbally, from friends, online...do you have other ways you reinforce those good habits?

Kerri: This might sound totally weird, but I know the day I was diagnosed with diabetes, so we call it my dia-versary. And people in the

> **Pajama delivery service?**
> Anybody reading or listening, if you know about a service that delivers cute PJs, let me know. Otherwise, I'm starting my own!

diabetes community kind of celebrate their dia-versary. I know, that sounds totally strange, right? I realize how counterintuitive it is to do this, but every dia-versary my family and I—now my husband and I—we get a giant cake, and it says something about diabetes: "Screw you, diabetes!"

And then we eat that cake. That is what we do. That's the reward for another year of good health. And it sounds crazy and so weird but there's something really really awesome, you know, about slicing in with a giant knife to a cake that says "Screw you, type 1 diabetes!"

Jenni: That's so funny. I love it. I think maybe we all need to take a moment and think about some kind of good, positive reinforcement, like a congratulatory "Screw you!" cake.

Kerri: It's kind of instinctual for people to want to reward themselves with food, and that's not a habit I want to make—because that's a disaster for someone like me. Sometimes I will buy a new camera lens or something as a reward for reaching a goal that I've set for myself.

I try not to constantly reward myself because—this is going to sound super cheesy—the reward of this work is to have good health in the first place. It's hard to kind of quantify if nothing's changed. "Here's another day, and nothing's changed." How do you really wrap your head around that, you know?

Jenni: Yeah, that makes a lot of sense. I understand it's a little cheesy to say the reward is good health, except it is a super-awesome reward. I've gone through months where I haven't been able to do much of anything because my health is so crummy, so to feel good and be able to be active and make creative things and help people, get out there, travel...all those things are awesome. And if I can do that, that is a great reward for taking care of myself.

Any last thoughts about good habits?

Kerri: You might be really focused on your health, and thinking about "Oh, my diabetes is making me do this," or "I have to do this and this and this," but it's not who you are. And that's such an important thing to remember. You have a condition, but it's not the core of who you are. Even on the days when it feels the crummiest and like it totally is. It still *isn't*, and you are way more than your disease. Remembering that helps put everything else into perspective.

This interview has been shortened and edited to fit this book. To read the full transcript or listen to the full recordings of this and all the Pep Squad interviews, head to ChronicBabe101.com.

Lesson 3

it's time to turn around negative thinking

Babe, you have enough forces working against you—you can't afford to add negative thought patterns to the mix. This lesson will teach you how to identify negative thoughts, and work with them to either minimize or remove them...and to make space for more positive thoughts.

The four most common negative behaviors in ChronicBabes

Over the years, I've identified some of the top negative behaviors among the women in our community. It's likely at least one of these will be familiar to you.

Isolation

Feelings of isolation wear you down. I mentioned in lesson 2 that isolation is also bad for physical health—it's associated with mortality rates similar to smoking and obesity.

If you're living with chronic pain, illness, or disability, you already feel different; isolation from others can reinforce that feeling.

When you're isolated, it feels like you have to do everything by yourself...and that's difficult and depressing.

Living in isolation means you miss reminders that you're not the only person dealing with your issue. Conversely, when you're connected to others, you gain a valuable sense of perspective—there's a whole world of people dealing with the same challenges.

Isolation can make you focus more on what's wrong instead of being distracted by fun, humor, and love.

Begin to release isolation:

If you're reading this and realizing you're feeling isolated, pledge to confide in someone today, preferably someone you know and trust.

Tell them as much or as little as you're comfortable with; the key is to *start* the conversation about the challenge of isolation.

Work on getting past thinking of yourself as "other than." You're pretty special, but not so special that you're the only person facing these challenges. There's a world of folks online with whom you can commiserate and develop new ideas.

Make friends with some of those folks online. Join a support forum or Facebook group and participate in conversations. If you want to remain anonymous, create an alter ego.

You'll also need to learn to release the misconception that everyone else is "normal" and you're somehow an oddball.

While you're at it, practice ignoring the temptation to feel like healthier people are the enemy. Even someone who's in "perfect" health has challenges you may not be able to see or understand.

Black-and-white thinking

Are you prone to thinking in extremes? That can be self-destructive. When you can't see degrees of success, everything looks like failure. It's time to accept a variety of positive outcomes.

Black-and-white thinking wears you down. When you accept a limitation as an absolute, you're not open to other possibilities or workarounds, so you feel you have no options. You may begin to see anything less than your best-case scenario as a failure.

If you have a narrow view of things, you may miss out on opportunities because they won't be "perfect" or "as they were before." (For some of us, "before" wasn't all that great anyway. But it was familiar, and we miss the comfort of familiarity.)

Begin to release black-and-white thinking:

Embrace compromise. To do so requires you to release resentment about things not being the way they once were, or the way you hoped. (Lesson 1 on acceptance is a great primer for this work.)

You'll need to stop holding up your "old" life as a model of perfection. When we look back in fondness, we may gloss over issues we don't want to dwell on. There is *no way* your life before chronic illness was perfect.

Get acquainted with others who have embraced compromise in their own lives, if you want to see examples of this practice in action. Online forums and support groups are perfect for this.

Get creative: Can you think of some compromises? Even one? Practicing this can flex some great muscles in your brain—and prepare you for bigger compromises to come.

When faced with a cruddy situation, resist the urge to think, "Well, this is a disaster! Everything is ruined!" Instead: Take a deep breath. Get pen and paper. Make a list of possible degrees of success: your perfect scenario; various outcomes that could be very good, good, or acceptable; and the worst-case scenario. Then ask yourself: Can you get okay with one of the options in the middle of the spectrum? Because babe, you can stay mad and grumpy, or you can make a choice to live in the in-between and have some peace.

Perfectionism

I hate to burst your bubble, but the idea of "perfect" is false. When you expect your progress to be linear—always upward—you set yourself up for failure. When you expect yourself to solve a complicated challenge on the first try, you set yourself up for failure.

Beating yourself up for nonlinear progress and other forms of imperfection wears you down. If you're always trying to attain the unattainable, you aren't able to celebrate any successes, even small ones (which are often just as important as the big ones).

When your standards for your body and health are the "perfect" visions we see in contemporary marketing and media, odds are good you'll stop loving yourself—and start hating yourself (and your body).

Perfectionism can lead to feeling that every tiny frustration is a major setback, instead of letting little mistakes or errors roll off your back.

Who said you must be perfect, anyway?

Begin to release perfectionism:

You wouldn't beat up your niece or your best friend for being imperfect, right? Don't hold yourself to the same impossible standard.

Your time is precious. Even if you *could* be perfect, you don't have time for that—perfectionism is not *living*.

Limit exposure to people who are critical of your imperfections. This means creating stronger boundaries with the people in your life...more on that in lesson 4.

Accept that all progress is nonlinear: Life is like riding the waves in an ocean, not like climbing a tall hill. Progress ebbs and flows, and if you can learn to surf those waves, you'll feel calmer even in rough seas.

Daily affirmations are a wonderful antidote to perfectionism. They may feel cheesy to you, but repeating something like "I am enough" to yourself every morning as you wash your face can become a powerful habit. Search on Pinterest for pretty (perhaps irreverent) affirmations that fit your unique style.

To reinforce the value of imperfect success, create your own success journal. Create a space to write every day, for a couple of minutes at least, about your successes. No feat is too small to celebrate! You don't have to show this to anyone—but refer back to it whenever you need to feel proud of yourself.

Deciding on a negative outcome in advance

Negative forecasting (or catastrophizing) is an understandable behavior in someone who keeps facing negative surprises. For years after I first got sick, I was a champion catastrophizer—I could spin a tale of disaster for every possible outcome. Why not? I'd already had so many negative outcomes that "shouldn't" have happened to me.

But that's a waste of energy, and it's fiction. Deciding on a negative outcome in advance wears you down in many ways. You're defeated before you even begin. You won't be open to positive outcomes; you'll just look for the negative, which means you won't see the whole picture.

Deciding on a negative outcome means you make it nearly impossible to plan for the future. For anyone, it can be scary to try to plan for the future—but add catastrophizing to the mix, and wow—there's no way to get excited about anything.

Begin to release imaginary negative outcomes:

If you find yourself catastrophizing, talk about your negative feelings with someone you can trust, who might be able to offer an alternate perspective. This might be a friend, family member, or even a therapist.

Trust in that person is important, because you're going to ask them to share an alternate view—and you need to know they're not blowing smoke.

Once you start talking about your catastrophic thinking with others, begin making a short list of possible positive outcomes to remind yourself there is an array of possibilities. They may seem highly unlikely right now, but with practice, you'll start to believe they're possible.

Practice positive visualization. When I want to achieve something a great deal, I sometimes meditate on it, visualizing the outcome I desire. I give it details and depth, and picture it as clearly as I can. I may never get everything I visualize, but allowing my mind to mull over potential good outcomes makes me more open to the possibilities.

Tapes (or MP3s?): Record over them

As you begin to work on overcoming negative thought patterns, you may realize the same negative messages play in your head, over and over. I used to call these "tapes"—back when people used cassette tapes. Now they would be MP3s, or a playlist, but let's call them tapes for short, okay?

These tapes replay on a loop in our mind. They may be based on an experience you had as a child, or perhaps something that happened to you in the early stages of becoming ill.

Have you lost your sense of humor?
Without humor, life is so *blah*. No one can blame you if chronic pain or illness has broken your giggle box, but you can do something about that. Google "Lauren Rowe YouTube" and learn from a master of ChronicBabe humor.

A few of my tapes: "You're not a good enough person" and "You're a burden" and "People are talking about you behind your back." Ugh! Those tapes are the worst.

I learned to record some new tapes I try to play whenever I catch myself playing the old ones. My new tapes include: "You deserve to have a beautiful life" and "You're effing awesome!" and "Your work matters."

Your challenge: Record some new tapes. If you taped over cassettes, hints of the old recordings would sometimes still be audible. It's the same with mental tapes: The old tape might never go away completely, but you can make a new one and turn up its volume.

Memorize your new tapes and sing them loud inside your head. Sing it, girl!

Guilt is for chumps

I say that with love, because I get it—sometimes, I feel guilty about some things. It's an effort to shrug off that guilt.

Here's what Dave Grohl (drummer for Nirvana, lead singer and guitarist for Foo Fighters) has to say about guilt: "Guilt is cancer. Guilt will confine you, torture you, destroy you as an artist. It's a black wall. It's a thief."

I couldn't agree more. Guilt will eat you alive, especially because so many of the things we feel guilty about—not being able to work as much or at all, not being able to travel as much or at all, needing help with all kinds of stuff, canceling plans at the last minute—those things are often completely out of our control. And yet we often feel like crap about them.

"No work or love will flourish out of guilt, fear, or hollowness of heart, just as no valid plans for the future can be made by those who have no capacity for living now." This quote is from Alan Watts, a historian and philosopher who helped bring Eastern philosophy to the West. It resonates.

How do we begin to shed guilt? I believe what Watts says goes to the heart of the matter. When we can stay present in this moment, it's hard to feel guilt. It's when we look backwards at what has already happened and feel regret—or we look forward with some sense of anxiety about what is to come—that we start to feel guilty.

When I look closely at guilt, I try to take the approach that Arthur Ashe spoke about: "Start where you are, use what you have, do what you can." (I talk more about this in lesson 2.) That's really all anyone can ask of us. It can be easy to respond, "Oh, that's too simplistic. Guilt is much more complicated than that." Sure, it is, but when we start to look at guilt and how to shed it, I think we must return to the basics.

Here are two exercises to try:

Grounding meditation to ease guilt

Get comfortable. Close your eyes. Breathe. Plant your feet on the ground, or feel the cushion underneath your tushy. Imagine you're a big, old tree with deep roots. Feel yourself being rooted. Feel the wind in your leaves. Feel the soil beneath you. Breathe. Feel the sunshine on your trunk. Feel a cool breeze. Feel how deep your roots reach. Breathe.

Stay here. It's that simple—if you can spend five to twenty minutes doing a grounding meditation a few times a week, you will begin to feel more rooted in the *now*, instead of dwelling in the guilt-inducing past.

Identify the cause to root out guilt

Try this simple exercise to weed through your thoughts and identify a source of guilt, so you can release it and make room for joy. Here's how I like to start:

Grab a piece of paper and write down the thing you're feeling guilty about. Example: I think I said something that offended my friend in an email exchange, because now she's not responding and it's been two days.

Now, get logical: Ask yourself if this is the only conclusion, or if there might be another reason. Example: She could be really swamped because it's a busy time of year for her. Write out other possible scenarios; how many can you come up with? (If you're going to use your imagination to cook up some guilt, might as well put that imagination to good use instead, yes?)

Approach the person about whom you're feeling guilty. Spell out your perception, and ask a question that helps you touch base with reality. Example: *Dear friend, I think I might have said something that offended you in my last email, and if I did, I apologize. I also recognize there are other reasons you might not be emailing me back. When you have a chance, let me know you're okay or if I can do anything. Thanks! Love, Me.*

Best-case scenario: You've started a conversation. Now you can get real about what's going on. Maybe she'll reply: *Dear Jenni, I am swamped, my friend, taking two days to return emails—I haven't even spoken to my folks in two weeks. When I resurface I'll text you so we can plan a coffee date. Love, your friend.*

This happened to me a few months ago. You can see that while I work to banish guilt, it's an ongoing process. Guilt often shows up when we take things too personally, or take on too much responsibility. Keep practicing this exercise to ground yourself in reality and stay connected with those you love in a healthy way—and make room for joyous emotions!

Apathy is just so, you know, meh

Apathy is one of those negative emotions that sneaks up on you slowly. When I experience a moment of apathy, it is often a side effect of other feelings:

- I'm depressed because things are hard, and I feel too worn down to do anything.
- I'm angry and have been without results for so long that I stop caring.
- I'm tired, or hungry, or disappointed in someone or some loss.

Can you see how many other negative emotions can turn us into apathetic creatures?

I implore you NOT to give in to apathy. I have a few things you can try.

Start by recognizing apathy for what it is. It is the lack of emotion—and it is most likely temporary. If you can recognize this aloud, you've already taken some of the wind out of its sails.

Make some small changes. Apathy is often a side effect of other negative emotions, so it's good to mix things up in your day-to-day in the same way you would if tackling those other emotions. This includes:

- Getting more sleep
- Eating healthier
- Drinking more water
- Reading something uplifting
- Spending time with someone positive
- Looking at art or listening to music
- Getting outside
- Washing your face or taking a bath

Once you start to jostle yourself a little, it's easier to take the next step: volunteer, even if it's just ten minutes a week. Maybe you answer someone's question on a forum with helpful advice, or call your sister to sing your niece a song each day after school. Make a commitment to volunteer in a small way and stick with it. Getting outside yourself is a great way to smash apathy.

Being a caregiver is a demanding—but rewarding—role

Tony's wife lives with migraine disease, including migraine and cluster headaches. She was diagnosed right after they married, and they coparent Tony's twelve-year-old daughter. Tony says he wishes there were more tools for caregivers, as it's extremely challenging—but worth the effort.

It's been a roller-coaster ride. She puts on a fantastic face. If you didn't know her and saw her out in public, you would have no idea the amount she suffers. I'm one of the few people in her life with whom she will break down her walls, and I've seen the worst of the worst.

My wife has been ill since birth. She was born with clubfeet; she's had multiple physical ailments throughout her life that she's been able to handle. But this is definitely something that has knocked her down.

My daughter is very understanding, and when my wife is having a bad day, we try to find something else to do. But sometimes, you walk on eggshells because we don't want to cause any additional things she has to deal with when she's in a really bad cycle.

I hate to say "caregiver." I know that's what I am, but it's [the] thing she feared the most, is that out of all of this, I have become that person.

I rarely ever get rattled. But when I do, it tends to manifest in a way that isn't always positive. [Those times are] few and far between—it's something of a normal relationship, but it's also kind of magnified by the fact that she suffers from debilitating headaches.

It's probably one of the more demanding roles you could possibly have because it's something you don't anticipate. It's demanding, but at the same time, you're helping someone try to work through their struggles, so when you do see that person having a more positive day, there's a sense of accomplishment.

> *I've struggled with how to reach out to other people. I know there are support groups out there, but I think if it's placed into a book, it's something people can access a little bit easier because it's tangible. It's not as easy to go find a support group and feel like a part of something, where with a book, you get to read people's stories and their trials and tribulations in the role as a caregiver. And I think in that aspect you can kind of gain some sense of "Hey, I'm not alone in this."*

How to face a fear of success

People really have this?

I know! For many of us, this seems like a ridiculous fear. I mean, don't we *want* to be successful in our efforts and endeavors? I sure do.

Mostly. Sometimes I'm freaked out by success, and it can put me on pause. Let's talk about some examples:

I'm a little bit afraid of how my life will change once this book comes out. What if tons of people buy it? And then I have to field tons of questions I'm not sure I can answer? What if it's so tiring to handle the post-launch book success that it takes me away from other things? What if it causes an increase in my symptoms?

These fears can sometimes cause me to procrastinate on this book, pushing it aside for something that's more of a known entity.

But that's self-sabotage, in the same way that fear of negative outcomes can be. If I let those fears dictate my behavior, I'll never finish this project. (Good news: If you're reading it, I finished! Woohoo!)

Who knows if any of that will really happen? Who's to say I can't cope if it does? After all, I've dealt with a lot in my life and I've got some mad skillz.

I'm not going to let fears of success dictate my behavior. As each one pops up, I try to look at it critically, step back, and observe. It helps me see what's rational as opposed to what's emotional, and then I can tackle the rational concerns with facts and plans and support.

That's one example. Here's another I think many in our community have encountered, in either their own life or that of someone they know:

What if I get well?

Let that one marinate for a minute.

What if I get well? What if I suddenly find a drug, an exercise and meditation combo, a dietary change, or a new doc, or scientists develop a new cure for fibromyalgia? What if I get well? Even mostly well?

My life would change significantly. I would have to suck it up and work longer days again, and I would have no excuses like "fibro fog" for when I forget things. I would also lose the very thing that drives my whole ChronicBabe project, which has also become part of my identity. I mean, I am *The ChronicBabe.* What if the *chronic* part were removed from that identity? Would I still want to do this work? Who would I be? I've been sick almost half my life—who am I if I'm *not* sick? And would I have to go back to working full-time hours?

Ugh, can you hear my mental gears spinning?

If I let this fear control my actions, I would not take positive action regarding my health. If I let myself be afraid of success, I would not take the self-care actions I need to do to maintain my baseline. I would stop seeking new treatment modalities that could bring me relief.

And let's be real: this work is vital to me. Essential. I don't think I could stop doing it if I wanted to. Even if I became perfectly healthy, this community is my second family—I would never give it up.

When these fears creep in, I have to step back and observe, to suss out what's reasonable and what's fanciful. The fanciful stuff—the ideas that are pure speculation—I can push aside. The reasonable questions I can address with facts: Yes, I would still think of myself as *The ChronicBabe.* No, I would never abandon this community. And yes, I could handle longer work hours.

If you haven't had fears of success yet, consider this: The same practice I'm using here can be applied to *any* work we do on our fears.

POP QUIZ

What's your talisman?

A talisman is an object you hold or wear that embodies a belief you hold dear. Some people also believe talismans hold good luck or fortune; that's not my jam, but to each her own.

I encourage you to find or make a talisman that represents your ChronicBabe-ness. Over the years, I've worn a locket, bracelet, and other adornments to remind myself I can kick ass even if I'm a sick chick. It can be anything you like—as long as you can wear it consistently.

How to talk to your inner naysayer

As you work on changes of any kind, your inner naysayer may show up to talk smack and get you down. Nope! Not happening! #ShutUpNaysayer! Here are some things you can say back to that no-good-lying-jerkface-naysayer:

- I've *totally* got this.
- Rock-star behavior is my default.
- I am good enough.
- Do, or do not. There is no try. (Thanks, Yoda!)
- I'm able to handle anything life throws my way.
- There's nothing wrong with me.
- There's always a simpler option.
- I've dealt with harder things and come out shining.
- Shut up, naysayer lady.
- Asking for help is a sign of strength and collaboration, not weakness.
- I'm not broken.
- The world holds mystery, hilarity, and joy for me.
- I'm not missing out; I'm giving myself permission to take a break.
- There is always another option to try if this one doesn't work.
- Much dumber people make it through life okay, so *I* certainly can.
- If I falter, there will be people to pick me up.
- Self-doubt is not indicative of a bigger problem. It's a hangover from past experiences.
- I am worthy of love, success, and peace.
- I have one job right now: to be kind to myself.
- I'm surrounded by people who believe in me.
- I'm not scared. Even if I am scared, that's not weakness—that's humanity, and that's okay.

You might need professional help: Identifying depression

This lesson is all about negative behaviors, so I need to mention that some of these behaviors can come from—or be indicative of—depression.

If you're feeling intense apathy, or having thoughts of self-harm, or struggling to manage the basic tasks of life each day (like bathing, eating, brushing your teeth), seek professional help.

Depression is very common in the chronic illness community. It can develop because you get sick, or if you're like me and are already prone to it, it can get much worse when you get sick. Some medications can also exacerbate depression and its effects, particularly thoughts of self-harm. And it's no joke.

If you have even a small suspicion you could be depressed, talk to your health care providers about a consult. Addressing depression can make tackling the work in this book much more doable.

Sometimes you just need to shut up

I say this with love: *Shut up.*

If you find yourself telling the same story in your head, over and over, about how much you're suffering because you're sick...shut up. Playing that tape on repeat all day is self-destructive. Find yourself a joyful distraction, like listening to music or playing with your friend's kids.

If you're telling the same stories about suffering, over and over, to your support team, you may be alienating them...so shut up. Your story matters—I'm not saying you should never tell it—but are you repeating yourself? If it's the sole focus of every communication, it eats away at your joy and peace—and the joy and peace of others.

If you're talking to a stranger who asks how you are, and you find yourself telling your long tale of diagnosis or suffering...shut up. You don't need to spend your precious energy on telling this tale again, and you don't have to have a sad interaction. You can choose to stay kind and pleasant...and have a break from the difficulty.

Anger and fear are closely tied together

Anger hurts. *Physically* hurts. Anger does all kinds of bad stuff to our minds and bodies: It releases chemicals that give us a rush, but then make us crash. It causes us to tense up, ready to leap, and again...crash. Anger causes pain—in our hearts and minds, too.

I used to get angry all the time. Throw things, break things, scream obscenities at people. I was the one driving home on the freeway after a long day at work, honking at everyone and hollering at folks who weren't going fast enough.

Hard to believe, right? It was a terrible way to exist. But I was raised to be angry, at just about everyone and everything. It's taken years of therapy and hard work to get cool. I still work at it every day.

One thing I've learned: Anger and fear are like twin little girls, holding hands, at the end of a long hotel hallway. They're not exactly the same, but they're awfully close. The next time you're really angry, try to go somewhere quiet and write down how you feel. I bet you'll see some things:

- That your anger is about something scary, like an emotion, a situation that's out of your control, or a person who isn't behaving as you wish
- That you're also afraid of how angry you are, that the anger is a rush you don't want to feel and you don't know how to stop it...which is scary
- That your anger often morphs into other emotions like rage, fear, or sadness

You are not alone in feeling these things. This is normal, and seeing it at face value is the first step toward dousing anger's fire. The next time you're angry, try to write about it. Examine the other emotions and thoughts at the root of your anger. If you can see them, you can start to address them...and reduce your anger.

Looking closely at these things can feel scary. Don't be afraid. They're just thoughts; they can't actually hurt you. Keep that in mind and keep writing.

Self-loathing drives bad decision-making

A driver behind our choice to *not* make healthy changes? Self-loathing.

On nights when I skip taking off my makeup before going to bed, it's mostly because I'm feeling lazy...but I also think it stems from not loving myself enough in that moment.

I'm not saying that to beat myself up, but to get real about my history and how it shapes my behavior today. By getting real, I'm able to see things more clearly and make changes.

My upbringing included a lot of negative influences on my self-image. Taking care of myself was never the top priority; my priority was always taking care of others.

As a result, I've got a long habit of neglecting some basic self-care, like washing my face before bed, or moisturizing. Once, I told a friend I had splurged on self-care time to moisturize, and she was *appalled*—she couldn't imagine an existence that didn't assume regular moisturizing. I was *mortified*.

One way to tackle self-loathing is to amp up our self-love. Grab an empty jar, a bunch of slips of paper, and a favorite pen or marker. Each morning, write down three things you love about yourself. They could be anything that comes to mind. Place them in the jar.

It will feel weird and forced. But it gets easier day by day. And by all means, put extra slips of paper in there throughout the day if you feel like it.

At the end of the week, dump out the jar and read through them all. Rejoice in all the ways you love yourself! Then stuff them all back in the jar and start again. Or hang them up around your bathroom mirror.

By practicing these tiny self-love acts each day, we build a habit that's physical, practical, and replicable. And we ingrain pathways in our brain that teach us to love ourselves.

POP QUIZ

Avoid comparison-itis

Do you spend time online? I know you do, girl! You've likely experienced comparison-itis because of it.

The images we see online—the carefully crafted profiles on Instagram, Snapchat, and Facebook—are mere slices of people's lives. Don't be fooled into comparing your life to theirs. It's a waste of your precious time.

When you see someone looking awesome, take a moment and express gratitude for something real in *your* life: a cuddly pet, a terrific friend, a unique skill. This is the way to combat comparison-itis. (Well, that and intermittent social media breaks, babe!)

Get out of your own head

Do you have perspective on your situation? Or are you too close to it?

One way to begin cultivating some perspective is to get out of our own head. I often do this by practicing "observing." This is an idea I tap into all the time; it harnesses skills I use as a journalist, which I started practicing almost thirty years ago, so I've had a lot of practice. I think you can learn it, too.

When our mind spins out of control about our situation, it's good to get a little disconnected. I'm not talking about disassociating—where you check out of the experience—but rather, disconnecting by taking a light step back. Some people like to imagine they are floating above and watching the scene play out. Others like to mentally picture themselves as a reporter, notebook in hand.

Disconnecting a little helps us to become more objective and gain perspective. It's hardest to be objective about our own behavior, but we can start practicing on others.

When you're talking about a fear with someone, observe how they respond. What's their body language? What advice do they give? Criticism? Resources? Do they make it all about themselves? Or do they stick with your concern? All of this is valuable data for you to use, not only in how you learn to cope with that fear, but also regarding the relationship with that person.

When we can step back and observe, it takes a little bit of the emotional intensity out of the situation. And when we do that, it's easier to think critically about the questions at hand. I encourage you to start practicing.

Hopefulness is a state of mind

This section will probably be the most woo-woo thing I've ever written. I know you're used to me offering lots of hands-on, actionable tactics, but this piece right here? It's all in your head. For once.

Hopefulness has to start within you. You must make a choice. It's like Luke Skywalker—he had a choice to make, and he had forces pulling him toward either option, but ultimately, he chose the good.

You must make a choice to be hopeful. You must make a choice to build systems and support into your life that *keep* you hopeful, too. Because it's easy to wake up tomorrow and just say "I'm hopeful today!"

and then get knocked over by bad news. Those systems and support methods will keep lifting you up. You can memorize all the tactics and check out all the resources in *ChronicBabe 101*, but truly: it starts with you.

When you remind yourself each day that hope and possibilities exist, you reinforce the hopeful nature within yourself. When you multiply that many times by building in habits and systems that reinforce hope, you are making sure you *stay* hopeful. Each time you light a candle, say a mantra, reach out to a friend for support—you are reinforcing that hope. And each time you reinforce it, you're building a stronger foundation for yourself.

Hope is not a permanent, linear, nonstop kind of thing. There will be days when you struggle. There will be moments when all hope is lost. You're not a bad person, or a lazy person, if you falter. You're a human being.

But only you can create a lifestyle that helps you be the kind of hopeful person who gets back up after she gets knocked down. Only you can make the choices that lead to that daily buildup of hope.

Make today the day you choose to be hopeful. Make today the beginning of a fresh approach. Take a moment each day to remind yourself of your commitment. And bring everyone you know along for the ride—you'll be helping them in the process, which also makes them better equipped to help you when the time comes.

HOMEWORK assignments

1) The power of gratitude

Make a list of ten things in your life you for which you are grateful. Post the list somewhere you can see it every day—in the bathroom, next to your nightstand, on your fridge, or where you hang your key ring when you come home each day. Fold it up and put it in your pocket.

Look at the list each day, and read it aloud. Recognizing gratitude every day will help you feel more positive on even the hardest days. *Bonus points:* If you feel like it, make your list longer than ten items! Who am I to stop you?

2) Yes, and...

Think back to lesson 1, when we talked about the concept of "Yes, and..." In this lesson, we talked about negative behaviors. The next time you're voicing a complaint, try it with "Yes, and..." to see if you can move from the complaint to the solution—something you can do to fix or change it.

PEP SQUAD

An interview with Steven Kvaal, Ph.D.

Past and current relationships and their impact on our self-assessment

Dr. Steven Kvaal is an associate professor in the Department of Psychology at Roosevelt University, where he has been the director of training and director of the Psy.D. program in clinical psychology, and currently focuses on teaching and training. He began his work in health psychology in graduate school, where he provided behavioral treatments to tension and migraine headache patients and support services for hospice patients and their families.

Steven has since been a member of several interdisciplinary treatment programs in Florida and Illinois providing treatment for back, facial, and other pain problems. He also works with patients with more general mental health concerns.

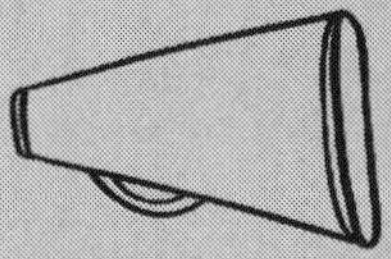

Connect with Steven:
Phone: 708-369-3802

Jenni: When we were talking about this call, you had a preference for how we started it. So I'd love to hear you just jump in with your thoughts and we can get started.

Steven: Okay. I was a little uneasy about the focus on negative thought patterns for two reasons, both the focus on thought patterns and the focus on negative and positive. I think the idea that we can separate our experiences into thoughts and actions and feelings is a pretty artificial separation, and I also think it's difficult to separate all of those thoughts, feelings, and action, from the relationships within which they occur—and other contexts, though I think relationships are really what's critical for most folk.

Jenni: That's an interesting perspective I had not thought about. I've actually never had somebody talk to me in that way about the relationship between negative thought patterns or beliefs and how intertwined they are...Obviously I've talked to people about how intertwined they are with relationships and how connected they are, but I think in our community, at least in this culture, a lot of people are used to thinking about negative or positive, or good or bad. I think about this a lot in mind-body questions; a lot of people are very disconnected.

"Sometimes problems arise [from] trying to impose those differences of negative or positive. 'Is this a good relationship or a bad relationship?' 'Is my doctor a good doctor or a bad doctor?' ***The reality is that it's going to be mixed."***

—Steven

Steven: I think, of course, they've been separated throughout history to make it easier to analyze them and think about things in different ways, but I think it's important for us to remember that our experience might not necessarily be divisible quite so neatly.

The same with the negative versus positive; it seems to imply a clear difference or separation that I think is not usually that clear. Maybe it's my age, but I think ambiguity, ambivalence, and compromises are more characteristic of reality than [are] negativity and positivity.

And I can see how it can be helpful, especially for some patients who are feeling very stuck, to talk about negative thoughts as a means of getting some leverage on how things could be looked at differently or starting to make some changes. But I think that forcing [thoughts] into negative and positive [categories] can become a bit tyrannical, and does violence to reality, just as the separation of thought and feelings [does].

I think as people start to become more reflective about problems and experiences or problems in living, the ambiguity in the mix tends to become more predominant or more clear. Sometimes problems arise [from] trying to impose those differences of *negative* or *positive*. "Is this a good relationship or a bad relationship?" "Is my doctor a good doctor or a bad doctor?" The reality is that it's going to be mixed.

Jenni: I don't think I've ever had very much in my life that's been very clearly good or bad, that's uniformly, "This is it, it's good or it's bad." There are a lot of shades of gray, and a lot of us live on a spectrum day to day.

Steven: Shades of gray, and a mix of good aspects, bad aspects, middling aspects.

Jenni: When we think about relationships, and how they impact our tendency to think negatively or have maybe unhealthy behaviors, can you talk about how it's important for people with chronic illness to look at those relationships? Or look at the behaviors and thought patterns and where they came from? What's the value of doing that?

Steven: I think there's value in two different ways.

Number one is, at least in virtually all of the patients I've worked with, the chronic illness has had a huge impact on their relationships. When I do an [intake] interview with folks, I ask them to describe their pain or other medical condition, but probably the most important part of the assessment for me is to ask about what impact it's had on their views of themselves and on their relationships. And that's what we usually spend a lot of time talking about. Most patients say they've never had the opportunity to talk about such things before, and many tear up, both because it's a tender spot in their lives and because they appreciate the opportunity to share such experiences.

Relationships often suffer when people have developed chronic illnesses, because they can't do the things they used to do, perhaps, which changes their views of themselves, and that can affect the relationship. People in their lives may not understand the impact of the illness.

Most of the people I've worked with have chronic illnesses, and their experience is that it's very difficult for others to understand what it's like to have a chronic problem. They will often say friends and family can be very patient for weeks, maybe months, but then many start to get impatient and wonder why you're not feeling better, *why aren't you over this yet?*

Jenni: Does that kind of experience then generate some kind of negative thoughts or negative self-perspective or behaviors?

Steven: I think so. Just the other day, in our pain group, we were talking about this issue. And even folks who've been working with a pain problem for a long time, and recognize that it's not their fault that their problems still persist, will also say that it's hard not to internalize those judgments, implicit or explicit, that other people are making, and at times wonder, *could I be doing more? Am I not exerting my will enough? Am I not motivated enough? Could that be the problem?*

Or, I've even had people go so far as to doubt whether they're actually disabled and wonder how much of their problem might be just in their mind. Even folks who've had five or six operations, transfusions, and hardware. It can be difficult not to see yourself reflected in other people's views of you.

Jenni: So when people have that kind of experience—and I know it's hard to generalize, because everybody's different—where do you start with your guidance for them on how to get past that?

Steven: I think it has to do with the second part of the importance of relationships, and that is the extent to which our early and most formative relationships have affected how we see ourselves and others and what we expect of others, especially when we're in need or in distress.

Often, people will have a more severe vulnerability to feeling at blame, or guilty, or as if they're not motivated enough, if some of their early experiences with parents and other people who were close in their life weren't very supportive—weren't as supportive as they could be—so they don't have as strong a sense of confidence in who they are and their value.

So the intervention then begins with reflecting on those experiences and the impact they've had. It takes a huge amount of emotional resources to cope with a chronic condition, and especially a chronic painful condition.

And if you've been through a lot of emotional difficulties early in your life, adding a chronic and painful condition can make those vulnerabilities come to the surface again, even though in some ways people might have learned to adjust and adapt very well, and develop a stronger sense of self-worth and value and confidence. [That sense] can be shaken even in folks who had a very supportive childhood with very loving parents.

*"**How one manages with chronic pain or other chronic medical conditions isn't essentially different than how one manages with any of life's difficulties.** I don't think it's different in kind from dealing with, say, a divorce, or the death of someone close to you, or a job loss, or other kinds of disappointments."*

—Steven

Jenni: I had a very rocky childhood and upbringing, and I've learned to be very resilient. I've written about this a lot at ChronicBabe.com and that's something I've worked on a great deal, but I still have moments where, you know, I'll feel like I've tried everything, I'm doing everything my doctors are telling me, and I'm working really hard on it...and even though I've surrounded myself with very supportive people, I'll have moments where I think, *am I just not doing this right? Am I not working hard enough on this? Why am I failing?*

I can still slip into that space of very intense self-judgment, and that's a tough space to get out of. I think a lot of us with chronic illness wind up getting our heads there.

Steven: Yeah, and I think what you just described also connects back with what I talked about earlier, with my problems with the emphasis on negative versus positive. In that some things are going to be negative and remain negative and can't necessarily be overcome. In my classes, the students always chuckle nervously when I say this, but we're all going to get sick and die.

Jenni: For example, if I observe something about myself—like, I'm having self-judgment, and I'm almost twenty years now living with fibro, and certainly many years with therapy and other advice. If I'm still having moments of self-judgment, then I know that's probably never gonna stop. But there's a difference in how I act when I have those moments, right?

Steven: Yeah, definitely. Especially if you can catch yourself in the act, and then of course that gives you another opportunity not to judge yourself for being self-judgmental.

Jenni: Right! Judging judginess is not the hottest idea.

Steven: Not so good. You were asking about how to work on these things. That's where in psychotherapy—and I don't really draw a clear line between psychotherapy and psychological pain management—that's another area where I think the boundaries are very blurred.

Jenni: For me, they have been one and the same, really.

Steven: That's where it can be helpful to look back and think about, *how did I develop this tendency to use judgment to motivate myself and to evaluate my experiences? And judging myself, in particular?*

Although some people may tend to be more judgmental of others, others are more judgmental of themselves. Some tend to wield that judgment stick indiscriminately. It's a tough one. It often has clear sources in that people learned to do that to cope with a difficult situation.

So for example, if someone had very critical parents, being judgmental could be one method of trying to avoid parental criticism, by judging yourself first, maybe even more harshly. At least that way you might be obviating your parents' judgment, or you might not have to deal with the anxiety and uncertainty of wondering when that stick of judgment is going to come down, if you're applying it yourself.

Jenni: So how can folks begin to consider their current relationships and their past relationships, and look for origins of some of these behaviors or thoughts to try to address them or at least become aware of them? How can someone get started if they've never been to therapy or they haven't thought about this stuff before?

Steven: One way is to think about how they're feeling in a particularly troubling situation and maybe think back to the times when they've felt that way before. Or another approach, not so very different, is to think about what they're troubled by or what they're wishing for from others, or are afraid will happen. What do they expect others will do in response to their need or their wish, and what has happened before? How did they come to expect those kinds of responses from others, and how did they come to act in a certain way in response to what they expect?

It sounds maybe too abstract or too contorted, but I think the basic point or premise for me is that we learn about ourselves based on how others treat us, and certainly when working with a chronic pain problem, you're interacting with others, with your family, with physicians, with people on the job if you're still able to work, so you've got those personal interactions.

But as you mentioned, dealing with conditions like that also can affect how you think about yourself, which can also lead back then to thinking about, *how did I come to see myself in this way? How did I come to act towards myself in this way?* Because my premise in working with people on their relationships—especially troubling relationships, and especially when people are puzzled by how they have trouble changing and continue to act in ways that don't seem very helpful—is that those ways of acting served a purpose at some point.

I don't think anyone willfully acts irrationally, or against his or her best interests. With everyone I've worked with so far, having ways of treating oneself or thinking about oneself or other people usually made sense at some point, and usually earlier in life when one was more vulnerable and had to adapt to circumstances.

I'd like to add a caution, though, in that some folks who've had very, very troubled lives may find their distress increasing as they start to think back about these things. In that case, it's very helpful to have a supportive, caring, therapeutic relationship with someone, to help work through those periods. And also someone who can say, *let's back off from this for a little bit; let's think about something concrete, about what you might do tomorrow or the next day.* To prevent those recollections from being overwhelming sometimes. It depends on the individual.

Jenni: That makes a lot of sense. For some people, things are so intense that the last thing they want to do is send themselves into a flare-up because they've spent the afternoon reliving terrible things that happened when they were a kid. That's not productive.

But I like what you're saying: getting some professional help to get through that process makes so much sense. And I'll speak from experience and say that it's a great idea if folks can do it. Because that person is your guide through the jungle.

"I would venture to say nearly all of the chronic pain patients I've worked with ***have at some point wondered whether they were different or crazy in some way*** *because of the things they were experiencing, which were in reality the most common experiences."*

—Steven

Steven: I think it also helps to see the fallibility of those guides; that's another way to learn, maybe, to be less judgmental about yourself, too—to see how a caring and well-meaning therapist or physician can also make mistakes.

Jenni: Yeah, because they're human too, it's not like they're impervious to flaws.

Steven: There's one more thing I wanted to say and that is, although it may sound like I'm encouraging people to feel worse about their situation, I hope it's not exactly that way.

That's not been my experience working with a lot of patients or working with myself; I also have a couple [of] chronic pain problems, although not very severe. My experience is that although people may, with reflection, understand how they've been shaped by important relationships, and that may lead to sadness or even grief, most people I've worked with feel that that feels more real and less frightening, in a way, than being anxious or worrying or having difficulty facing uncertainty. It provides a little more solid sense of reality than having avoided thinking about those incidences for a long time.

Jenni: That makes sense. I can imagine being alone in the middle of the night and really not feeling well and then starting to get really self-critical. Instead of swirling in that storm of fear or anxiety and *Where's this coming from? What do I do? I don't know why I'm like this!* I would prefer to think, *you know what, I'm being self-critical because I have a history of that that stems from this long relationship.*

Then, I can start to tackle that, I can start to say, *Okay, I see that about myself.* Awareness is so much a part of caring for ourselves. Now I see that, I can think about how I want to be different, or remind myself of what's in the past and that I'm in the present. And in the present I have a lot of tools to take care of myself, and people who love me and support me, you know?

Steven: And think about the troubling relationships as well.

Jenni: I'm wondering if you could give us your best advice for those folks to get started on a journey of self-exploration that might lead them into more positive territory.

Steven: I'm assuming you mean besides the obvious psychotherapy, both individual and group?

Jenni: Well, that's a great place to start, for sure.

Steven: Especially group. And I'm saying that because many—I would venture to say nearly all—of the chronic pain patients I've worked with have at some point wondered whether they were different or crazy in some way because of the things they were experiencing, which were in reality the most common experiences of someone who's coping with a problem of pain that doesn't go away and that interferes with life in all its aspects.

Jenni: So being in a group of people where you can say that and everyone nods their head and says, "Yes, I've been there too," that's got to be very empowering, I think.

Steven: Yes, I think so.

Jenni: If someone wants to ask themselves: *What's something I could do tonight with a spare twenty minutes of my time, or hour of time... what can I do right today to get started on this and start thinking about it?* Do you have any tips for that?

Steven: A way to start might be to think about one's thoughts and feelings, not just specific to the chronic pain or chronic problem, medical condition. And think about: *Am I feeling frightened? And what am I frightened of? And am I feeling that I need help from others? And am I afraid I'm not going to get it? Am I afraid that I might lose others' love? Or am I afraid that I might*—and this is a big one, I think—*I might lose myself or who I am?*

Jenni: And identify those, because those feelings are there whether or not they're caused specifically by your illness or something else, right?

Steven: Yes. And I think it can be more productive to work with some more general questions. Because these days I—maybe I'm oversimplifying, maybe my memory is deteriorating so I'm trying to reduce what I need to keep in mind to be helpful—but more and more, I think that how one manages with chronic pain or other chronic medical conditions isn't essentially different than how one manages with any of life's difficulties, although it can be among the most severe of difficulties and the most intense. I don't think it's different in kind from dealing with, say, a divorce, or the death of someone close to you, or a job loss, or other kinds of disappointments.

This interview has been shortened and edited to fit this book. To read the full transcript or listen to the full recordings of this and all the Pep Squad interviews, head to ChronicBabe101.com.

Lesson 4

ESTABLISH healthy boundaries TO CREATE confidence

Women often let their boundaries go all blurry, and that's dangerous. We're conditioned to satisfy the needs, demands, and expectations of others—and in doing so, we often let them into our heads and our physical spaces.

Have you heard the phrase "good fences make good neighbors"? Good boundaries in our relationships provide safety. They free up emotional and physical energy, and give us space to blossom as unique individuals.

Mesh tank top or suit of armor?

Boundaries sometimes get a bad rap. Many people mistakenly believe putting up boundaries simply means blocking people. Not true! Boundaries protect you, yes, but they can also strengthen relationships.

Boundaries are the words and actions we use to create space between us and others. They may be spoken or silent, intense or subtle. They change all the time, depending on the circumstances.

I envision boundaries as a wardrobe of ever-changing clothing. For a phone call with someone I dislike, I mentally adorn myself in a suit of armor. I'll be reserved, not offering up any personal information. Businesslike, professional, or courteous, depending on the situation. I will mentally shield myself from anything negative they say.

For a conversation with a client I've known for years, I may wear a cardigan and jeans, and slip off my shoes. I can be more relaxed, revealing more of myself and listening closely as they do the same. It's casual but not too familiar.

When I hang out with my best friends, I get crazy: I put on a mesh tank top, sparkly leggings and nothing else. I let my hair down. I stretch out on the floor. I'm free, barely protected, because I know I'm safe. In my mind, I'm wide open to hearing their input because I know anything they say will come from a place of love and respect.

Boundaries can be physical—perhaps you limit one-on-one time with people with whom you don't get along. Boundaries can be verbal—perhaps when an acquaintance begins to discuss a challenging topic, you gently change the subject to something less difficult. Boundaries can be time-sensitive; I often set an alarm on my phone to vibrate after fifteen minutes when I'm talking with difficult family members. (I do this for them as well as me; after fifteen minutes, we're *all* likely to be getting on each other's nerves.) The alarm helps me end the call while we're still enjoying each other's company.

I encourage you to stock your mental wardrobe well. Keep a variety of outfits handy for all occasions. Be prepared for a quick change; you may need to throw on a Kevlar vest for someone who's surprisingly jerky, or slip into something soft and cozy when a friend pays a surprise visit. Have fun with it! #MeshTankTops4Eva

So many ways to say *no*

Sometimes, you've simply gotta say *no*. It's not your job to make the other person agree with you; you're not obligated to explain why it's okay for you to set boundaries. But you can help ease discomfort about *no* by saying it with a bit of grace.

Try weaving a few of these *no* statements into conversations and see which ones feel natural:

- That's not going to work for me.
- I prefer to go another route.
- That's not really my thing.
- That's not a good option for me; can we explore a different approach?
- No, thank you.
- I don't think my spiritual guru would go for that.

- Not at this time.
- That's never been my cup of tea.
- That might work best for you, but it's not a good fit for me.
- Let's try looking at this another way.
- How nice of you to think of me; I wish I could attend, but I'm booked.
- Can we explore other options?
- In another universe, maybe, but not on this planet.
- If I could help you I would, but I'm not able to today.
- Thank you, but I'm not interested.

And sometimes, you just have to say *No. Nope. Nah. No way.* If the situation calls for it, put your foot down and move on.

How are boundaries set?

A good boundary can be so many things, but most important: a boundary protects you. Physically, emotionally, spiritually, legally—boundaries can offer you protection in many ways, especially from people who (intentionally or unintentionally) smash your spirit.

It's good to keep our boundaries a little more flexible and fluid, so as our relationships change, we can take good care of ourselves.

A good place to start defining boundaries is with someone who's being a jerk. Let's say you're living with your dad, and he says "Suck it up!" whenever you talk about your symptoms. Your dad loves you, but wow—he sure doesn't know how to support you or be kind with his words!

You could start by limiting how much you tell him; this is a self-directed boundary. When you give him less material to work with, he's less likely to say thoughtless things.

You could choose a time when you're not feeling very symptomatic (and therefore not as vulnerable) to talk to him about how much it hurts when he says stuff like that. (Be prepared that he may not get it, okay?)

You could consider limiting the space you share with him physically; maybe instead of watching TV together every night, you can read a book on the porch, or watch Netflix in your bedroom.

You could enlist the help of another family member, asking them to jump in and change the subject when he goes on a "Suck it up!" rant.

You could use his behavior as an additional motivator to get your own place.

You could create an inner mantra, to drown out his words: "I got this!"

Can you see how boundaries can work in many ways? They help *all* parties involved, because they reduce conflict and damage to relationships.

Five ways to set boundaries

Deflect. Say things like "I hear you, but I prefer not to discuss that. How 'bout those Cubbies winning the World Series?!" It may feel awkward to be so direct in deflecting; it's easier if you bounce to something everyone can agree on.

Change the subject. Practice before a family gathering: "Oh, you don't say! By the way, I meant to ask for your turkey roasting techniques; can you show me?" Change the tone by steering to another topic—especially effective if it compliments the other person.

Set physical boundaries. If you're staying at someone's house, it's okay to excuse yourself to read in your room or take a walk. If you're at a party and a jerk is walking toward you, it's okay to maneuver behind another person to avoid them. If you're at an event where someone is being nasty, leave. It's okay. If you must call a taxi because your ride wants to stay, fine. Protect yourself.

Set emotional boundaries. If someone is upset because you refuse to talk politics, don't own their feelings. If someone is sad because you need to leave the party early, don't own their sadness. As you set boundaries, you will challenge others' perceptions of you; they may share some intense emotions as they grapple with things changing. Don't own their feelings. You can be compassionate and patient without taking responsibility for making them feel okay.

Ask for backup. Bring a friend to a party, someone who will change the subject if you freeze. Start a text/phone tree with friends to stay connected. Get your favorite cousin to help you maneuver around your nosy aunt. Ask trusted confidantes to help you reinforce boundaries.

PTMO, baby!

Have you heard of FOMO—the Fear Of Missing Out? It can make us say yes to things we know in our gut are not healthy, especially if people tell us how awesome they are and try to talk us into participating.

FOMO can be very unhealthy! The next time FOMO strikes, consider giving yourself some PTMO—Permission To Miss Out. My pal Leah and I came up with this years ago at a conference, where I was feeling FOMO about attending a fancy dinner...but my body was telling me to go sleep. She gave me PTMO (I needed someone else to tell me it was okay) and I never forgot it.

Give yourself PTMO, babe. It can wipe away fear, guilt, and sadness when you honor your needs. It's an important part of setting boundaries with others, too.

How are boundaries enforced?

Through clarity: When you are crystal-clear with yourself about your no-go behaviors, and you remember the benefits of honoring your boundaries, it's easier to enforce them when people push back.

Through repetition: You may have to be a broken record and repeat the same boundary-setting phrases many times before it finally sinks in. This is true for the other person *and for you.*

Through hard lessons: If you set a boundary and then let it slip—and incur someone's crummy behavior as a result—that hard lesson will help you learn to enforce the boundary with more force in the future.

POP QUIZ

Pick a boundary to strengthen

If you haven't worked on boundaries before, you may be tempted to put up walls to everyone at first, but that can be counterproductive and exhausting. You may also be tempted to tackle the most complex, challenging relationship first—but it may be too much for a beginner. Start small, with a nosy neighbor or an annoying acquaintance. Ease into it. These things take time.

The benefits of healthy boundaries

ChronicBabes reap many benefits from enforcing boundaries:

- Fewer unwanted conversations about embarrassing symptoms
- Less criticism from others that might otherwise seep into your psyche
- More time to rest, heal, and pursue things you love
- More time to spend with people who nourish your soul
- Less conflict in relationships
- More focus so you can get things done
- A feeling of greater independence and autonomy

These are broad-ranging; in your life, there will be many more specific benefits to enjoy. For example, firm boundaries help me avoid talking about the specifics of my illnesses with other ladies in the gym locker room. They ensure that I don't feel guilty about not volunteering with a neighborhood organization. And they provide me with cover on days I don't feel like attending a garden club meeting. How will boundaries help *you*?

What happens when you don't have good boundaries?

A lack of healthy boundaries can result in many negative impacts. Among those I've experienced:

- Thoughtless, groundless advice from people who don't understand your condition or situation
- Criticism from people who have not walked in your shoes
- Self-doubt stemming from the criticism and unwanted advice of others
- Physical fatigue from doing things that you don't enjoy or that aren't healthy for you
- Emotional fatigue from dealing with jerks
- A lack of time to be creative or to use the arts as a way of coping
- Physical danger from proximity to people who don't understand or care about your physical needs

Does this sound dramatic? That's because *boundaries are serious business, babe*. In my life, they've had an enormous positive impact.

Thinking about our family as acquaintances

You know that acquaintance of yours, the person you bump into at church or at the grocery store on double coupon day? The one who's super-annoying?

You know how, because they're an acquaintance, you accept that your conversations will be uncomfortable but have no bearing on your decisions? How you can talk with her, listen to her crap, nod politely, and disconnect completely when you walk away? Because she's just an acquaintance?

Take that feeling. Imagine your most challenging family member is that person. Imagine how conversations might be easier if you could disconnect like that.

This is my secret weapon to handling difficult conversations with family members. I'm not always good at it, but I keep practicing.

Family relationships bring decades of baggage, adding layers of meaning to simple sentences. They can really sting. They can feel judgmental. They can sway us to make big decisions we don't *really* believe in, because *they're family*.

I invite you to try thinking about a family member as an acquaintance. Let's imagine you're preparing for an uncomfortable conversation with your sister about planning the holiday reunion.

Now, imagine your sister is an acquaintance. She might say things that are annoying, but it's okay—they don't carry any weight. You might need to push back on some things, but she's not your big sister anymore—the one who feels like the boss of the family—now she's an acquaintance, so it's easier.

If you can prepare for interactions like this, otherwise-difficult conversations get easier. You'll be calmer, and you'll take things less personally.

Thinking of your family as acquaintances doesn't take caring out of the equation; I still love my family dearly. But this perspective releases you from overburdening responsibility.

Some of my favorite boundary-setting strategies

Set a kitchen timer nearby when you're on the phone with someone challenging. When the conversation goes bad, make the timer go off. "Oh, goodness—that's my pie in the oven. Gotta go!"

If you're invited to an event you're not excited about, say, "Thanks for thinking of me, but that won't work for me this time." It's kind, simple, and hard to argue with.

Use your caller ID.

Don't let the insistent beeps, vibrations, and visual alerts on your phone trick you into responding to someone who isn't healthy for you. Turn off your ringer and notifications.

A simple "Will you excuse me for a moment?" works great at events when you're stuck in a bad conversation.

Get some physical space. When you see that one weird guy who frequents your favorite café, steer yourself to a seat with no nearby vacancy, or take your chai latte to go.

Cultivate "resting bitch face." Practice at home in the mirror. It comes in handy on the street and public transit.

Try this: "I can't talk about this right now. Can we discuss at another time?" And...don't reschedule.

Be a broken record. As weird as it feels, repeating the same *no* phrase multiple times in a conversation is powerful.

POP QUIZ

Is this a boundary violation?

If you're setting new boundaries with someone and they push back a little, that's natural; it will take time and repetition for them to learn the new rules. When you've set a clear boundary and someone blasts through it, that's a *violation*. As you develop new boundaries with someone, ask yourself: What's your no-go?

If you tell your mom, "Stop asking about my sex life!" and the next time you speak, she asks about it, that's a violation—a no-go. Swallow your discomfort and remind her of your previous chat. If she does it again, well, babe—you may need to set a firmer boundary. "If you continue to ask me about my sex life, I'll take a break from speaking to you, Mom." That may set her straight.

This work is uncomfortable, but worth it. Reward yourself for being strong. And forgive yourself if you're not always able.

Your boundaries will be tested, but you are strong!

Will some folks reject your boundaries and push back? Yup! Will people take offense? Probably! Will family members say things like "What's wrong? This is not like you." Oh yeah! Will their complaints make you relent sometimes? Sure!

The firmer your new boundaries (and the longer it's been since you had any), the more uncomfortable you'll make others—and they're gonna try to put that discomfort back on you.

It's okay. I swear: You will make it through.

At first, it may seem scary and awful and nauseating. But over time, the benefits you enjoy from firm boundaries will be so wonderful you'll celebrate. When I first got caller ID in college, I would watch the little box light up for each call, and sometimes run to the bathroom to be sick—that's how anxious I was about screening calls. But by the end of my first quarter freshman year, I didn't even flinch—sometimes I would even do a little happy dance because I had avoided yet another abusive phone call. It was *divine.*

Be strong, girl. The rewards are liberating!

A note about social media

Many folks find social media frustrating, draining, and downright depressing. I feel the same way some days. It has become ubiquitous, and if you're like me and must be active on social media for work, too, it permeates practically every minute of life.

But you *can* set some boundaries on social media, and you should—because jerks abound online. Here are some of my favorite strategies:

- Set a timer on your computer (I like BreakTime) and honor it. Spend a finite amount of time each day on social media.
- Unfollow or unfriend anyone on Facebook who doesn't make you smile or think or laugh.
- Quit Facebook groups full of complainers, whiners, and naysayers. Don't waste your energy arguing with people.
- Set your privacy settings so your Facebook or Instagram account is private.

- Take breaks: Uninstall social media apps from your phone for a week (or even a day!) and see how it feels to spend less time online.
- Use the "lists" function in Twitter to curate your feed, so if you want to spend just five minutes, you can hop on and look at your "health" or "makeup" or "pals" list.
- Walk away. It's cool to put your phone down sometimes.
- Remind yourself to not take personally someone else's jerky behavior, which is more about them than you.
- Seek out people who spread joy, humor, facts, and whatever else you seek.
- Ban anyone who's a jerk to you, who trolls you, or makes you uncomfortable.
- Turn off notifications so you're not constantly getting beeped at or buzzed at.
- Excuse yourself from conversations that make you uncomfortable. You don't have to participate just because someone calls you out or tags you.
- Opt out. It's okay to turn off your phone.

Is it worth the risk to relax your boundaries sometimes?

I'll never forget the time I shared a van to the airport with a handful of acquaintances. These women were fellow attendees of a health care conference; we had socialized a little, and they were becoming brand-new friends.

We talked about orgasms. The whole ride to the airport. We ignored the driver, and we gabbed about sex and chronic illness and sadness and pleasure. I don't know who started the conversation, but I know I didn't hold back once it began.

One woman told us she sometimes felt suicidal because the connection she once shared with her partner had fizzled, and she felt so deeply disconnected she didn't think it was fixable.

One woman talked about how exhausting it was to think up new positions and scenarios that might coax an orgasm out of her. And how she sometimes faked it because she didn't want her partner to feel inadequate or disappointed.

One woman talked about how she had learned to not be as goal-oriented during sex, which took some of the pressure off, and how (paradoxically) that sometimes made it easier for her to orgasm.

One woman talked about how frustrating it was that her antidepressant rendered her unable to orgasm, which made her sad; when she tried to go off the antidepressant, she *could* orgasm...but then she was depressed. She was frustrated at the tradeoffs.

Did I plan to hop in a van and talk about orgasms with near-strangers? Nope. But these women are now friends for life. I feel such a deep connection with them. If they came calling for help, I would do everything in my power. I'm not embarrassed for them, or for myself, or for the driver of that van, for that matter. I'm proud that we could all open up and share our struggles. It made me feel strong, supported, connected, and happy—in spite of all the bad stuff.

Sometimes it's worth the risk to let down your defenses and get closer to people.

Developing strong communication helps caregivers and their partners thrive

Will and his wife married just a couple of years ago, but they've known each other for about a decade. Years before, she began her ChronicBabe journey; she has Ehlers-Danlos syndrome (EDS), fibromyalgia, and chronic fatigue. They've developed great communication patterns to manage some of the physical limitations she faces.

We try to balance how we push each other, and especially how I push her when we're trying to do things. There are cases where she can do more and just needs to get past a little bit of funk about it, versus when she needs to push back on me, saying, "No, really, if I do this I'm not going to be able to do these other things I need to do." And then we'll rebalance.

I'm very cognizant when we're planning stuff that we plan an adequate amount of down time. We went to Dublin a couple of years ago, and we walked a lot more than we normally do, but then we would find a place to sit down for a couple hours. I think it's a matter of day-to-day checking and body language.

When we're out doing things together, I regularly check in with her to make sure she's still okay. There are definitely little physical signs that indicate she's probably lagging more than she wants to let on, or is aware of. I think it helps, too, that we're both pretty introverted, so when the question of "Hey, do you want to go home and get back into bed?" comes up, we're both like, "Yeah, that sounds great!"

We have this concept of companionate silence. That could be the two of us reading a book in a room, and I find that to be a very gratifying experience. We do occasionally talk about having lives outside of each other because it's healthy for a relationship to not have 100 percent overlap in the interests, because you might get sick of each other.

It is a key factor in any relationship to be able to ask for the things you want. It's especially important when you've got chronic illness as kind of a third party to a relationship, because [illnesses] can get pretty demanding and you can't really ignore them.

HOMEWORK assignments

1) Send your dinner back

Do you settle for undercooked burgers or salads that have too much dressing? Knock it off, lady! Practice sending your meal back if something's not right. This is a low-stakes way to work on boundary-setting.

But watch your tone. *Please* and *thank you* work wonders.

"As a waitress, it sucks bringing food back to the kitchen, but I get it—I want the customer to get the meal they want," says a friend who works in food service.

The first time I did this, I had an anxiety attack. But it got easier, and it's a great way to practice boundaries.

2) Break down your own boundaries

Have you seen the Jim Carrey movie *Yes Man*? In it, he can't say no to *anything*. You, too, can practice relaxing your boundaries in a low-stakes way by saying *yes* to a few things this week that are normally a *no* for you. Usually don't like tacos? Try saying yes to a new flavor. Usually turn down invites to see sci-fi movies? Try saying yes to a new flick. You just may find something new to enjoy, and it's great practice.

3) Imagine your boundaries wardrobe

In this lesson, I shared some of my boundaries wardrobe tips. What would your boundaries wardrobe look like? A fuzzy robe and slippers for hanging out with new friends? A bikini for chillin' with your BFF? Consider making a secret Pinterest board or a magazine collage to get a clear visual. #FashionIsMagic

PEP SQUAD

An Interview with Caryn Feldman, Ph.D.

Creating boundaries to strengthen relationships and protect your precious energy

Caryn Feldman, Ph.D., is a licensed clinical psychologist at the Shirley Ryan Ability Lab (formerly Rehabilitation Institute of Chicago) Center for Pain Management. She is also an assistant professor at Northwestern University, Feinberg School of Medicine, department of physical medicine and rehabilitation.

Caryn received her Ph.D. in clinical psychology from the University of South Carolina, where she became interested in health psychology. For twenty-seven years, she has worked with those suffering with chronic pain and comorbid conditions. Professionally, she is interested in the application of mindfulness strategies to chronic pain. She is a huge fan of *ChronicBabe*.

Connect with Caryn:
Website: sralab.org

Jenni: Let's start with the basics. What are boundaries? What does that word really mean, and why do we need them? Why are they important?

Caryn: The simplest definition is that a boundary is a limit. It provides us with structure and order and safety in a world that can be quite unpredictable.

Boundaries are everywhere; we take them for granted. We have physical boundaries that define the limits of my office, this building, this city; the physical boundaries remind us there's a separation between your chair and my chair, and between you and me—and that's when it really gets interesting.

We're talking about personal boundaries, and they're harder to see, but they're also everywhere. They include relationship limits, role boundaries, emotional time [and] energy boundaries.

You ask why we need them. Personal boundaries help us define what is physically or emotionally safe for us in any given moment. They are a necessary tool for our health.

Jenni: I think there are a lot of people who, if we said that word to them, they wouldn't exactly know what that means, but I love the idea of thinking that it's something essential to our health.

Caryn: Both our physical and emotional health and, of course, the interaction between the two.

Jenni: Can you give us an example of setting a healthy boundary around chronic illness? Like something someone might do to take good care of herself?

Caryn: Sure! Let's say your cousin, Shirley, is constantly giving you unsolicited medical advice, and it drives you crazy. Every time you talk, it's the same conversation, and it's a shame because, otherwise, you love your cousin Shirley, so how do you respond?

You might get angry and make a snide comment, after thinking to yourself, *I've told her a hundred times, I don't need her to be my doctor.* This is obviously not a great solution. Or you might smile, nod, and secretly plot revenge. Neither of these situations are obviously health-friendly or relationship-friendly.

Setting a boundary in this situation means finding a way to respect your own preferences without sacrificing your health or your relationship with Shirley. One possibility is to recognize your own ongoing annoyance with *Shirley just being Shirley.* If you've already nicely asked her to stop the advice-giving, maybe find a way towards softening your heart to her. Remember, she loves you and this is her clumsy attempt [at] showing it. Can you just accept Shirley as she is? Maybe you could ask her for her chocolate cheesecake recipe.

Jenni: Like a diversion.

Caryn: Well, it's something else to talk about, without it being a fight.

Jenni: I love the idea of softening your heart to someone, because so many of us with chronic illness and chronic pain [get constant] advice, criticism, or just weird comments from people who don't know quite what to say.

Caryn: People genuinely don't know what to say, and it's an interaction to help them find a way to better communicate with you.

Jenni: I love the idea that you're turning it back by asking her for her chocolate cheesecake recipe; that's so cool, because you're also bringing them into the conversation instead of it being one direction, like her just talking at you. It's more of a sharing conversation experience, which to me sounds more pleasant and more beneficial to both people.

> *"**Boundaries let you have more emotional safety and honesty.** [They help] you not to go where you don't want to go."*
>
> —Caryn

Caryn: Exactly, because when we are talking about healthy boundaries, it really is about a balancing act. On one hand, how do you set this limit, and on the other hand, how do you maintain the relationship? It's easy to get too focused on one of those sides.

Jenni: I think some people might feel some resistance to this idea, because it means changing the dynamics of some longstanding relationships. I mean, some people, like my family, have known me my whole life, and that's been challenging for me.

But I think it's important to remember that boundaries don't have to result in a negative outcome, right? They really can improve relationships for everybody involved.

Caryn: The question is, do you want them to change in a healthier or unhealthier direction? It's funny—it's paradoxical—setting limits can really allow for greater intimacy. Boundaries let you have more emotional safety and honesty. [They help] you not to go where you don't want to go.

Remember, there is no intimacy when you have pent-up resentment toward someone. That leads to poor emotional and physical health, and distances you from the other person.

Jenni: Sometimes I've found that in those situations when I'm feeling really resentful, it's almost like I cut myself off and I'm being less authentic with people.

Caryn: Exactly.

Jenni: I hate that. It seems the opposite of how to have a good relationship with someone.

Caryn: Right! Then you're inadvertently disrespecting yourself and distancing yourself from the other person, so that's a lose-lose situation.

Jenni: When I was first starting to think about this concept, I had the tendency to want to tell someone, "I am setting a boundary with you," and I think that was an overexplanation. I don't think I really needed to actually say that. What kind of language do you think we can use to set a boundary with someone without explicitly stating it?

Caryn: Overtly stating that you are setting a limit may be necessary, at times, especially if we are talking about violence or physical safety. But I'm not so sure that's where you generally want to start. If someone said to you, "I'm setting a limit with you," would you like it?

Jenni: No, it would feel so uncomfortable.

Caryn: Yes, not so much! There are more effective and friendlier ways of setting boundaries, so in general, the best language is assertive language. Language that is respectful of you and the other person. For some of us, learning the language of assertiveness is almost like learning a foreign language. The thing to bear in mind is that it requires practice, practice, practice.

Jenni: I know that from experience. This is not something I just sat down one day and talked with Caryn about and the next day—boom!—I was good at it. This is something I've continually worked on for years. Not to say this is some agonizing process or anything, but it takes practice and sometimes it's a big change for us.

Caryn: Yes, and I really appreciate that you are emphasizing that, because what often happens is, people will learn like five words in Spanish and then they expect that to be an excellent communication tool on their trip to Barcelona. You can learn a few assertiveness words or phrases with really negative results and come to the conclusion that boundaries don't work, or *I can't be assertive.* There are some common pitfalls to look out for.

Jenni: What are the kinds of things we want to avoid?

Caryn: People who are newly attempting assertive communication may overshoot the mark and come across as aggressive. This is especially true if there are longstanding pent-up emotions. So, obviously, that's backfired, and other people believe they can't set a limit because the consequences could be so dire; they convince themselves they can't risk it. You know: *So-and-so is going to hate me.*

Setting limits and being assertive: these are both skills to be learned, and you want to start small and work your way up, so you can practice with anyone. You can practice at the restaurant; you can practice with your best friend. Practice with your best friend who loves you unconditionally. Practice with the taxi driver, a coworker; practice until it feels more natural and you can find your own voice.

Jenni: Are there other ways we can set boundaries, other behaviors that aren't necessarily verbal or written? Like instead of saying no, we write to someone? Are there other things we can do to set boundaries?

Caryn: Absolutely. Going back to cousin Shirley, what did we do? We practiced acceptance, compassion, and non-engagement, and those are all internal processes that can keep us grounded, solid, and clear about our limits. If you anticipate a problem, it's important to be prepared. That's what caller ID is for. Use it.

Jenni: One of the best inventions ever!

Caryn: It's fabulous! But of course, you have to be able to honor your own needs in that situation and not sort of automatically answer the phone, and also you want to be ready with just a few words that are short and sweet. Bullet points. "More words" does not mean "more clear."

"For some of us, learning the language of assertiveness is almost like learning a foreign language. ***It requires practice, practice, practice.****"*

—Caryn

Jenni: That's a good thing to remember.

Caryn: That's a common mistake people make: they overexplain, they overtalk, and then the message is confused. If they just keep it to a couple of bullet points—that's the homework you would do up front, if you can anticipate a difficulty.

You might also be prepared to use the so-called "broken record technique." That's where you keep repeating yourself in a calm manner until the other person doesn't have a choice but to hear you, and that is very effective. Not an easy thing to do, but sometimes necessary.

If you want to be prepared, you can also stick to a timeframe. You can use a meditation timer or just decide there's only a certain amount of time you are going to allow for certain conversations.

Jenni: I love setting a timer like that. I think I have four kitchen timers in my house. I have fewer phones now, but there was a time when I had a phone in every room and I had a timer next to every phone, and sometimes I had a sticky note that said, *if this person calls, don't answer*. Because when caller ID came out I would do that thing where I said, *I'm not going to answer it if it's them*, but then out of habit, I would see it and I would still answer it. I had all these sticky notes and egg timers everywhere.

Caryn: I think sticky notes are fantastic. I use sticky notes before I go in to see my physician; when I go in for a medical appointment I make sure I've got my bullet points because those are my needs. And it's very easy to get caught up in other things and in conversations that may not be negative, but they are not what you are there for.

Another thing: If you're face to face, it's important to be firm, and standing up to end a conversation can be pretty powerful. If you just keep moving toward the door, you know, extending a handshake, you're setting a clear limit.

> ***"Be prepared to use the so-called 'broken record technique.'*** *That's where you keep repeating yourself until the other person doesn't have a choice but to hear you."*
>
> —Caryn

Jenni: When I first started setting boundaries, I thought it kind of meant like, I'm building a wall against everyone...and that's so *not* how you need to use them.

I have set a boundary for myself for the past month where I only spend fifteen minutes on email a day. I am limiting my exposure and limiting my time, because I am protecting my time as a valuable resource so I can work on other things. It's been great!

Caryn: That's the beauty of setting boundaries. You've discovered that, and you raise a really important point: A lot of people think of boundaries as walls. It doesn't mean drawing a line in the sand; when you think of setting a boundary in that way, you're gearing up for a fight, which probably isn't where you want to go.

Jenni: I don't think any of us wants to do that. Do boundaries change over time? How [do] we know when to change the limits of a boundary?

Caryn: Boundaries definitely need to change, because we change, relationships change...everything changes. I like to think of boundaries as needing to breathe; as we said, healthy boundaries are not walls, not rigid.

You don't need to put on a suit of armor because you are going into combat. That will leave you lonely and cold and uncomfortable. Boundaries that are too soft can leave you enmeshed with another person; you lose your sense of self, you're naked, no protection. A healthy boundary is flexible and permeable, like a nylon stocking or a mesh tank top.

Jenni: Mesh tank top! I always laugh when I think of the mesh tank top, because it's such a funny idea. I'll think of meeting with someone or talking with someone and imagine myself putting on a mesh tank top, which, in and of itself, is a great visual.

Caryn: It's a fashion mistake, but a relationship advantage!

Jenni: I love the idea of permeability. I want to be able to let in the good stuff you love about someone like cousin Shirley—her recipe is great, she probably has a great jewelry collection she wants to loan you sometime, and you want to get the [love] that she has for you—but you want to block some of those things you don't like.

Caryn: Also, bear in mind that sometimes things can get through that mesh tank top, and it can hurt you. But again, it doesn't have to be so extreme that it means you immediately need to rush to the suit of armor.

Jenni, have you ever learned how to dance, like ballroom dancing?

Jenni: I took ballroom dancing when I was in middle school.

Caryn: I think dancing is all about boundaries. You have a partner; your partner is not you. And if you are a woman, usually you don't even get to lead.

But the beauty is, you learn to live in the moment. You don't second-guess your partner, anticipate or control their moves—you just relax and respond. You move forward, you step on a toe. *Ouch! Sorry! Not safe.* Step back, not too far, not too close.

You keep practicing and keep dancing until it feels more intuitive and you can experiment with a sense of kindness toward your partner, and a willingness to get it right. So, your dancing experience will come in handy.

Jenni: I love that comparison. It makes so much sense. I'm totally envisioning myself right now in my poofy pink taffeta dress, with dyed-to-match shoes...and I had a perm, I mean this is middle school in Texas. And I had braces.

Caryn: There you go!

Jenni: It's such a great visual. In dancing, our partner might be more receptive, or sometimes you get the geeky guy who has two left feet and he's irritated because you aren't doing a great job.

I think in day-to-day life, some people are going to resist our boundary-setting. I'm wondering if you have any suggestions for how we can persist.

Caryn: In general, you want to start small and, if necessary, escalate. It is really important to recognize that others won't necessarily accept or understand our boundary settings.

If you've been saying yes for twenty years and then one day you say no, that takes some flexibility on the other person's part. Not expecting an instant change from the other parties is really important.

You also don't want to start from a position of defensiveness. The other folks you are talking to are not opponents, and you want to try not to view them that way. It's not their fault you haven't known how to set a limit for twenty years. Try to remember that the other party has their own fears, [their] own frustrations, and their own hurt, and like you, they have both effective and ineffective coping methods. Try not to own their struggle and just focus on having compassion for both of you.

It's like you are juggling. One ball is the get-your-needs-met ball; the other ball is the maintain-the-relationship ball. And it's very easy to drop one. It's very easy to get your needs met at the expense of the relationship, and it's very easy to maintain a relationship at the expense of your needs. The trick is keeping your eye on both balls.

If you need to escalate, use the "broken record technique," or disengage and politely end the conversation. End the conversation when it stops being productive. The emphasis is on *politely* ending the conversation. Because you won't want to come back to it.

Jenni: Also, you won't want to end that conversation with either party feeling negatively about it, like, *That was bad, I don't want to engage with that person again.*

Caryn: Remember, especially if you have been saying yes for twenty years, the other party really has a disincentive for you to say no, because that's really shaking things up a bit. That can be challenging for everyone. Remember to have some compassion and understanding for that other person. This is going to be challenging for them, too, and that's okay.

Jenni: What do you think is the greatest benefit of creating healthy boundaries in our lives?

Caryn: Healthy boundaries offer you so much. They offer you less stress, more intimacy, more compassion, sensitivity for yourself and others—and with chronic illness, you already have challenges and struggles on a daily basis. The beauty of a boundary is that it can always be changed, and it's really only limited by your willingness to grow and change and learn. I'm reminded of a Native American saying, "No tree has branches so foolish as to fight among themselves." We're all connected.

This interview has been shortened and edited to fit this book. To read the full transcript or listen to the full recordings of this and all the Pep Squad interviews, head to ChronicBabe101.com.

Lesson 5

learn to love your body again

We sick chicks sometimes hate our bodies. They seem to defy us at every turn! In reality, our bodies are trying their hardest *to serve us despite all the health issues they face.* It's time to start loving our bodies again.

Let's start with RuPaul

"If you can't love yourself, how in the *hell* you gonna love somebody else?!" If you've ever watched *RuPaul's Drag Race*, this catchphrase is stuck in your brain.

On days when I'm really being mean to myself, I can close my eyes and imagine RuPaul saying that to me—and my sense of self-love starts to come back. (Find RuPaul on YouTube for the full effect.)

Metta: Loving-kindness as a starting point

For a gentler exercise in reinforcing self-love, try a *metta* meditation. *Metta* is the Buddhist concept of loving-kindness. A *metta* meditation starts with yourself, and ripples out to everyone else in the world.

Find a quiet place and close your eyes. Breathe deeply, inhaling and exhaling, and find your natural breathing rhythm.

Say these phrases to yourself: *May I be safe. May I be peaceful. May I be at ease.* (You can also make up your own simple phrases.) Repeat these a few times, while maintaining steady breathing.

Now, imagine someone you love dearly, picturing them clearly in your mind. Repeat the same phrases to them a few times: *May you be safe. May you be peaceful. May you be at ease.*

Continue the practice by addressing the phrases:

- to someone you like
- to someone who's an acquaintance
- to someone you see occasionally but don't know personally (like your bus driver)
- to someone you dislike
- to all living creatures

To finish, come back to yourself and say the phrases.

When I feel disconnected from others—when I'm feeling isolated and unlovable—*metta* meditation always helps. A quick online search will yield guided meditations by Tara Brach, Pema Chödrön, and others.

How to make friends with illness

Part of becoming a ChronicBabe is making friends with your illness. Standing clear-eyed, face to face with your illness and all that comes with it, and saying, "Hello, illness! Let's get acquainted. I want to understand you so I can be the best friend to you."

I know that sounds weird. Maybe you're thinking something closer to *I want to punch my illness in the face.* I get it. But I'm here to tell you: Violence won't make you feel any better.

You may be asking yourself, "How the heck am I going to make friends with my illness?" I use a simple practice. For example, if I wake up in the morning and I'm having a flare-up—which can include pain, fatigue, and cognitive difficulties—I start by taking a moment to observe. What's happening in my body? My mind? What's the reality?

Then I try to remind myself that while having a flare-up sucks, it's part of me. It's my friend. It's a challenging friend, to be sure—we all have those, right? That girl you see around who's not the most fun, but she's part of the gang? For better or worse, this friend—illness—is part of my life.

I ask my annoying friend: "What are we going to do today? How can we collaborate and get it together, babe?" I look in the mirror and say those words aloud.

I try to imagine holding my friend close, recognizing how hard it is for her to be in pain every day. The compassion I feel for her—for the FibroBabe part of me—helps take the edge off, and then I'm able to think about workarounds to make the most of my day. I apply this practice anytime I'm flaring up.

This is how I begin to make friends with my illness. Ignore the part of you that feels silly talking to yourself, and give it a try.

Create your personal mantra

Step 1: When I say "personal" mantra, I mean it—you don't have to share it with the world. Don't let shyness about your thoughts, feelings, desires, or needs keep you from creating the most kickass mantra possible.

Step 2: Keep it brief. Mine is three words. Are you ready?

"I am awesome."

Yup, that's it! Sometimes I mix things up and add a different word or phrase, but that's the one I try to think about every day.

Step 3: Leave out the judgment. When creating a personal mantra, you might be tempted to say things like "when I" or "if I could" or "sometimes"...try to keep this light, fun, and positive.

Step 4: Keep it in the present. Don't project; don't wish. This is not about thinking "what if" or hoping for something. This is about telling yourself, *right now*, that you love yourself. This is about taking just one second of your time to get rock solid. Resist the temptation to say things like "one day, I will be X" or "in the future, I will be Y."

Step 5: Make it personal. Mine might sound generic, but when I sing it to myself it adds a level of silly. That makes me smile...and makes me *believe* what I'm saying/singing. Consider including a nickname, a word that makes you giggle, or a made-up word. This is just for you, no one else.

Step 6: Break my rules if you want. Who am I to dictate your inspiration?

Fall in love with yourself again...with a self-love letter

You love your friends, right? They're flawed, sometimes unreliable, annoying on occasion...but you love them. You love your family, right? You may get frustrated with them at times, but generally, you appreciate their support, and you love them even when they're being pains in the tushy.

So why don't you love yourself that way? If you're like me, there are moments when you do NOT love yourself, when you do NOT love your body. You feel like it's betrayed you. You feel ugly because your illness or disability has changed you. You don't feel lovable.

Girl, lemme tell you: I love you. You're my sister of a sort, and I adore you. Especially because you're here—committed to making your life better.

Try this exercise with me, because I think there's a lot to love about you. I want you to get reacquainted with your lovable qualities, *which will help quiet the voice that tells you all the things you don't love.*

The exercise:

Write down at least one thing your body still does well. Do your lungs breathe themselves? Do your feet keep you walking? Do your eyes see well enough to read, or make art? Is your hair luscious? Write it down.

Write down at least one thing about yourself that's pretty. Are your toes cute? Are your earlobes adorable? Do your eyes shine when you're speaking passionately? Does your booty curve in a fun way? Write it down.

Write down at least one quality of your personality for which you've been complimented. Do you have great judgment about the character of others? Are you helpful? Do you cook beautiful meals? Have you said something lately that made a friend laugh? Write it down.

Write down at least one part of your body that is sexy. Is the curve of your breast soft and supple? Do your lips get fuller when you're turned on? Do you have a long, strong neck? Write it down.

Write down at least one thing you've done well lately. Have you been great about taking out the trash? Have you won a new client? Is your meditation practice growing stronger? Were you a good friend to someone in need? Write it down.

What's your favorite outfit? Put it on: The dress, or the pants and blouse, or the leggings and sweater...whatever you love most.

It's time for a dramatic reading.

You're going to take these five things, and while wearing your favorite outfit, stand in front of the mirror and recite them. This will feel weird. But trust me: This is a first step toward loving yourself fully again.

Here's me: in some adorable leggings, a flowy top, my hair styled, mascara. Here's what I say:

> *My body still serves me by getting up every morning and going through my yoga routine, even on flare-up days.*
>
> *My smile is pretty. My teeth are a little crooked, and my lower lip curves down sometimes because I once had Bell's Palsy, but still—my smile is pretty.*
>
> *I was recently told that I really helped someone find new enthusiasm for life, via my YouTube videos. I'm proud of that, because I work hard at it.*
>
> *You know what's sexy about my body? My breasts. They are knockout big, and in the right bra, they are VA-VA-VOOM.*
>
> *A thing I've done well lately is maintain a strong working garden all season long, shared with friends, and provided for my little family.*

Just typing that makes me emotional! Some days, I forget how lovable I can be.

Now it's your turn. It may be challenging, but practicing this once a week will shift your mindset to self-love.

Can you hear your gut?

My gut gives me problems. I have irritable bowel syndrome, so I sometimes have unpleasantness that's unrelated to emotions and energies I experience. I also have anxiety, which means I sometimes feel a sense of danger even when there's no real danger to be found.

In the past, when people have told me to trust my gut, I always struggled with that idea, because much of the time I simply *can't* trust my gut.

If this is you, take a moment. Remember there are other places in your body that send signals when something is wrong. Even if your chronic stuff makes your fight-or-flight response go off at the wrong times, there are still ways your body can tell you when it's time to take care.

(If this topic feels extra-impossible, I recommend talking to a therapist; it took working with a professional to really get it myself.)

Even without the help of a therapist, you can begin to tap into (and learn from) your body's wisdom. Let's give it a try.

Your "gut" is much more than your gut

People say "trust your gut" because, of all your body systems, the gastrointestinal (GI) system is one of the most common sources of signals that something is emotionally charged. When you're crushing hard on someone, you get "butterflies in your stomach." When you have stage fright, you may throw up. When you feel nervous about something bad, you may say, "I feel a pit in my stomach."

If you've done any reading on anxiety, you also know that many people with the condition (myself included) get insane GI symptoms with anxiety attacks. Just this morning I was having an anxiety attack about a work project and had to run to the bathroom, barely making it to the toilet! My body and mind are intensely connected.

If you feel like you can't trust your GI system, consider some other ways your body may send signals:

- Your palms may get sweaty
- Your vision may get blurry
- You may feel yourself breathing faster, and more from your chest than from your diaphragm
- Your back may tighten up
- Your feet or hands may tense up
- Your mouth may go dry
- Your skin may begin to tingle
- Your heart may start beating harder
- You may feel a little lightheaded
- You may get a headache
- You may hear a little voice inside your head saying *nooooooooooo*
- Your neck may tense up

These are just a few of the more common physiological symptoms you may experience when your mind is trying to tell you something—by expressing that something through your body. (Dangit, mind! Just tell it to me straight!)

You must stop and listen

Tuning in to those signals is crucial for learning to trust your gut, and trusting your gut is a *big* part of being a strong, confident ChronicBabe. When you don't trust your gut, you ignore signs that you need to make a decision or change course, and that can hold you back—or get you into unpleasant or harmful situations.

But how do you listen?

On any given day, my palms may sweat, or my neck tenses up. That doesn't necessarily mean my body is giving me secret signals.

The skill of listening to your gut is challenging because you only get to practice it when things go wrong. But you can start now by looking back to past experiences.

Let's say you had an uncomfortable conversation with a colleague or family member last week. Do you remember any physical feelings you had at the time? Can you recall if there were any words or phrases they used that made your stomach turn, or made you feel tense? Try to recall the physical feelings you had. Those may be signals to watch out for in the future.

The next time you're faced with an uncomfortable situation—perhaps you're in a doctor's office to talk about a potential new treatment and start to feel a little dizzy, blurry, and tense—ask yourself: Is something upsetting me right now? What may be causing this reaction? Perhaps you don't feel heard by the doctor and you're afraid you won't leave with clear next steps. You may need to raise your hand and say, "Excuse me, doctor, but we need to go back to my earlier question, because I'm not satisfied and want to talk about this option again."

Does this kind of listening (and taking action) require strength? Yes! But you can cultivate that strength. Learning to read your body's signals can really help. It's a true act of self-recognition and self-love.

POP QUIZ

What works well in your body?

I mentioned in the self-love letter section that it's important to recognize what *does* work in your body. Take a moment each day and do a "review of systems"—what works? Are your lungs breathing easily? Do your eyes see clearly? Recognize and give thanks for what works.

Is loving yourself "selfish"?

Nope!

...Oh, you want me to say more about this? Hmm...

Anyone who tells you it's selfish to prioritize self-care is flat-out wrong.

Of course, I would never advocate that you get a mani-pedi for self-care when that money should be paying the gas bill. Self-care should not come at the *expense* of basic necessities. But if you decide the most loving act you can commit today is to skip a party and stay home to rest, including a DIY face mask and painting your toes, go for it.

Some people—many women, especially—feel pressured to take care of everyone else before they care for themselves. That's not fair. If you're ever on the fence about doing some self-care, just imagine me popping up on your shoulder and whispering in your ear: *Go for it, babe. You're worth it!* #SelfLoveIsntSelfish

Make a sparkle list

You know that tiny thing you do each day that makes you feel more human? Like putting on lipstick to go get groceries, or changing into fresh underwear even if you must stay in bed all day?

Those go on your sparkle list: A collection of tiny things that help you feel like your boldest, prettiest, most awesome self.

To make a sparkle list is easy; to enforce it is much harder. I encourage you to do at least one thing a day.

My personal sparkle list has a ton of things, including:

- Painting my toenails
- Listening to a favorite song
- Putting on lip gloss
- Wearing a piece of jewelry I've been neglecting
- Lighting incense
- Eating a piece of fruit
- Moisturizing my hands

POP QUIZ

What are you into?

Girl, we are conditioned to be freaked out by anything, well...*freaky*. But no one is pure vanilla! If you want to spice things up, consider investigating an online forum like FetLife.com, where you can learn about many sensual possibilities. If you're feeling extra-brave, open an incognito tab in your browser and go hunting for kinks. (Incognito *not* because you should be ashamed, but because this stuff is private—and if you share your computer with anyone, things could get *awkward*.)

Day-to-day sensuality: Yum

If you have chronic pain or illness, a decent part of your day is taken up with self-care and managing symptoms. Sometimes, you can get lost in that process and forget you're also a sensual being.

For me, feeling sexy is all about sensuality. Because I have fibromyalgia, my senses are always heightened to the max—you probably know that's a huge aspect of the condition—so I often feel like I'm on overload for *bad* sensations.

Embracing sensuality is about turning on your senses to all the *good* sensations. It's like pointing your little radar dish toward deliciousness.

Here are a few ways I embrace sensuality in my day-to-day:

- When I wake up in the morning, I sometimes stretch and roll around in the bed like a cat. I embrace the languid nature of the wake-up time, enjoying the feeling of being in between sleep and wakefulness.
- I always put on essential oils. You can go exotic, floral, bright, and citrusy. I carry some in my purse, too, so I can refresh. Having a delightful scent in my nose all day keeps me feeling beautiful.
- I moisturize. Seriously, sometimes just slowly moisturizing my whole body reminds me of what *does* work and gets me feeling pleased with the parts of my body that *don't* hurt.
- I embrace a mindful eating practice. Especially in summer, when my strawberries are coming in. I'll pick a berry and slowly

bite into it, letting the flavor fill my mouth. I pause and savor. I take another bite. In this way, I truly enjoy the taste, texture, and sun-warmed beauty of the fruit.

- I get lost in music. We're bombarded with media all day in our culture, and it's exhausting our senses. It's a beautiful thing to turn down the lights or close your eyes, pop in your headphones, and get lost in music. It can be relaxing, invigorating, luscious...whatever you need.
- I spend some time on Instagram, which is eye candy for me. Without worrying about "catching up" (because you can't ever see *everything*), I browse pictures and enjoy the sights. Especially on days when I'm unexpectedly stuck in the house, it helps to get immersed in beautiful images.
- I take some measure of beauty for myself. This might mean doing a fun face mask, painting my nails, or moving to a favorite song.

I'm sure you have something you can do—even if you feel awful—that helps you feel more beautiful. Put on a favorite blouse, apply a vibrant lipstick shade—do something that gives you a little zing. Enjoy that feeling of beauty.

These are the things I do every day to help myself maintain sensuality, to keep my senses alive to all the *good* feelings I can access, even when I otherwise feel crummy. This practice helps me feel sexy and alive, awake to all the amazing sensations the world offers.

What kinds of small things could you weave into your day that feel, smell, look, or taste good? The possibilities are endless.

If you get stuck, ask your girlfriend, your honey, or your online friends for ideas. You may be surprised by what they suggest. The sensual world awaits!

For some caregivers, it's about helping—but not enabling

Morgan's significant other has chronic pain from undifferentiated connective tissue disorder, which is likely related to Sjögren's syndrome but still lacks a firm diagnosis. They live together a few days a week, and Morgan tries hard to be encouraging, supportive, and accepting—without enabling bad habits.

My significant other is my number one focus, but I grew up with a parent who had chronic pain. I kind of feel like "caregiver" indicates the person I'm working with is somehow completely incapable. I would think of myself more as a "pain partner," where I'm the support function. I'm not a nurse; I'm here to help.

We're both nerdy academic types, so we're information-fueled. A lot of the conferences I've been to with her were to learn about what she's going through.

Caregiver resources
For a list of caregiver-focused resources, head to the Extra Credit section at the back of the book.

One of the things I've been asked as a caregiver is to help push her along some. She doesn't want to give up, so it's an encouragement function, to know what a red line is versus a perceived red line. Like, "Have you hit the wall and you just need to run a little further to get past it, or are we really done?"

Sometimes I see other people in the community with their partners, and I feel like [the partners are] more on the enabling side than the helper side. I understand why the instinct is to be the enabler, because that's what I was growing up, but I think it's also okay to work with your partner to say, "I'm not living inside your body, so I can't be sure, but I think you can do this."

Body image is part of "You don't have to just retreat." I would put that in the same category as "We can still go out this weekend, we just have to plan to have some down time" or "We can still do that social event, we just need to think about where we can take rests on the way." I would say, "Hey, I know you're feeling a little stressed out about how you're looking, but we can just take it easy this weekend and just do the yoga pants day."

It's none of my business, really, how she looks unless she's specifically asking for my opinion on it. I don't feel like, "Oh, that's too tight or that's too loose" or "I think you're gaining weight or you're not gaining weight," or any of that stuff. It's not my place to comment on it unless I'm being asked about it.

Generally speaking, there's not a lot of stuff for the caregiver. At a recent medical conference, there was nothing for me—I spent the whole weekend in the hotel room. We're not just there to hold the bags.

> *I'm not looking for a medal or something—but for a way for caregivers to either get involved in these situations, or just acknowledgment that we're there too, and a couple courses just for us would be helpful.*

Masturbate. Yup! I said it.

Odds are good that, like me, you've struggled with masturbation. Whether you have mental blocks, or were shamed for enjoying it in your childhood, or because your hands hurt too much to hold a vibrator, or...you get it. There are many things that can stop us from enjoying ourselves.

But masturbation is lovely! And it's healthy. And natural. Pursuing a practice of self-love is a wonderful thing.

Here are a few bits of advice that have helped me get my personal mojo back. Keep in mind: You will have ebbs and flows. Sometimes you'll feel horny every day, and then go weeks without that feeling... it's okay.

Research lubes that work for you (there are many organic, vegan, chemical-free options that work for those of us with skin sensitivities) and then USE THEM. You can't use too much. I promise.

Create a ritual of intention. Turn down the lamps, light a candle, turn on some good music, put on a pretty piece of lingerie...it may feel forced at first, but creating a ritual for masturbating can help break mental blocks.

Don't be shy about toys. There are shops online that can help you pick ergonomically correct toys. Early2Bed.com and GoodVibes.com are two of my favorites. You may have to try a few before you find one that works.

Remember: This is an act of love. You are worthy of love and pleasure. Don't let anyone tell you otherwise.

Speak with a therapist. If you're having trouble getting past mental blocks related to previous sexual abuse, shaming by anyone in your life, or body-image issues—talk to an expert who can help.

Watch porn. Yup! There is a TON of porn online to get your juices flowing. Open an incognito tab on your browser if you want to keep your searches secret. Explore.

Start out non-goal-oriented. Some women have a harder time reaching orgasm than men, and we can sometimes get hung up on speed—slow down. Enjoy it. Maybe you orgasm, maybe you don't. Start with being okay with either outcome and you'll feel less pressure to "succeed." Don't psych yourself out.

Learn to love "pacing"

Are you in a hurry? Slow down, lady.

Pacing is a skill that will serve you for life. Whether you like it or not, your body may need you to take your time now with things you used to breeze through.

I love to write. Some days, I'm so filled with things to say, I could write for ten hours straight—as I did when I was twenty-five.

But my body is entirely different now. If I spent even one day like that, I would pay for it for weeks.

Instead, I pace myself. I've found tools (like the BreakTime app) that help me manage my computer time. I've learned to plan my projects over longer stretches of time, including time cushions in case I flare up, so I can work in small chunks daily.

It was frustrating at first. But pacing is worth it; without pacing, I would not be able to work *at all*.

What task do you need to pace? Can you break it into smaller pieces? Are there tools that could help? Can you delegate part of the task?

Practice pacing.

Develop a "no shame" policy

In my house, we've instituted a "no shame" policy. If I say anything self-critical out loud with my husband around, he stops everything and grabs my hand, looks into my eyes, and says, "I can't validate that statement." I do the same for him.

The "no shame" policy means I don't have to apologize for my pants being too tight because I ate a bunch of rich food on vacation. It means I get pushback if I mention that my face looks extra-wrinkly today.

We've had this policy long enough that when I hear myself say something self-critical while alone, I can almost hear his voice countering me: *"I can't validate that statement."*

When I'm tuned in to my inner monologue, it's shocking to hear how many unkind statements I can make in a day. It's like all the mean girls from junior high live in my head.

The "no shame" policy helps counteract that crud. If you don't have someone in your house who can be the enforcer while you learn to adopt your own, imagine my voice, saying with kindness: *"I can't validate that statement."*

HOMEWORK assignments

1) Create a self-care ritual

Make a list of five things you want to do daily, like flossing, washing your face, brushing your hair...simple things that help you feel better. Commit to doing all five of them every day for a week; set aside fifteen minutes or so for this new self-care ritual.

2) Post a selfie

As sick chicks, we sometimes don't feel selfie-worthy. But babe, I want to see your beautiful face! Play with filters and apps, try a funky angle... have fun with it. Post your selfie with the hashtags #HospitalGlam or #SickLooksLikeMe to be included in larger sick-chick self-love movements, and for sure add #ChronicBabe so I see it. Smooch!

PEP SQUAD

An Interview with Ev'Yan Whitney

Exploring sensuality and sexuality can be liberating and healing

Ev'Yan is a writer and female liberation artist. Her mission is to help liberate others into loving themselves and manifesting their sexualities, and to encourage them to be beautifully mindful...if only to teach herself the same lessons. She spins unadulterated truth and provokes self-actualization over at her blog: *SexLoveLiberation.com.*

Ev'Yan believes that exploring those three things, while maintaining an open and vulnerable heart about them, is vital to our existence. She empowers her community of budding sensualists with a newsletter, e-book, coaching, podcast, and much more.

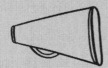

Connect with Ev'Yan:
Website: SexLoveLiberation.com
Facebook: Facebook.com/sexloveliberation
Instagram: @evyan.whitney

Jenni: When I think about being sick for a long time, to a lot of us, the idea of sex and our concept of sensuality sometimes really gets shoved under the rug. We may be too tired, our body may feel unfamiliar to us, for some of us our libido diminishes because of some of the medications we're on. There are any number of reasons why this happens. I feel like our sensual side is an essential part of who we are; do you agree?

Ev'Yan: Absolutely, our sensuality keeps us connected to our bodies. It's like an awareness of our senses—even the ones that have been diminished through illness. It's about mindfulness, I think, being mindful that we have these senses.

It's really important; it's an intrinsic part of our lives. Without this awareness, we can't live a fulfilled life and we're starving ourselves from actual genuine pleasure, and that's what living is about—having pleasure and loving our lives despite the things that are holding us back.

Absolutely, sensuality is huge; it connects us to a lot of things spiritually and the way that we express our sexuality. I don't think we could actually be human beings fully without the expression of sensuality.

Jenni: Without getting into a lot of detail, I can say comfortably that throughout my life, as a ChronicBabe—being that I was diagnosed almost twenty years ago with fibromyalgia—my libido and my sex life has been a roller coaster. Things come and go, the seasons come and go, and everything kinda changes back and forth and it's confusing.

But when I'm taking good care of myself and really loving the things that *do* work about my body, I feel much more grounded and much more like myself. So if we really neglect that, it's a problem. When we neglect that side of ourselves—or maybe *let lie dormant* is a less-judgmental description—what price do we pay in our day-to-day life?

No judgment.
Just to be clear: I'm not judging anyone who has not been good about honoring their sensual side, because I've gone through times when I have not. I really don't want anybody to feel judged here. Smooches!

Ev'Yan: I think we become disconnected from, not just our bodies, our physical bodies, but that spiritual side of us that requires human contact, whether that's one on one or with our partners. We were born sensual, sexual human beings, so to not express this side of us is like ignoring a part of us that is really, really important.

It's like cutting off your arm, but that's a little bit too dramatic—but you're missing a chunk of yourself. Something within you isn't getting fulfilled and you might even feel like something is missing in your life, on a deep level...not necessarily like *Oh, I have a craving for this and it's not in my kitchen*, but more like something in our bellies that is saying *Feed me, feed me, I need sensuality, I need the expression of that, I need the manifestation of that.* It's kind of miserable and I can speak from that because I've experienced that shutting it off; it's definitely miserable.

Jenni: I think a lot of people can relate to that.

Ev'Yan: I think the best saying about this is that *everything is undoable*. You can have forgiveness and you can forgive yourself for the impression you put on yourself; you can move forward. It's not like where you are now is where you will be for the rest of your life. You can help it and, definitely, you can express your sensuality, without question. You just have to do the inner work.

Jenni: I'll just jump in and say one thing to people who have issues that are medically related, perhaps related to medications or procedures. I urge people to talk with their health care providers about that. I know how hard it is to walk into the doctor's office and say, "I can't orgasm anymore; what's wrong with me?" but you've got to say it!

Ev'Yan: Absolutely! I don't believe doctors would look at you funny, because I feel like that is just common sense. The orgasm and the expression of your sexuality [are] part of human nature, and if you go into your doctor and say, "I am not living the life that I want to live, can you please help me?" they're not going to look at you like you're crazy—they'll say "okay."

If anything, you will be admired because you are taking control of your life: *I recognize that this is essential in my life and how I'm living it*, so they are going to want to do something about that.

Jenni: I hear what you're saying when you say that perhaps the doctors will admire you for standing up for that. I totally agree with you. The times I have been freaked out about asking questions like that, the reaction has been so positive.

What are some the health and wellness benefits of a healthy sex life?

Ev'Yan: You feel better, you feel more connected to not just yourself but everything that's around you, all the blessings we have been given.

Sex—not just with another person but even sex with yourself—is a really great way to be reminded you're not alone. That's what I feel like when I'm involved in some sort of intimacy—whether it's with me, or my partner—I feel incredibly connected to the Earth. It's kind of difficult to describe.

Jenni: I understand what you are saying because I feel very much grounded...

Ev'Yan: Right, yes, that's the word!

Jenni: And that's grounded like rooted, not the dug-in way, but in touch with my most primal nature, my most natural state. I'm no expert, but when I am open to that side of myself I feel more like myself, like I'm a full person. I know also that orgasms release endorphins, which are great for pain management.

Ev'Yan: And it makes your skin glow...

Jenni: Depending on what kind of sex you are having, that can sometimes count as aerobic exercise.

Ev'Yan: Absolutely! You can burn a lot of calories, depending on the kind of sex you are having.

One thing I like—and the people that I work with through my writing work—is that we were born from this innate sexuality, born from an orgasm, so in that way, to pleasure ourselves or to be intimate with someone, it kind of brings you back to what you were created from. That's the kind of groundedness and the rootedness that I was speaking of.

It's so overwhelming, but also it's a really great reminder that you came from that kind of carnality that you have in you. You have it in you because you were born from it. It's not something that needs to be learned—[it's] probably been neglected and that's okay—but it's already within you, you were born from it; you just need to express it.

Jenni: I hadn't really thought of it that way, but I love thinking about that, because you are basically acknowledging where you came from and staying in touch with that, especially for a lot of us whose bodies don't quite work the way we wish they would. [Sex is] a really nice way to take us back to this part of us that we *can* still get to work, or at least *I can work on that*. You know, we are all in different stages of where we are on the spectrum.

For those of us who maybe have not really embraced or have been neglecting our sensual side, do you have any advice on how to get back in touch with that?

"You came from that kind of carnality that you have in you. ***You have it in you because you were born from it."***

—Ev'Yan

Ev'Yan: I think that expression of sensuality is different for everyone. I could list things, but I don't know if it would resonate with people.

I feel that starting with the awareness of your senses is a really good place to come from. Starting with touch. Caressing yourself. Self-exploration. Self-pleasure with your own body. Reacquainting yourself with your own body, your skin, and your pleasure spots. It's a really great way and it puts you there, automatically. I'm not saying necessarily in a sexual way, maybe you can just run your fingertips over your own arms, or cradle your belly in your hands.

Things like that show love and tenderness and care, and that's really what sensuality is all about. It's accepting a part of you that is so accepting of who you are, and your journey, and what that looks like.

It is about listening, too, to your body—and feeding that inner hunger that is in every one of us. I think it is acknowledging and recognizing that we are sensual creatures, sexual creatures. Just that, in and of itself, is a really great way to thrust yourself into sensuality.

And practicing that on a daily basis, even if you have to write something on a sticky note that says, "I am an orgasm." That will immediately put you in the state of mind that says, *Yeah, I am a sensual being, I am walking, breathing, I am sensual.*

Jenni: That's the kind of sticky note that I would totally forget to put away, that everyone who visits my home would get to see! I love that idea. Everyone would remember you have that sticky note. Maybe you *want* people to see it?

Ev'Yan: I'm sure that would be an interesting conversation. I'm sure they'd be like, "What are you talking about?" and you could say, "Actually this applies to you as well; we were literally born from orgasms." I think it's a great thing to remind everyone. Even if it's a little bit hard to latch onto, to be taken back to that, to remind us that's where we came from.

Jenni: Maybe I will write that on a sticky note and see what happens next time I have people over.

Ev'Yan: You should put it on the refrigerator.

Jenni: Right next to "buy eggs and milk and beer" and all that stuff I write up there. I'm actually going to do this when I get off this call. That's going to melt people's circuits, but that's fine; I like to do that. It's difficult for a lot of us to talk about that stuff. I think that's a great thing, to start a conversation.

I want to talk for a minute about how sensuality doesn't necessarily equate to sex or orgasm; they aren't necessarily the same thing, or it isn't necessarily a linear process that sensuality absolutely leads you to having sex or having an orgasm.

Ev'Yan: I believe that sensuality is a spiritual experience. Like going inside of ourselves. And what we were talking about earlier, acknowledging that we are an orgasm, that we came from orgasm. Realizing that we have this need to connect and express our sexuality. So, I feel that sensuality is emotional, it's the most spiritual, and it's internal, not necessarily tangible, like a physical thing.

For me, it's just about inner awareness. Realizing that we have these senses and these desires, and we were born with them. I think that's what encompasses sensuality to me.

Sexuality is an expression, a physical expression, of sensuality, so it's like sensuality in motion. It's a manifestation of sensuality.

When you feel like you're in touch with your senses and you're in tune to your body, you are very aware of that. Usually amazing things come from that, and whether that's having sex or self-pleasuring, usually something physical happens, and it doesn't necessarily mean that it has to deal with sex or an orgasm.

It's really good to recognize where they are different because I feel a lot people can say *sensuality* and *sexuality* in the same breath, but a lot of people don't understand the difference between the two. There really isn't a huge difference between the two; it's just about the way you express it, what area you come from with it.

> *"I feel that sex is a really great way to be reminded that* ***you're not alone****."*
>
> —Ev'Yan

Jenni: I have chronic pain, and I have pain every day. Sometimes something will hurt, say I've done a little too much cardio one day and the next day my thighs hurt, so maybe when I wake up in the morning I start to move and stretch and I'm like, "Man, my thighs are really tight and sore!" I may quietly caress them for a minute and get calm, and be like, "It's okay, this sensation feels good. Let's focus on that sensation." That's showing myself I love myself even though I am in pain, that I am not angry at my body—I'm actually showing it some tenderness.

When I do things like that—just that simple act of getting back in touch with what feels good to my body—[it] does a couple things. It helps me reduce pain, because I get less focused on what's bad and more focused on what's good, and then I'm in a better place to attack the rest of my day. Instead of getting out of bed saying, "Man, my thighs hurt!" I can remember, "They hurt, but I also am able to touch them in a way that feels good." That can change your outlook in a big way.

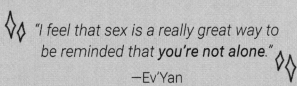

We're talking openly here about sex and sensuality. For a lot of people, it's a bit more taboo, and especially in some parts of our country and the world, it's *really* taboo. I have found that sometimes it's even more difficult to talk about the specifics about what we need or desire when we're sick. Maybe we don't know how to express, how to work around, "My butt muscles really hurt, so I can't be on top!"

It's sometimes challenging to express that when we're not coming from a place of total confidence. I'm wondering if you have ideas for ways to start a conversation with a partner or even to discuss issues with a friend, to try to get advice?

Ev'Yan: I definitely think anyone who has a partner should talk to their partner, as embarrassing or uncomfortable as it might feel. I think it's really important to acknowledge that discomfort and transcend that, then say to yourself, "Okay, I really need to talk to my husband about the way sex makes me feel when I'm having sex with him."

It's not going to be a fun conversation, and then you'll do it anyway, because communication is key in expressing your sexuality, especially if you are with a partner. So much progress and understanding can happen when we are honest not only with ourselves, but also with the people we are sharing our bodies and our life with.

[I've] had a lot of moments in my marriage where I'd actually have to sit down with my husband and say, "Sometimes when we're having sex, it's not like this and I would prefer it to be." It's not fun, it's not comfortable, it's actually kind of humiliating, but if we can get past the discomfort and realize that speaking and communicating with each other gives us the best intimate life possible, ultimately that's the life we want. I can live with the discomfort. Ultimately that's what's going to bring us closer together.

I think it's great that you, Jenni, have this community where people can come and speak about their difficulties and their uncertainties. Speaking with like-minded people is a really great way to get your voice heard, and I think you've created a really safe place for people to do that.

We're not always going to be able to have that same kind of response from people who aren't on the same page. People who aren't sick may not be able to relate to the issues we are going through.

Aside from that—finding that level of communication with people at an outer level—I think it's really great to step inside of yourself and take some time and have an internal dialogue with where you're at, where you're feeling, and have a great way to do that. There are so many different ways that you can speak about sex, there are a lot of safe places for you to do that—I think a lot more than people think there are. My blog is one of them.

It is about moving past the discomfort and the taboo of sex and realizing that ultimately, we are sexual beings. I hate how people feel like, *Oh, sex is so gross or Maybe it's something I should be ashamed of,* when it's part of who we are.

It's like breathing. I don't think there should be any shame surrounding that. The more we can speak about it openly, we bring awareness to something so essential in all our lives, like a heart beating, air in our lungs.

> *"With such a touchy subject as sex and intimacy, **it's really easy for us to get caught up in beating ourselves up.**"*
>
> —Ev'Yan

Jenni: It's asking for what you need, and sometimes that's a little difficult. I know I've been to a bunch of parties with girlfriends, or brunch or something, and I say something and everyone stops for just a second and sort of giggles...Like, *Oh yeah, we actually all want to talk about this, but somebody had to break the ice.*

Ev'Yan: That's totally how it is! It's not like everyone is sitting in their houses like, *I don't want to talk about sex, I don't need to talk about sex.* Everyone needs a voice on that, and sometimes that's what it takes: *I'm having sex and I want to talk to someone about it.* That will bring other people into that awareness, and they will be able to speak about it openly too, and it's good to know they have a safe place to do it.

Jenni: We've talked so much about many different things. Do you have a favorite all-time tip you give people exploring their sensual side that we haven't talked about yet?

Ev'Yan: Probably the best tip I give people on a daily basis is forgiveness. Forgiving themselves for oppressing their body and not expressing their sensualities. Forgiving themselves for being hard on themselves, [for] personal expectations, [for being] angry with their body for the way it *should be* responding.

There is a lot of growth in our ability to forgive ourselves, and with such a touchy subject as sex and intimacy, it's really easy for us to get caught up in beating ourselves up. I should have been tackling this stuff years ago; I'm totally not there yet. I'm speaking personally because it's an ongoing battle with myself to not be hard on myself.

Starting to reach a place of forgiveness is probably the best way to move forward, explore your sensuality, and express your sexuality, and have conversations with people—and I think it all starts from forgiveness.

This interview has been shortened and edited to fit this book. To read the full transcript or listen to the full recordings of this and all the Pep Squad interviews, head to ChronicBabe101.com.

Lesson 6

build your "team" to maximize support

Throughout *ChronicBabe 101*, you've been working on *yourself*. Now it's time to reach out, to build *Team You*. Who's on your team? How will you let them know? What techniques will help you stay in contact with your team? You can't do this alone, babe!

What makes a great team?

Just like in sportsball, a great team has a bunch of different players from varying backgrounds. You want a mix of confidantes and acquaintances; folks you know in person and folks you know online; friends who are grounded and friends who can think creatively.

When people with chronic illness begin to think about their team, they often think that *every* person must be their BFF, and that every member should know all the gory details. But that's unrealistic; if you depend on every person to be your everything, you'll be disappointed.

How to start assembling your team

Look at your Rolodex! (Or iCal or your smartphone or your phone tree...you know what I mean.) Who do you know? Start closest to you and move outwards:

- Spouse/partner/girlfriend/boyfriend/lover(s)
- Family (the ones who don't drive you crazy, anyway)
- Friends
- Colleagues and coworkers
- Fellow volunteers from a nonprofit you love

- Fellow worshipers/parishioners from your faith
- Health care providers (including nurses, receptionists—the whole office)
- Neighbors
- Members of your favorite online forums
- Housekeeper
- Service providers you see often (like hair stylists and manicurists)
- Local business owners you support
- Acquaintances at your community garden
- Fellow parents at your kid's school
- The bus driver you see daily

I think our teams must comprise people from all over our life; all these people have the capacity to help us in some way.

Team Jenni: An example

If I listed my entire team here, it would take *pages*. But here are a few examples that may surprise you:

- *The nurses at my pain care center*—not just because they're all competent to the extreme, but because over the years, they've made an effort to get to know me and go out of their way to solve problems (like medication access).
- *The woman who owns the housecleaning service we use*—like me, she's an avid gardener, and she sometimes surprises me with treats she's grown or seeds from faraway places.
- *The manager at my local UPS Store*, where I get my business mail—he's always extra-friendly in an authentic, I-like-to-know-my-customers way.
- *A family of refugees who gardens alongside me at my community garden*—we only know each other's first names, but we share food and gardening advice, and their kids are adorable.
- *A Canadian sewist I met online who also copes with chronic health issues*—her work is inspiring, and her honesty in her posts has

led to many fascinating conversations. (I hope to meet her one day!)

These are just a few people on Team Jenni. Could I survive without them? Yup. But would I want to? No! They make my life richer, and I'm thankful for them every day.

As you work on *Team You,* I encourage you—nay, implore you!—to think outside the usual suspects. By expanding your idea of *team*, you increase the ways you feel supported.

Use your words

Should you tell people they're on your team? Yes!

Now, if I walked up to my community gardener friends from across the globe and started talking about them being on my team, we would face a serious language barrier. But I *have* told them they're my friends, that I care about them, and that I will help them in any way I can.

It's my experience that most people like to feel helpful. Telling the people on your team that you appreciate them is part of solidifying your bond. Even telling your regular bus driver that you appreciate how he always announces your stop is important—not only for him, but also for *you* to take a moment to appreciate the support. Which reminds me:

The care and feeding of your team

Your team is not going to sustain itself. It's up to you to maintain connections, as often as appropriate. While it would be grand if everyone reached out to you, it's important that you initiate contact, too. (This is vital if you're stuck in your house most of the time and don't see people in person.)

First: Say *thank you*. It's impossible to utter those two words too often.

Second: Ask *how are you?* You never want your team members to feel like the relationship is one-sided.

Third: *Surprise them*. Your interactions shouldn't just be about your needs. Make an effort to treat them; even the smallest gestures matter.

Take care of your team. Feed their souls with kind words and gestures.

When to call in the team

Are you prepping for a big surgery? Call in the team.

- Ask your housecleaner to add an hour to her usual appointment for laundry.
- Ask your postal carrier if they can bring packages up the flight of stairs to your door instead of leaving them in the foyer.
- Ask your church friends to sign up for MealTrain.com so you don't have to cook.

Are you experiencing severe depression? Call in the team.

- Ask your best friend to text you every morning with an inspirational quote.
- Ask your friends from the illness forum to check on you daily.
- Ask your spouse to bring home flowers.
- Ask your psychologist if you need new meds.

It's appropriate to ask for help from individuals on your team anytime, really—but when the shiznit hits the fan? Call *everybody* in for support. You don't have to explain why to everyone, but you *do* need to make the most of all the team-building you've done and get that support, girl.

POP QUIZ

Who's on your team?

Have you started working on your list? Get busy! Start your list today.

Educating your family and long-time friends: Start the conversation

The people closest to us are often the ones best at pushing our buttons. They're the mom who says "Can't you just get over it?" when we talk about our umpteenth flare-up. The sister who gets frustrated because we can't travel to visit as often as we once did. The friend who keeps inviting us to go clubbing, when we've told them over and over that we're only game for a glass of wine in a chill restaurant.

If an acquaintance did these things, we'd tell them to buzz off! But when a dear one does it, it pushes our buttons.

There are two main components of getting our friends and family to understand us.

The first component is kind of sucky, and universal: they may never "get it." That's it. No matter how much we want them to—or feel they should be able to—they may never fully understand what we're going through.

So *you* have to do the hard work of beginning to accept that. Ultimately, it only matters that *you* get it, that *you* know how to live this ChronicBabe life.

I know that's probably hard to hear. I still grapple with this sometimes—why can't my family member accept it at face value when I say I can't do running-based sports?—but we can't force people to change. The sooner you start to breathe in acceptance of this, the easier it will be to stay cool when they say ignorant, thoughtless, or ridiculous things.

The second component regards how we talk to them and what we share. Your family and close friends have so much history with you—they knew you before you were sick—so they may have a hard time wrapping their heads around this new version of you. They will also be dealing with their own mourning process.

I have a family member who *still* tells me how sad it makes her that I've been sick for so long, and while it's a drag to hear (get a therapist!) it's also a good reminder that she means well, and that she holds grief for me.

No matter how well someone knows us—and how deep our history runs—that bond does not exempt them from learning about what we're going through, and understanding the illness(es) we face.

While some dear ones will do their own homework and meet you with understanding, others will do their own homework and come up with garbage Internet articles and an old wives' tale about how tart cherry juice mixed with garlic cures all. Blergh! Still others will do no homework at all.

So: Try to meet them where they are. It's unfortunate that this task falls on your shoulders, but if you really want to teach them and create deeper understanding so you can enjoy the relationships more, it's worth the effort.

Start by collecting all your favorite resources on your illnesses. This could be a small pile of books, a list of links, or a couple of anecdotes about friends with the same conditions.

Talk to each individual about what you'd like them to understand; be prepared to share your resources: "Mom, I know this has been hard for you, but I think you'll feel less scared once you understand my condition better. It will also help me, because sometimes I want to talk about it. My favorite book about it is available at your library, and I'm emailing you a list of five links to read. I would love for you to review those, and then we can talk more."

If someone is reticent to learn things, get your talking points ready—the top three things you want someone to understand. "Cousin Jadah, I know it's hard to understand why I'm so different lately. It's because of my condition:

"One, it's chronic, which means I'll have it for life.

"Two, I'm under the care of some amazing doctors and we're working to improve my day-to-day health.

"Three, for now, what I really need is to manage my energy and be chill. Let's do something fun and simple, like watch a football game."

And if your dear one wants to learn more, yay! Invite them to attend a support group, join your Facebook support group, or watch some instructional videos with you. Maybe you can turn them into an advocate!

Start simple, and keep your expectations low; there will be people who just don't get it, and you can handle that—because you'll also surround yourself with badass friends (a.k.a. family of choice!) in person and online who *do* get you. Over time, your family and oldest friends just may get it together and come along for the ride.

What's an accountability buddy?

My pal Cece is a professional singer and speaker. Although our businesses are different, we're accountability buddies, and it helps us a great deal.

We structure our accountability this way: Each week, one of us leads a text conversation around midmorning. We ask each other a few predetermined questions about the challenges we're currently facing in our business. We cheer each other on, comfort each other when we're struggling, and offer ideas. Once a week, we have a phone call to talk through some of the meatier challenges we're facing.

Having an accountability buddy makes me work harder. I know she believes in me on the days when my self-confidence falters. She's full of interesting ideas because she's creative. We can use similar marketing strategies, which helps—and because we're not competitors, we feel comfortable talking about the nitty gritty.

There are days when I don't feel like texting Cece, because I'm tired, or I'm frustrated, or I worry she'll think I'm slacking. But those are the days I need her most—and I know she feels the same way.

My friends Sarah and Stacey are also accountability buddies. We created a six-week challenge for ourselves to work out and eat healthy a set number of times, and when we met our goal, we treated ourselves with a visit to the local Korean spa for a few hours. It was divine!

Throughout the challenge, we texted each other when we hit milestones. We cheered each other on, offered encouragement, and (gently) called B.S. when someone was slacking.

Knowing these two babes were cheering me on helped me stay active, and I loved supporting them, too. Having a common goal helped; we were flexible about what "counted" as exercise or eating healthy, because we each had different needs and abilities. And we re-evaluated (and changed) our arrangement whenever necessary.

Accountability buddies are a huge part of my success. Think about how you could structure an accountability relationship with someone else: What would you need? What could you offer? How would you both benefit?

PEP SQUAD

Kevin Rynn, Pharm.D.

Say hello to your pharmacist friend!

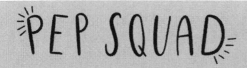

A good relationship with a pharmacist can make a positive difference in your health care experience, and I'm not just saying that because my friend Kevin Rynn is a pharmacist. Kevin is currently vice dean and clinical professor at the University of Illinois at Chicago College of Pharmacy, and has worked in the industry for years.

People used to think of the pharmacist as being on a pedestal, says Kevin, because pharmacies were constructed that way—with the pharmacists on a level above patients. "Newer models of pharmacies are trying to get pharmacists out there and talking to patients, and being patient advocates, because the latest in health care is more patient-focused and patient-centered care," Kevin tells me.

You may not know it, but pharmacists receive the same training as doctors and usually study between six and eight years—so their experience level is high. BONUS: they're on almost every corner these days.

"I think pharmacists are the most accessible health care professionals," says Kevin. "Certainly, there's a pharmacist somewhere working a twenty-four-hour shift." It's true in big cities, in particular. Right now, in my city of Chicago, I can walk right up to a counter and talk to a pharmacist—I can't do that with any of my other health care providers.

A broader shift toward patient-centered care

Those extra-accessible pharmacists are part of a broader shift in health care, one that means pharmacies are offering more chronic illness education to patients—and many are connected to clinics with nursing staff, which means you can get more services in one place, like vaccinations and physical exams.

Kevin says building a relationship with your pharmacist means they can help you jump hurdles to care. "They can be in touch with your provider...because when you call the office, sometimes it's hard to get through to people. To be honest, when a pharmacy calls an office, they're probably going to get called back sooner than a patient." So for any drug-related issues, your pharmacist is really your friend.

Pharmacists can help you decipher potential drug interactions, drug-food interactions, and medication-related dietary issues. Pharmacists learn about all the same disease states as doctors and nurses, so once you're diagnosed, if you have a question about your condition, pharmacists can often provide guidance.

"Pharmacists are trained in physical assessment as well," says Kevin. "Showing [a pharmacist] a rash on your arm or other parts of your body certainly happens." (Whoa, babe—careful which body parts you show! Let's not get crazy!)

If your insurance changes, your pharmacist can help ensure you stay on the best medication or get moved to the most optimal medication for you. If you're like me and your insurance provider requires you get your maintenance medications from a mail-order pharmacy, make sure your *local* pharmacist also knows what you take. Kevin says to keep a detailed list of your meds with you and always review them with your local pharmacist when you add something new.

Girl, you better tell the truth

"Most people drop it off, pick it up, and hopefully there's not a problem. But if there is..." Kevin says most problems can be headed off at the pass with a conversation. Some patients tell pharmacists want they think they want to hear instead of the truth about what they're taking and how often, he says. This can cause BIG problems.

Let's say you're not taking your asthma medication faithfully, and you tell your pharmacist you're having more symptoms. She may call your provider and request an increase in dosage. But when you take the larger dosage, you have side effects—which could have been avoided if you had taken the medication properly in the first place, or at least been honest.

"Financial reasons...belief systems...problems they've had...there are a lot of people who have medications but don't take them, for whatever reason," he says. Honesty is crucial. You can be real with your pharmacist.

Kevin also says your personal medication knowledge shows pharmacists you're compliant. When a patient can't name their medications, it raises a red flag for him and other pharmacists that they might not be compliant—which can make it harder to get the treatment they need for future issues. Don't let ignorance of your meds get in your way, babe!

Next steps: Make friends with your pharmacist

How do we begin to build a relationship with a pharmacist? I asked Kevin if it would be weird if I walked into my local pharmacy one day to say *hi*. "If you came into my pharmacy, I would definitely appreciate that," he says. And not just because I'm cute. (Kevin adds that usually people just breeze in and out, and it makes a real impression when someone shows up with a smile and a kind word.)

Today, pharmacists are also able to perform medication therapy management (MTM). That means you can schedule a consultation to sit down with a pharmacist to review all your health care conditions and medications and get advice on optimizing your regimen. You may be able to spend more time on this with a pharmacist than with your primary care physician!

Make friends with your pharmacist, lady. Take a moment to say hi, and ask for your MTM consultation. This is one relationship you can't afford to let fizzle.

For a more detailed conversation about making friends with your pharmacist, head to ChronicBabe101.com and listen to the full recording of my conversation with Kevin, or download the transcript.

Creating and nurturing relationships with health care providers (HCPs)

You've likely had at least one health care provider who didn't really listen to you or respect you. I've had a handful. They can ruin it for the rest of the good ones—and there *are* good ones!

The key to building a relationship with the good HCPs is communication. Here are a few things I do to make sure my communication is clear and effective:

- When I meet a new HCP, I ask how they like to be contacted if I have questions or information to share. Sometimes they have an online patient portal; sometimes they answer direct emails, or even text messages. Respect their boundaries.
- If I want to discuss research with my HCP, I reach out first and ask if they've read it—this way, I don't look like I presume they're not up on the latest studies. If they haven't, I offer to send them a link to it, or ask if I should bring in an abstract to my next appointment. They do *not* need us to mail entire journal articles or bring printouts to the office—they have services that provide access to research. (Also, reviewing research during a checkup can eat into time that's better spent on urgent needs, so ask ahead of time if you can either extend the length of the appointment or if you can chat about research on the phone.)
- Say *please* and *thank you*. Even if you're feeling frustrated, scared, or irritated, remember your manners. Politeness rules.
- Respect the nurses. They are often the keeper of the sample meds, your communication records, and your doctor's time—so making friends with nurses can really increase access to your HCP. Plus, nurses know a *ton,* and they are often as helpful as the HCP.
- In fact, respect all the office staff. Each one of them cares about your health, is working hard—and is a gatekeeper.
- Come to the appointment with questions prepared, either on paper (don't forget a pen to take notes) or in a digital device. Review your questions one by one so you don't forget any; if you're alone and can't take notes fast enough or don't trust your memory, ask if you can record the appointment. (Most phones

come with built-in recording apps now.) Make sure the HCP understands why you're doing this—it's also important for them to understand that not only do you want to be thorough, but that your memory isn't awesome lately. (It could be a symptom they want to check out.)

- Bring a trusted friend or family member with you to appointments. Introduce them to your HCP and explain that they're present to ensure you absorb all the information. Prep the friend or family member in advance, so they know the questions you need answered and the topics you prefer not to review at that appointment.
- Keep thorough and time-ordered records of all your appointments, exams, test results, symptoms, and procedures. Add a list of all your current medications and contact info for all your HCPs into your phone for easy access at any time, by you or by someone else. If you have a friend or family member you trust, give them digital access to those files, too—you can use secure programs like Evernote, Google Drive, or Dropbox to share and update.
- Periodically ask your HCP if there are any other broader concerns you should be thinking about, like side effects of long-term use of medications, disease progression, or hopes of treatments in the pipeline. This shows them you're seeing the big picture.
- Make sure your HCPs know how to contact each other. If they're not all in the same medical system, provide them all with updated contact lists including phone, fax, and mailing addresses. When you get a test result, ask that HCP which of your other HCPs should get a copy of the results—and follow up to make sure it happens. You may have to chase down paperwork, and that's annoying, but your health care team will appreciate your help.
- If your HCP is not respecting you, is questioning you unfairly, or isn't addressing concerns you have, make an appointment to discuss your goals. Do *not* go in ready to be pissed off—go in with the goal of improving the relationship. Ask for what you need done differently; ask if, together, you can shift the focus

of the care to address a specific need. If they won't make that appointment, or they aren't receptive, find a replacement. Ask your other HCPs for referrals.

You do *not* have to tackle all this alone, and you do *not* have to settle for a cruddy relationship with your HCP. It may take work, time, and patience, but it will pay off in a more collaborative relationship.

The need for more caregiver support is very clear

Tom's wife has primary biliary cirrhosis, or PBC, and recently went through treatment for breast cancer. Pregnancy and an acute illness coincided with an uptick in her symptoms and subsequent diagnosis. He has recently found more support for caregivers because of his wife's secondary diagnosis—a positive outcome from a terrible situation.

[The U.K.] health system is very different from the U.S. health system. Here, it goes, "You seem fine to us because we don't want to spend the nation's resources and get off our bums to overstudy you." They didn't diagnose her until our daughter was six.

Once she'd been diagnosed, in a sense the worst was over, because it was more like, clearly this has affected all sorts of physical stuff from the walks along the beach to the bedroom, so it was much easier to talk about it then.

The cancer thing has been a revelation because PBC can affect younger people, but most of the people with it around our area tend to be older, whereas there's a network here of people living with cancer in their twenties, thirties, and forties. We went to a disco on Saturday night, which was fantastic, because the partners were there as well. With the PBC, it was very hard to meet partners because caregivers don't come to the meetings—it's the sufferers who come to the meetings.

I think what's nice about this carer network is that it cuts across all those boundaries and you're sort of in a different space. This is a key part of your life, whether you come from a more conservative or liberal background. You're a member of the human party rather than the left or right parties.

The big shift that we've noticed is having gone from one chronic illness to cancer, the sympathy level from the "well" population is on a logarithmically different scale. You know, at work you can say, "My partner's got a chronic illness," and it's like "yada yada." No one is like, "Oh, that's terrible." But thanks to Richard Nixon and his war on cancer, everybody's got that on their mind.

Build community through creative action

Let's talk about the resource of *creativity*.

I know you have it in you. I'm not just talking about your ability to paint, draw, knit, or write a story. I'm talking about the ability to walk through your life every day, approaching things with a creative mindset.

Fatigue and pain can eat away at creativity; I know this from experience. To rekindle creativity, we need to make a daily exercise of nurturing it.

An exercise to boost creativity

A good way to start exercising your creativity is with ten minutes, a piece of paper, and a pen. You've got ten minutes, right? Set the timer on your phone and spend ten minutes describing an item in your house. Describe its looks, smells, textures, what it makes you think of, how it helps you—everything you can think about this item. It could be as obvious as a doorknob, or it could be a brick in a wall, or it could be a piece of fruit on your counter.

The more you practice, the more things you'll see. You'll see that doorknob not just as tarnished brass that's a little bit loose on your side of the door; you'll see it as a reminder that you have a home, a tool to use to access fresh air, and a thing that allows you to let in helpers. You'll see the piece of fruit as not just a mango, with a delicious smell and red and green skin; you'll see it as nourishment, a reminder of a vacation, and a good reason to go get more at the international market down the way.

This exercise helps you tap into something deeper in yourself: the ability to see things, to recognize them for what they are, *and* to see their potential.

Why creativity matters

When your creative brain is turned on, you can start to problem-solve. Obstacles don't look as scary because you can see ways around them. You can spot the possibility in everything, and you're able to put things together in fresh ways. Let's talk through a couple of examples:

Let's say you're flaring up and don't feel much like making dinner. You're standing in your kitchen—and nothing is coming to mind. You scan your freezer but you feel blocked. You're sure you have the makings of a meal, but you just can't puzzle it out.

When you're tapped into your creativity, you can scan your cupboards and see possibilities. That can of tuna fish, that jar of capers, that small hunk of cheese. You have rice, so you can cook that and stir in the other ingredients, season it with salt and pepper, maybe a drizzle of olive oil, and you've got a meal.

Here's another example: Let's say you want to give a thank-you gift to a friend who helped you. But you've only got five dollars, and that feels like nothing—you really want to give a personal thank-you gift.

It's spring, and that means people are gardening; your friend mentioned she wants to grow some herbs. You can stretch that five dollars into a truly meaningful gift. Start at the thrift store, where you can pick up a used pot for two dollars. Head to the hardware store, where you can pick up a couple seed packets for another three dollars. Scour your wrapping paper or craft supplies and find some ribbon and pretty paper to wrap around the pot, and place the seed packets inside.

Then go online to find local gardening resources; in Chicago, for example, we have a group that creates pop-up gardens all around the city, and they maintain a treasure trove of info on how to grow herbs on city porches. Grab a short list of websites your friend might like and write them down on another piece of paper to put in the pot with the seeds, along with a personal note of thanks.

There's five dollars well-spent, to create a deeply personal, unique, thoughtful gift for your friend, which can help her enjoy fresh herbs well into the fall.

You may be thinking *I've never been creative—I don't make things.* Maybe you're more left-brained, and creativity to you has always meant being wild and free and audacious and weird. It doesn't have to be. You make your own brand of creativity. It doesn't have to mean *making* something. Even if you've never painted or drawn or written a thing, you can still be creative.

You may be a little afraid of what may come out of your creative efforts. To be honest, it's a little scary for me sometimes; my mind is a wild little creature, and the ideas that come out of it are sometimes frightening and challenging. But that's okay—we need to face that fear. You don't have to act on every thought or idea that comes from your creative process. Creative action is simply a tool to help you think in new ways.

How does creativity connect with community?

Your community is made up of all the people with whom you share time and resources. Your community can be as diverse and wide-ranging as you wish; with the Internet, we're not limited to people who are physically near.

I'd like you to start thinking *bigger* about who is part of your community. And I've got an exercise to help you start thinking that way.

An exercise to broaden your idea of community

The first part of the exercise is all about list-making. I'd like you to think of this is an ongoing exercise; in fact, you may want to start this list in a document on your phone so it's always handy when you get a flash of brilliance.

List all the areas of your life where you know people, or encounter them with some regularity. Start at home and work your way out geographically. Here's a portion of what I wrote in five minutes of focused list-making:

- Home—my husband
- Condo building—my neighbors; the surrounding buildings; my mailman and other delivery personnel I see daily
- Neighborhood—my alderman and his staff; the farmers market; the local shops I frequent; the café where I like to work; people I see regularly at the parks; regulars on the bus
- My city—farmers markets; shops; music venues; theater; comedians I know; writers groups; spoken word events; radio hosts and podcasters; volunteer groups; city-run educational events; block parties; the lakefront where I walk
- My friends in Chicago—my friends; friends of friends

- My friends all over the world—we keep in touch on social media, FaceTime, Skype, and WhatsApp
- My family—not physically close, but we use social media, phone calls, texts, FaceTime, and snail mail to stay in touch
- My spiritual practice—local practitioners; friends who also study Buddhism; spiritual teachers around the world who blog and create podcasts
- ChronicBabe—website comments; social media; speaking events; meeting people through consulting work
- Quilting and crafting—local supply and craft shops; Instagram; the Chicago Modern Quilt Guild; a local shop owner and her friends who have invited me to sew with them; online communities where we share pics, swap fabric and talk strategy; bloggers
- Northwestern University—alumni relations folks; hanging out on campus; meeting people who work there in my field; speaking at their events; reading the alumni magazine to keep up with changes

...And that's just a small portion of my list! If you put some time into it, you can think of tons of places you meet people. All those people are part of your community—and many of those relationships have the potential to grow stronger if you choose to nurture them. Keep adding to your list.

2 The second part of this exercise is to use the creative muscle you've been flexing to come up with ways to make deeper connections, or new connections, with people in your community.

Start by choosing one area in which you wish to have more or deeper connections. Let's say you want to know your neighbors better. Starting there, think about ways you can connect with them. Consider an entire day: When do you see your neighbors?

When you're walking your dog...are they also walking a dog? Do your dogs play well together? Could you suggest a weekly doggie date for them (and you)? Could you ask where they like to buy supplies, or suggest splitting a bag of kibble—to buy in bulk and save? Could you ask if they know a good dog park nearby, and if it's not that close, could you schedule a date where they drive all of you together?

When you collect your mail...do you see neighbors in the lobby? Do you introduce yourself? Compliment them on their hair style or their new holiday wreath? Ask them if they know a good Thai place that delivers to your building? Ask if they caught *The Great British Bake-Off* on TV last night? Do they know about the building improvement committee, are they on it, and can you join or help out in any way?

When you open your blinds in the morning, do you spot neighbors across the courtyard? Do you wave hello? When you're taking your trash out at the same time, do you ask how they are? When you're both mowing the lawn or watering your plants, do you walk over and ask what's new?

This practice is ongoing, meant to help you make more connections week by week. If you have social anxiety, my examples of meeting people in person may not resonate, and if that's the case, try to think about another community of people with whom you could apply similar strategies.

If you get stuck, take a break! This is a creative stretch, and might feel weird or scary. But don't give up. Your health depends on it.

Get crafty

Making things gives us a sense of accomplishment. It also helps us flex our mental muscles, making it a terrific companion to our work on making change.

Crafting offers social benefits: If you belong to a crafty group of friends, you may teach each other skills. If you belong to a formal group (I'm a member of the Chicago Modern Quilt Guild), you gain access to experts and a supportive community.

Crafting can improve your hand-eye coordination and dexterity, and help boost your creative capacity. Making things forces us to use parts of our mind and body that may otherwise be neglected.

Crafting gives you something to share with others, a creative outlet for things you need to express.

When we're struggling with our career—or if we have to leave the work force altogether—developing a creative hobby can fill some of the void.

If you're coming back to a craft you loved before you got sick, be prepared to change your approach. You may need to work on it in smaller chunks of time, or break a project into smaller tasks. You may want to research ergonomic approaches that make the craft healthier (there are lots of knitting videos for this, for example).

And if you're new to a craft, do your homework. Find the online forums where creative folks hang out (Textillia.com, for sewists, is a great example). Search for articles about "*X hobby* and chronic pain"—there are *many* crafty ChronicBabes writing about how to stay healthy.

Tracy Mooney is a great example. Her SewSupportive.com project aims to collect all kinds of healthy advice for sewists with chronic pain and illness. And my pal Terry, despite chronic pain and disability, has not given up his love of hiking. In fact, he runs an incredible website and Facebook group about his experience at bit.ly/DisHiker.

There are endless resources out there for us #craftybabes who are determined to keep doing the things we love. If there's a blank space in your life, get a hobby, babe.

POP QUIZ

What can you do for your team?

We ChronicBabes have to spend a lot of time thinking about what we need to be our best. When's the last time you thought about your team members and what *they* need to be their best?

Could you babysit a friend's kids once a week so they can have a night off? Could you copy edit a colleague's blog post when they need a fresh perspective? Could you walk a neighbor's dog on extra-hot days?

Your team is there for you; it's important you try to be there for them, too. Open the conversation with them about ways you can be supportive.

Caregivers and "caregiver fatigue"

Our relationships with the people who are our caregivers—our spouses, partners, girlfriends, boyfriends, parents, and more—are among the most important.

Some of us need much more daily care than others. Some of us need to rely on caregivers to do many things for us that healthier people can do for themselves. This can make us feel dependent, and that's difficult.

We are entitled to feel frustrated, pissed, irritated, or whiney at times...but as I was creating this book, I realized we ChronicBabes sometimes forget about the weight our caregivers *also* carry. Healthy relationships are two-way streets, and it's my experience that many folks who aspire to be ChronicBabes are missing a part of this equation: recognizing "caregiver fatigue."

When we are sick for a long time, we may get bitter. We may start to believe the world owes us something. And we may begin to take that out on our caregivers.

Our caregivers are managing all the pieces of their own existence, *plus* a big chunk of ours. And yet...we sometimes forget to cut them some slack. We get pissed when they don't read our minds, we get frustrated when they say they need a break, we feel like they're deserting us if they need alone time.

Babe, those people need to rest and recharge for two reasons:

1. They are humans with their own lives and existence, and they deserve to feel as well as they can. And:
2. They can't be great caregivers for us if we never give them the chance to rest and recharge.

There are many women in our community who have to become caregivers themselves, taking care of aging parents or children with special needs. It's a huge weight, one that takes away from your ability to care for yourself. You may begin to feel guilty for wanting your own time and space, and you may quietly resent the person you're caring for, even while knowing they've done nothing to deserve it.

What if you made a concerted effort to talk with your caregiver(s) and ask what they need to be happy and healthy? What if, at a time when you're not feeling your *worst*, but when you're both rested and fed and calm, you started a conversation about how you can support their needs?

Do they need one night off a week? Do they need to know that in the first fifteen minutes after they walk in the door after work, they can have a break from hearing about what ails you? Do they want to have a signal they can raise—a sound, a face, a phrase—that lets you know when they just don't have the mental energy that day to be your shoulder to cry on? Will it help them to see a list of *Team You* so they know you have others' support when you're in need?

What can you come up with together to help your caregivers feel less intensely responsible for you, to feel independent, to feel like you respect them and understand their needs?

If you're reading this and thinking, *But this puts more space between us!* I can practically guarantee you that doing this will improve your relationship and bring you *closer*.

Start a conversation with your primary caregiver. Even if you have a spouse or best friend you always rely on and you *don't* think of them as a caregiver per se, talk to them about this anyway—they may have concerns or needs they've been hesitant to share. #CaregiversRule

Think you can't make new friends? Think again!

As adults, it's harder to make new friends. And chronic illness can isolate us! Still, there are endless ways to meet people. Here are ten to get you started:

1. *Plot a yarn bombing.*
   If you're a knitter—especially in a city—find a group of like-minded folks who share an interest in knitting. Google [your city name] knitting club or hop on Meetup.com to find groups that craft together. Then help plan a yarn bombing—a gathering where tons of knitters get together and cover something unexpected with yarn. Just try not to get yourself arrested.

2. *Do your dry cleaning.*
   Years ago, I lived in an apartment building with a dry cleaner on the first floor; I saw her every day. I would wave, sometimes bring her my clothes, and always compliment her on her plants. One day, she gave me clippings from one of her plants; a couple of weeks later, I returned the favor. Now, years later, I still pop in to say hi and admire how much the plant cuttings I gave her have grown! She's great. A close friend? No. A nice lady who always gives me a hug? Oh yeah.

3. *Put an ad on CraigsList.*
   A friend of mine moved to Chicago years ago from Minnesota, knowing no one except her beau. She put an ad on CraigsList announcing a search for young women who like to read fiction and drink wine. She culled the responses and collected a lovely group of gals who, today, still get together, have stood up for each other at weddings, and happily sit for each other's babies. And still drink plenty of wine.

4. *Say hi.*
   Radical! Just say hi to everyone. You never know who you might meet.

5. *Start a #hashtag.*
   My pal Veronica started a project called #365feministselfie. She asked feminists to tag their pics on social media with the hashtag, to show the world the myriad faces of feminism. She's made tons of friends through this project.

6. *Open a spa.*
   Have a friend who sells Mary Kay or Arbonne? Know anyone who's good with essential oils? Have friends who like to paint nails? (Ahem, I *love* doing that...) Invite them all over, and ask each of them to bring a friend or two, for a spa day. Pamper yourselves and each other, get to know some new folks, and bond over shared experiences. (Alternative: Buy some cheapo nail polishes at the drug store, make yourselves homemade sugar scrubs, and keep it low-cost but still super-fun.)

7. *Be a DJ.*
   Love music? Passionate about a pop culture topic? Ask your local college or university if they have spots open for their radio station DJs. In some big cities, radio and TV channels are reserved for the public, and you need only put in a request. Then: Host your show! You'll learn new skills, meet new people, have fun talking to guest callers, and share your light with the world.

8. *Plan some hang time.*
   You've got at least a couple friends online, right? Plan a Google or Zoom Room online hangout with them once a month, perhaps with a specific topic to get everyone started. Open it to friends and friends of friends. Don't let being stuck indoors keep you from meeting and seeing friends.

9. *Pet something furry.*
   If you love animals, volunteer at the local animal shelter. Many facilities are happy to have volunteers spend time with animals, take them to nursing homes, or run adoption days. You'll get the benefit of some awesome furry-creature bonding time, and meet folks with at least one shared interest.

10. *Go all-out.*
    Make these ideas your own. Create your own club. Invite folks over for a night of inspiration board creation. Staying connected with others is *essential* for your wellbeing, so make a daily effort to reach out.

How's your friend-dar?

Are you looking for the signs that signal someone is good or bad friend material? Is your radar—um, your *friend-dar*—working correctly?

Friend-dar is an essential power for you to cultivate. It's the ability to spot the telltale signs that someone is going to be an awesome person in your life, or that they may wind up being a drag. You can start practicing it right away, and you can apply it to existing relationships as well as use it to evaluate potential new friendships.

Step 1: Make a no-go list

These are the behaviors or beliefs that disqualify someone from being your friend. Some of mine include:

- Perpetual tardiness with no apology or real reason
- Judgmental attitude or discriminatory behavior or language
- Inflexibility when it comes to rescheduling
- Narcissism or a high degree of self-focus

I'm clear about the things I can't tolerate. Make your own list; say what you really feel and believe. *Memorize it.* Know it to be true.

Step 2: Keep this list in mind whenever you meet someone new, or perhaps reread it before going to church, book club, or a support group meeting so it's fresh

Cultivate a state of awareness. This state of awareness does not mean you're hypervigilant and questioning everyone; it looks more like a gentle openness to signals. Watch people, and listen to them. They'll give you signs. To use my example, these would be red flags:

- Someone shows up late to lunch and doesn't acknowledge that I was kept waiting

- Someone makes an off-color comment or says something nasty, then tries to make like they're just joking
- Someone offers no options for when they can meet, insisting their schedule has no wiggle room
- Someone talks endlessly about themselves and doesn't ask about me, or barely listens when I talk about my experience

Are you catching my drift? I pay attention when someone does these kinds of things, because they're a signal that the person is not going to be good for me.

I'm not deciding they're a jerk, or that I never want to encounter them again. I'm not writing them off forever. But my friend-dar does tell me to watch out—they are going to be frustrating companions. Why would I choose to spend time with someone who's gonna drive me nuts?

Step 3: Assess, re-evaluate, regroup

Maybe you work on this for a couple of weeks and realize your list is a bit harsh, or too narrow.

Maybe you realize you thought you couldn't tolerate *any* tardiness, when in fact you're cool with a new friend who's always five minutes late—because she's so fun it makes up for it.

Maybe you realize you're not being as strict with your no-go list as you could be, and someone snuck past your friend-dar...which means you need to reinforce your system.

Your no-go list is not a forever list; it's a "what works and doesn't work for me *right now*" list. Keep an open mind, and change the list over time to work for your current situation.

The bottom line: Don't waste your time hanging out with anyone who doesn't bring you joy. Sure, sometimes family connections or workplace obligations force us to hang with people who are jerky. But when you get to choose, then *choose*. Be proactive; if someone isn't being a good friend, gently set some new boundaries and step back.

The choosier you are about your friends, the stronger your support system will be. When you hang with a posse that rocks, you get stronger, happier, more creative...they'll bring out the best in you. And you'll do the same for them.

HOMEWORK assignments

1) What are your ideal qualities?

Have you ever tried online dating, or looked over a friend's shoulder as she created her profile? You have to spell out the ideal qualities you look for in a mate. The same goes for friends! Take a little time to write out some of the best qualities you could hope for in a friend, and use that list to guide your friend-making efforts.

2) Pretend you're a social media guru

The best social media accounts ask their audiences lots of questions and engage in conversation. You can practice doing the same, in person and online. Make a list of questions you can try on people, like "What's the best action movie you've seen recently?" or "If you could travel anywhere, where would you go?"

The best social media accounts *also* curate great content. That means they choose the most interesting, quirky, timely things to post. You can do the same on your own social media accounts, or in person, by staying current informed about news and current events. Seek out a few new sources, babe, and broaden your experience.

PEP SQUAD

An Interview with Lisa Copen

Building a reliable support team means you're never alone

Lisa Copen founded Rest Ministries, Inc. after being diagnosed with rheumatoid arthritis at the age of twenty-four. It's a nonprofit Christian organization that exists to serve people who live with chronic illness or pain, and their families.

Since 1996, RestMinistries.com (and its associated blogs and social media efforts) has reached hundreds of thousands of people. It continues to grow through the help of its volunteers, who keep it going every day.

Lisa also founded Invisible Illness Awareness Week, an annual observance that brings together a huge variety of people who share their stories and experiences with each other, in service of creating a supportive community for all.

Lisa and her husband, Joel, also own Gutsy Goodness, a jewelry company they began in 2015. Combining Lisa's love of design and passion for encouraging others, Gutsy Goodness pendants and keychains offer hope to those who face challenges, yet who know life takes guts! You can find them on Etsy or Amazon Handmade.

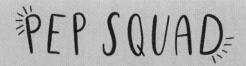

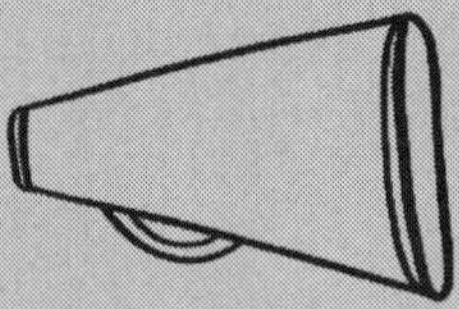

Connect with Lisa:
Website: RestMinistries.com
Facebook: Facebook.com/InvisibleIllnessWeek and Facebook.com/RestMinistries
Twitter: @LisaJCopen

Jenni: Lisa, can you give us an idea of who is on your team, like who is on Team Lisa—the people who support you and are in your life in a big way?

Lisa: I probably represent a lot of people out there who are living with a chronic illness because I have some wonderful friends, and I have family, and I have friends across the country, and I have acquaintances. I have a lot of layers in friendships that would make up my team, and yet at the same time there's also that feeling of "Gosh, who could I call right now to help me out with this? I can't think of a single person!"

As I was writing something the other day, I was asking this question about when you are a parent, does your child feel this way? Explaining it as a person with a chronic illness, we have a lot of friends who we can call in the middle of the night in an emergency. But sometimes we crave those friends who we call because we need a cup of coffee, or we need someone to come by and open a jar for us and hang out with us. Sometimes those are the hardest friends for us to find.

What I find is a lot of times, it is me telling myself, *I should be able to handle this. I don't need to bug them right now, they are really busy, they have kids too, they have a family, they have their own illness, they have issues, I am the lowest priority on their list.*

That's not necessarily true. Lots of times, people really do want to help, they just don't know how. Sometimes people are literally in your neighborhood only a mile away, and they find out later that you could have used them either for a gallon of milk or just a friendly hug. Then they feel disappointed that they didn't know it.

I have a wonderful family, and I feel extremely blessed for that. But they all live at least a thousand miles away. My mom would say, *In an emergency, I can get there in two hours on an airplane ride,* but in reality that's four hours to the airport. And so I find myself sometimes wishing that I did have family living closer.

For someone with a chronic illness, it's very, very hard to ask for help, and that's a whole other show unto itself. There are people who fall under the category of our well-known acquaintances, maybe people you are getting to know that you kind of clicked with, at maybe a meeting, Bible study, support group, or a kids event, and it's so hard to take that extra step and say, "Hey, could you pick my kid up after school this week or could you do this...?" It's so hard to go from being that acquaintance to [being] someone who needs something, and I try to push myself.

Jenni: It is really hard to admit that you need help, to ask people you really don't know that well for help. But what I've found is that simple requests are, for the most part, met with enthusiasm.

Most of the people I bump into in my life, even when they aren't very close friends, if I need something small and I ask for it in a gracious way, I can usually get the help that I need. I think the flip side of that is, I make sure that people know I am available, and if they need something they can call on me.

The more open we can be about it, that really sets a precedent, helps people know it is okay to ask for help. Sometimes it's the smallest things. I have written before about the guys at my UPS store, where I get all my mail. They know sometimes I don't feel good and it's really hard for me to lift a box, or sometimes I am waiting for a package or a paycheck and I am really excited, and they will call me and let me know, which is not part of the standard service at UPS stores.

When I think about my team, I include all those people. I include the manicurist who does a really great job on my pedicures. I include my cleaning lady. When I think about Team Jenni, it's full of people; I am thinking about my health care providers. My team is majorly big...we have the major league team and the minor league team.

Lisa: Well, you just expanded mine! It does take a village sometimes just for one of us. I think you learn what you want to do with your time and energy, and what you need to either ask for help with or pay someone to do.

We have a gardener that comes and clips plants and cuts our grass. I have a husband who is perfectly healthy who could do it, but that is not a joy to him. He would rather do anything than gardening. And about the third day that he tried it, we wound up in the ER for seven hours on a Saturday...and the copay alone would have paid for the gardener. I made the choice then [to get a gardener] and he's perfectly happy with it. He is happy to come home and see the prickly thorn branches from the palm trees all bagged up; it's a gift.

It does take a village to keep us all put together.

Jenni: Yeah, I include them, and here's why: A lot of times, I've gotten stuck feeling like I couldn't ask for help or I didn't want to ask a friend for something really big, when in fact maybe just a small assist would have made my day easier.

So I've started to try to think about moving through my day. Are there small ways I can ask for help and get it? And will that help my day go better? For example, today I was riding the bus and my knees and legs were hurting really badly, so when the bus pulled over to pick me up, I said, "Hey, can you lower the bus?" Because the buses here in Chicago go up and down to make it easier for you to step up.

That's a small thing. Normally, I wouldn't ask for it. It's a really small thing—it's part of the bus driver's job—but I thanked the bus driver and was polite and friendly. For years I thought I had to be so independent, do everything on my own, that it wasn't a good idea to ask people for help...and now I've gotten over it because I need assistance with different things.

"From an acquaintance, a relationship can actually form. And then ***it becomes more and more easy to ask for help*** *from those same people."*

—Lisa

Lisa: I think that happens with age and experience. When you start doing little things like that, it becomes a little simpler every time you do it. The first time, if you're someone who lives with a chronic illness, and you've never asked someone for help, it's hard. Every time I'd buy a Snapple at the store and was going to drink it, I'd have to ask them, "Will you please open the bottle for me? Because I can't get it open." I'd just briefly explain, "I'm sorry, I have rheumatoid arthritis so it's really hard for me."

But every time you do the tiniest thing like that, it does get easier, and you'll find most of us with chronic illness are real fighters. We will fight to do everything we can possibly do. When you ask for help, it's not a sign of weakness—it's a sign of conserving your strength for the things that are important in your day and saving that for the things you really value.

And maybe you knew you were going to do a certain amount of walking later in the day, and if you stepped on that bus and your knee went out, it would stop you from doing something healthy that you had planned. So it is a mindset we have to take on, and sometimes you have to claim it before you feel comfortable with it, and with time it does get simpler.

Jenni: It turns out that most of the people in my life just want to be helpful and get satisfaction out of being helpful, the same way I do. I mean, that's why *ChronicBabe* came to exist. It makes such a big difference.

Lisa: I think the first time you ask any person it can be difficult. Then their response, a lot of times, will encourage you to do it again. I think what you said is important too, about how you can do things for them too.

My son is in taekwondo and he's been at the same studio for three years, so I've gotten to know a lot of the moms over the years. Our personality, our outlook, our willingness to say, "Oh yeah, that's going on in my life too," or "I'm stressed about the holidays too," or whatever—they kind of get to know you to a certain level.

When you have to actually ask them for help, like when I had a splint on my hand for about three months...I had joint replacement surgery for rheumatoid arthritis, and I couldn't drive. It was really hard for me to find a ride to the studio because everybody's lives are chaos. To find someone who's going the same day, same time, that's in your kid's same class—that's nearly impossible. But I could take a taxi down there for about ten dollars, and then I could beg a ride back off anyone who happened to be there. Everyone was more than willing to give me a ride home.

You find that the act of even getting in someone's vehicle and having three minutes of conversation on the ride to your house, or whatever it is, creates a new level of relationship that you didn't have before. Even if you've known that person for years. And part of that is getting in their car and seeing the chip wrappers, and the spilled drinks, and that they're human too—and part of it is making ourselves vulnerable enough to say, "I need some help with this."

It does create a new kind of relationship, and we in turn can also be willing to help. When they're sitting there trying to help their kid with homework and they're saying, "I don't know how to do that math problem," if you do, you reach out and say, "Oh, I could help you!" It's the tiniest things. What happens is from an acquaintance, a relationship can actually form. And then it becomes more and more easy to ask for help from those same people.

Jenni: With fibromyalgia, I don't have visible symptoms. Besides the fact that I may walk slowly some days, or my eyes may look tired because I didn't sleep. So people tend to think of me as a really healthy and vibrant person, and that's great—I want them to think of me that way.

But sometimes, I will ask people to do something and they look at me a little funny, like, "Why do you need that?" The classic one is asking someone to get up from the handicapped seat on the bus, for me, because that is so hard. I don't look like I need a seat, but some days I can't stand. That's really challenging. I don't suggest that for first-timers—it's a tough one.

The biggest thing I've gotten from having a team is staving off isolation. For myself, living in a big city, in a high-rise apartment, I can feel like I'm just in my little concrete cube up here, all by my lonesome. Knowing I have all these people on my team really helps. *(Author's note: Since this interview, I've moved into a much cozier place with my husband. Whew!)*

Isolation is a big issue. Sometimes when you're flared up, you're kind of on your own—you have family in the house, but sometimes you've gotta feel isolated, right?

Lisa: Yeah, I think there's a misconception among a lot of people that if you have a family, you're not isolated. I feel blessed to have a husband and a son, and they're good guys, but I still feel very isolated.

There are a lot of people in marriages who are really hurting or that are abusive, and that's much worse than living alone, but I think that the most lonely times can be at two a.m. when you're sitting in the dark and your body is throbbing in various places and the rest of the house is quiet, or else they're snoring. And everybody's content, and no one knows you're hurting.

I went through a period of having some reactions to a medication in August; I was throwing up just about every night. From three o'clock until midnight, I was basically nauseous. There is no more lonely feeling than throwing up by yourself. You don't honestly want someone in the bathroom, but you want someone standing outside with a washcloth, saying, "Are you okay? Can I get you anything?"

Jenni: And at that point, you're like, "Do I need an air horn in the bathroom so I can notify people that...?"

"The most lonely times can be at two a.m. when you're sitting in the dark and your body is throbbing *in various places and the rest of the house is quiet, or else they're snoring. And everybody's content, and no one knows you're hurting."*

—Lisa

Lisa: Right! It's that feeling of, *you don't want anyone there, but you don't want to be by yourself.* You want someone to care. Via the computer, it's an amazing tool for being able to connect with people, and some people would say that prevents isolation. Because you can literally log on at two a.m. and find someone who's up, who also understands.

We can really be at risk of depending solely on the computer and our friendships from around the world. Even if, like you said, your connection is just with the doorman, or the mailman, whoever—I always see the UPS driver when he comes to visit me; he knows more about my life than some of my friends. All they have to do is look at what's being delivered some days.

Jenni: So when you make "Team Lisa" T-shirts, he's totally getting one.

Lisa: Right?! Sometimes it's just having a conversation. I always feel sorry for the people who come to the door to sell me something, because half the time they walk off with one of my brochures.

The other day, [a missionary] came and I ended up giving him my *Beyond Casseroles* book and a brochure. *God bless you, thanks for doing what you're doing.* I gave him a glass of ice water. It's connecting with the people that are brought into your life, wherever they're brought in, however you're feeling. It doesn't have to be major; you don't have to do something earth-shattering in their life. Sometimes just talking to them—you might be the first person who has acknowledged them as a person today. And there's something about that, that can refresh you as well.

Jenni: I think we have a lot of those moments in our lives that we don't realize are opportunities to connect with people. That moment of acknowledgment that *we're in this together, we're having a shared experience,* whether you're at work, at church, on the bus, at the grocery store, whatever. Connecting with people and sharing something with them is so simple.

It feels difficult sometimes for people who are shy or haven't done it before, but when you start doing it, you build these great connections. Even if those moments are fleeting, even if it's just for two minutes while you're in line at the checkout and you're both giggling over a magazine cover that's ridiculous, or whatever. Those moments are incredible.

When you think about the idea of a team—it reminds us that we're involved, we're part of a community—can you think of other places ChronicBabes like us could look for people who could be team members? We've talked about our family, we've talked about health care providers. Can you think of other places? You're very active in your church community, right?

Lisa: I am. Actually, my husband and I just started going to a small group last week. We haven't been involved in one for years, because for some reason a lot of them didn't seem to have child care. When we took our son to one, they had child care, but it was basically us sitting in the living room listening to fifteen kids in a bedroom wondering who was going to be killed first...it was not the relaxing environment we were looking for.

This year, our dearest friends for over fifteen years—their group started up again, and they have child care down the street at someone else's house with a babysitter. *We are so there.* And there's something wonderful about sitting in a room full of people with whom you have something in common. For those of us that live with illness, it's really important for us to have an outlet to speak about what we're going through with our illness.

On the other hand, don't box yourself in so that it is your entire life. You may be able to get the support you need for your chronic illness online because there's not a meeting everyone has to go to, you aren't dragging yourself there. And then you might be able to find a group or some different thing going on in your community that has another interest.

Maybe you've started taking up photography. Maybe you're no longer able to participate in team sports, or something that you've done like played softball for years, but suddenly you can become the photographer. So don't think just about illness but also think about other things you might want to be involved in and how those people can become your support network.

Let's be honest: Those of us with chronic illness, we reach out, we take meals, but if everyone on your team has a chronic illness, you're going to be cutting yourself off from a lot of the world. The reality is, most people out there still don't understand aspects of invisible illness.

I also think support groups for those with chronic illness can be amazing tools, but there are seasons we will go through in our life where we really crave that [support], and seasons where we don't really need it. And there are some really spectacular support groups, and there are some really awful support groups.

Jenni: I've been to some of the really awful ones!

Lisa: So if you're in a season where you're thinking, *You know what? This would really be helpful for me to sit down with some people and talk about what I'm going through, because I'm not being a great spouse or I'm not dealing well with my job right now, with my illness.* If you're in that season in your life, then go for it, and plan on visiting two or three different groups, maybe for your specific illness, maybe at your library, maybe at your church...we have different groups through Rest Ministries.

Try to check them out; if you go to one and you don't leave feeling better, my advice would be don't go back to that one. Because you should leave feeling somewhat uplifted. If you're coping with your illness, and all your family and friends are saying, "You need to join a support group. You need to join a support group"—if you're not feeling the call right then to do that, it's okay. We go through seasons.

I've had rheumatoid arthritis since I was twenty-four, and there have been times when it was really helpful and I wanted that, and times when I had things I'd rather do than go around and talk about feeling bad. Especially if I'm feeling decent that day. Now, with the Internet, there are some great tools, with Facebook, FourSquare, check-in features, Meetup.com, and more. Think beyond looking at your Starbucks bulletin board or your community newspaper.

"Support groups for those with chronic illness can be amazing tools, but ***there are seasons we will go through in our life where we really crave that,*** *and seasons where we don't really need it."*

—Lisa

Jenni: It's valuable to look for support groups for illness-related stuff, but also look for groups that are related to some of your other interests. Making everything about your illness and making everything with your team about your illness—that's boring, and people are going to get frustrated. You're going to get frustrated and tired of it. We can't spend 24/7 on illness. Well, we can, but we shouldn't, in my opinion, spend 24/7 obsessing about our illness and only relating to people in regards to it. I think the best thing we can do is fill our lives with as many other interests as possible.

Lisa: We need to think of our illness as a tool in order to help us find our passion, or what our purpose is going to be. Everything I do through Rest Ministries has to do with chronic illness. But I really get rejuvenated when I go to a Christian women's mastermind group. There's a book marketing conference, national writers and speakers association groups that I go to, and that's where I'll meet other women who have a lot in common with me. A certain percentage, maybe five percent or so, will also have a chronic illness, or maybe they're a cancer survivor or something, and we'll have that in common.

You come away with a new perspective and you're able to take it back to the illness community. You have to get out of your little circle to be able to grow and use [your illness] as a tool to reach out to other people. Not everyone who has a chronic illness wants to be an advocate for it the rest of their life, but if you have a chronic condition, you now understand suffering in a way that you probably never did before.

Illness is a tool, and it teaches you suffering like no one else. You can go out and encourage pretty much anyone who's hurting, because you definitely understand, even when *not* to say anything. So if your best friend is going through a divorce, if your sister is diagnosed with cancer, if someone's going through a really rough patch with their child who has a chronic condition, you have the ability now to know when to say, "I'm here for you; if you need to vent, put me at the top of your list. Pick up the phone." You get the honor of being someone who *gets it*. And that's a great place to be.

> ***"Don't be ashamed of your disease.*** *Use it in a positive light, to let people know that you needed that help and you appreciate their help and it really makes a difference in your day."*
>
> —Lisa

Jenni: What a great concept. I don't want to say we're ambassadors of suffering, but we kind of are.

Lisa: We kind of are. Every time you ask the person at 7-11, "Could you open my Coke for me?" Every time you do that, and they give you a look, and you say, "I'm sorry, I have such-and-such condition and I just can't do it today," you have now educated that person.

They give you this look like, *hmm*. And if you come back two weeks later and the same person is there, they're really gonna remember. But they may never give someone else that look again, of *Why would you possibly need help?*

It's the same way when you park in the handicapped spots legally, and you get the looks. If someone pulls over and says something to you, it is so hard to remain calm, and most people do not want to be educated on it. If they're the ones standing there telling you something, they just want to vent. But...

Jenni: The thing is, in those moments, you're taking care of yourself, like asking at the 7-11 to have someone open your soda. By getting your needs met, you're educating that person so they are more knowledgeable and more compassionate, and they are going to take that along, like you said, and share that compassionate perspective with other people, we hope. In the best cases, that's what happens. We are using our illness experience almost as a tool to help the world, to help everybody live in a more compassionate place.

Lisa: Yeah, so when you have to ask for help, don't mumble it under your breath and act embarrassed. Give them a smile and say, "Would you mind opening this for me? Because I have rheumatoid arthritis." Or whatever you have. "And my hands aren't working today." I can even hold up my joints, and my hands are pretty obviously deformed.

Have a sense of humor, smile, and that's what they'll remember. It's a great feeling.

Jenni: He may not know it, he may not know your name, but he then becomes an advocate for you.

Did you have any final thoughts you want to share?

Lisa: You and I know how hard it is to ask for help. We're not trying to do anything that we have not struggled with and still struggle with sometimes today.

But in our hearts we know it's the right thing to do, and so we practice. I think you can find the joy within yourself and go out and experiment and when you need to ask for help, put your chin up, and say "thank you so much." There are people that have jumped up to open a door for me, not realizing I had rheumatoid arthritis.

I had someone once see me trying to carry a huge mail bin out to the car from the post office, and he helped me carry it out. I said, "I've been doing this for fourteen years, and I've never had someone offer to carry it out for me. I have rheumatoid arthritis, and you'll never know what a difference that just made in my day." It was one of those horrible flaring days, but I had to get mail. And he said, "You're kidding! I can't believe no one's ever offered to help." It made *his* day.

If your illness exists, don't be embarrassed by it, don't be ashamed of it—it's a tool you can show now and then as part of your

ID to people, to say, "You really made a difference in my day today." There are people that will do something out of the kindness of their heart, and they don't realize how much you needed help that day.

Don't be ashamed of your disease. Let people know that you needed that help and you appreciate their help, and that it really makes a difference in your day. It makes a difference in our attitude and our outlook on the world. We feel like there are some people out there willing to go the extra mile. I know it's hard, and there are days I don't want to appear ill, and days I need help—don't deny it if you do.

This interview has been shortened and edited to fit this book. To read the full transcript or listen to the full recordings of this and all the Pep Squad interviews, head to ChronicBabe101.com.

Lesson 7

Strengthen personal relationships to WEAVE A SAFETY NET

Our personal relationships can take a big hit when we get sick. Creating a deep bond with someone is challenging for anyone. Add the complications of chronic pain or illness and it's even tougher. This lesson will help you repair and strengthen relationships that are ailing.

Being an equal player is not optional

One of the most powerful things we can do to strengthen our relationships is to say "thank you," "how can I help you," and other helpful phrases. It's not always about us...we need to be equal counterparts in relationships. Here are twenty-six questions you can ask and statements you can make to help strengthen bonds. Get real: When was the last time you said anything like this to the people on your team?

- How are you?
- I'm super-thankful for you.
- Is there anything I can do for you?
- How can I support you?
- You have a smokin' hot bod and I can't wait to smooch you later.
- What would be fun for you?
- You have amazing fashion sense.
- Is there anything you need from me?
- Our friendship is important to me.

- Is there anything you would like to talk about?
- What's new with you?
- I'm so thankful for your support and I'm always here for you, too, even if I can't be present in person.
- Is there anything you've been itching to tell me but have been holding back?
- What's your favorite color?
- You're such a creative problem solver and I appreciate how you always try to come up with a fix for issues that we face together.
- Is there anything about my chronic illness that's confusing for you?
- I can tell you're frustrated and I feel your pain.
- What can I do to help you feel more supported today?
- You're a great hugger.
- Would it be helpful if I called tomorrow to see how you're doing?
- Thanks for always being here for me when I ask for help.
- It sounds like you could use a pick-me-up. Want a quick phone chat?
- You're one of the coolest people I know.
- Can I get you anything?
- You're a pretty special person.
- Want to just chill at my house tonight?

Disclosure creates intimacy in all kinds of relationships

Deciding whether or not to disclose your chronic illness is tough—there's no one-size-fits-all answer. In some relationships, disclosure can foster intimacy and vulnerability. But sometimes, disclosure leads to more distance.

Family: Some will be cool *(I see you, Aunt Carolyn!)* and some will be jerks *(not gonna name names!)*. That's the breaks—just because they're related to you doesn't mean they're going to be awesomely supportive.

Before you disclose, think about what you hope to gain by doing so. Do you want their support? Sympathy? Advice? Do you think they'll be able to step in and help in some way? Or are you just considering disclosure out of a sense of obligation?

Get clear about your goals for disclosure; it will help you decide how much to tell, and to whom. It will also help you manage your expectations.

If your family dynamic is, ahem, dysfunctional: Consider sending a simple email with an update and a link or two to helpful resources. Then let them get weird about it, if they must—but don't own their dysfunction. (In some families, word spreads quickly, so sending a mass message like this can help you get out in front of it.)

In almost all cases, I recommend keeping things simple and leaving out the gory details. Telling your uncle all about your colonoscopy is just unnecessary—and the more details you share, the more likely they'll ask more probing questions at a time when you don't feel much like answering.

Friends: When I meet someone new and they seem cool—friend material!—I usually dive right in. This stuff permeates just about every area of my life—they should know what they're getting into.

I understand why you may want to wait. You may have fears of being judged unfairly. You may be a more private person, who prefers to share that information when you feel more secure in the friendship. By all means, take your time...but not *too* much time. For two reasons: one, the longer you wait, the more nervous you'll be about when and how to disclose; and two, if the new friend turns out to be the judgy type, *you don't need them.*

Romance: I think the same advice for disclosure in friendships holds true for romantic relationships. Again, take some time to think about your goals: What do you want from the disclosure?

Romantic relationships can bring the extra awkwardness of sexual encounters. Maybe you have trouble getting into certain positions because of pain or immobility; maybe you have an ostomy; maybe your medications make it difficult to orgasm. Maybe you simply haven't had a sexual partner since diagnosis and you don't know what's going to be different now.

Remember that the other person may also be facing these fears—you don't know what's going on in their head. They may have already dated someone with chronic illness or disability. They may surprise you with their knowledge and comfort with the situation.

I believe disclosing earlier is better. It's a lot easier to have a complex, revealing conversation over coffee than it is when you're naked for the first time.

Sometimes, disclosing your condition to a romantic interest or potential sexual partner creates an intimacy that adds a layer of depth to the relationship. When you show trust, that may release them to do the same. It can be quite beautiful.

And as with new friends, if a new romantic interest judges you or is turned off when you disclose your illness? *You don't need them.* You ain't got time for that. Save that love you have for someone who recognizes how badass you are *in spite of* chronic illness, and maybe even finds you sexy *because of it.*

POP QUIZ

Do YOU know how to ask, "How are you?"

This may seem overly simple, but girl—when was the last time you asked someone, "How are you?" and really listened to the answer? When we're in the daily grind of ChronicBabedom, it can be easy to forget to check in with others. But it's essential.

Seven ways to be a better friend

In my life, the love of my friends may be the most potent love of all—it's always there, growing and evolving. But to be a good friend is not easy, and ChronicBabes may feel like we can't be the kind of friend we most want to be. This situation requires us to get creative and think about new ways to be a good friend. Here are some of the things I've tried:

Make your home a welcoming space. If it's hard for you to go out, tidy up and stock your friend's favorites so they can come over and hang out.

Offer to figure out a way to babysit. If I can't physically pick up kids because of pain or fatigue, I co-babysit with another friend; if I can't drive them around, we plan a date that involves the parent dropping off and picking up.

Try new things. We can get stuck in a rut, right? Our friends may want to introduce us to new things that are a little scary: Ethiopian food? *But is it gluten-free?* (Most places can make it gluten-free if you call ahead.) A new workout dance class? *But what if I can't do half the moves?* (Ask the instructor for modifications; make a plan so if you need to leave early, you can meet your friend in the locker room and get lunch.) Friends bring us new sources of inspiration and fun—trust your friends to support you in stretching yourself.

Stay connected, and be proactive. We sick chicks often need our friends to reach out and check on us. But we need to reciprocate. Set a repeating alarm in your phone or calendar to text friends every morning or evening to say hello and ask how they are. Don't always wait for them to initiate.

Be flexible. If we ask our friends to be flexible for us, we need to be as flexible as we can be for them, too. Try to accommodate their schedule.

Tell them you love them. A few years ago, I started doing this spontaneously—it was like a dam burst. Now, I tell anyone I love them if I'm feeling it. One friend told me it makes her immensely happy to hear it; she feels as though I give her permission to do the same, which is new for her. How great is that?

Forgive. Even best friends screw up sometimes. Life can be hard without friends; don't push them away. Do your best to forgive, learn, and move on.

There's no such thing as the "everything" friend

When we're alone all the time because of illness—or even just more alone than we once were—we can start to get a little, you know, clingy. Then, when we meet someone who seems awesome, we can be a little, you know, overeager about planning get-togethers or texting or calling or...

As you get out there and make new friends, remember that not every friend is the "everything" friend. We shouldn't pressure folks to be that person.

I've got *one* everything friend. We've been pals for about eighteen years, and we can tell each other anything. We text every day, we talk at least once a week on the phone, we try to hang out weekly, I babysit her kids once a week, she checks on my mental health when I go quiet...we've stood up at each other's weddings, shown up at the hospital for each other, shared our darkest fears. No one can take her place.

I can't expect the new friend I met last summer at the community garden to show up when I'm in the hospital, even if she sees me post about it on Facebook. We're just not that close.

And when I posted on Facebook recently about my mother-in-law's passing, I didn't expect every person to comment with condolences.

Then again, it's kind of great that in an emergency, I could ask a neighbor friend to watch my place for two weeks—to check my mail and water my plants. I may not have known we could do that before, but she stepped up, and it was a welcome surprise.

Our friends fill different roles. It's good to remember those roles also change over time; maybe the girlfriend from the community garden will become someone I hang out with more after this summer season. Maybe I'll cook communal dinners with the neighbor friend. Who knows?

You may want to make yourself a list of the things you'd like your friends to do for you, *and* a list of things *you're* able and willing to do for your friends. Write their names next to the items they fit. This is not something I recommend sharing with your friends, and it's not permanent—it's an exercise just for you, to get you thinking.

Below are a few ideas for your lists. Adapt them to your needs and see how it feels. Write the names of friends next to each item; for example, my "everything" friend would fit almost every item on the top list, but my garden buddy may only be the last item. On the bottom list, I'm willing to go to the hospital for a handful of friends—but not everyone. But I would help just about any friend or acquaintance with copyediting.

We can't be everything for everybody, either—but we should try to be as giving as possible.

Things I'd like my friends to be able to do for me:

- Visit me in the hospital
- Bring me home-cooked meals when I'm too sick to cook
- Babysit my kids occasionally

- Listen when I need to vent
- Text me daily to see how I'm doing
- Touch base with me weekly to see how I'm doing
- Give me a ride to a party we're both attending
- Tell me when I'm being a downer and help me think of ways to find positivity
- Be reliable about hanging out (cancel infrequently)
- Share a laugh when things are rough out there in the world
- Answer my text messages within twenty-four hours, usually

Things I can do for my friends:

- Visit them in the hospital (I'm so good with the staff!)
- Send them food delivery when they're too sick to cook
- Be their ear when they need to vent, and their shoulder to cry on
- Help them by copyediting their résumés and cover letters as they search for a new job
- Teach them about gardening
- Return their text messages and emails promptly (but realness: I'm not so good with voicemails)
- Be compassionate when they need to complain about their own health challenges

These are just a few ideas. Start playing around with your own lists; they'll help remind you how much support you have—and help you identify things you need.

How do we know when a friendship could be ending...or is over?

Not every friendship is meant to last. If we're feeling a bit lacking in the support department, we may cling to friendships that are no longer healthy for us. Read the signs, and take meaningful action.

Signs to look for

There are many ways a friendship can run its course. It's important to learn to read the signs and signals that a friendship is no longer serving you. Sometimes it will be obvious—a friend tells you "We're over!" or they do something truly disgusting. Other times, the clues are subtle: you feel uncomfortable after every interaction, or the other person has slowly drifted away.

Here are some signs that a friendship may be on the downswing:

- You feel exhausted or drained, physically and/or emotionally, after every interaction with the friend.
- Whenever you see their posts on Facebook, you're annoyed (or even angry) with the tone, language, or content.
- You look at your text and phone call history with the other person, and you're the one who initiates—every time.
- When you plan an event, you feel uncomfortable inviting them.
- Despite your repeated requests to the contrary, they always bring up your illness and want to talk about the latest "cure" they saw online.
- They keep starting arguments with you, mostly about things you've done wrong—that make no sense to you.
- You keep trying to schedule with them and they keep putting it off, with no clear reason.
- They aren't polite or compassionate to your friends, family, children, or pets.
- They aren't polite or compassionate with strangers or acquaintances.
- You get a funny feeling—anxious or uncomfortable—whenever they show up on your caller ID, or when they send an email.
- The other person simply isn't that fun to be around anymore.
- You have a sense you've outgrown the other person—perhaps they have very different aspirations for their personal life or career.
- They do something dramatic—like use a racial or homophobic slur, or say something otherwise hateful—either privately in your company, or publicly among friends, or online.

Meaningful actions you can take

Any one of these may be familiar. And almost all could be, at least in part, the result of *your* actions—they're not just caused by the other person. That's important to keep in mind as you consider what actions to take.

If any of these seem familiar, or if they spark an understanding that something else is wrong in a friendship, now's the time to consider your next steps.

Do you want to end the friendship? Is the thing that's wrong so bad you can't even stomach being friends with them? You may need to block them on your phone, unfriend or block them on Facebook, unfollow them on other social networks, and set a filter so their emails go straight to the trash.

You may need to set other strong boundaries, too—like finding another book club to be in, or asking them to not call anymore.

Should you be dramatic? Nope! I almost never recommend this. Declaring "Our friendship is over!" is a surefire way to fuel someone's animosity. Most times, it's good to just quietly cut things off. If the person has truly been horrible, then consider sending a message saying, "I am struggling with the thing that happened, and I need to take a break from hanging out for a while so I can regain clarity."

Do you need to set some things in motion to create distance? Probably. You might want to quit their book club (gracefully), or unfollow the other person on Facebook so you don't see their posts. It's okay to quietly create a little space between you and the other person.

Do you want to work on the friendship? Sometimes this makes sense; sometimes, if you tell someone you no longer want to be friends, they will be willing to work on things.

Is there a chance? Are both of you willing to try? Are there things you could change, things they could change, that would make it better? You're not obligated to work on the relationship, but it may be worth the effort if there are good things you can still recognize.

Caregivers learn compassion—as do their ChronicBabes

Lisa's sister was diagnosed with Crohn's disease when they were in their teens (Lisa is one year younger), so in a way, they both grew up with chronic illness. They continually work on their communication to ensure they *both* feel supported.

I travel with her a lot—so you sort of run into various issues when you're traveling. She lives out of [the] country, so we always have passports, because one never knows if something comes up. We ran into problems because she was in the hospital on September 11, 2001, and we couldn't get to her.

At various times when she's been sick, you sort of take a little bit of that onto yourself because you want to help her, you want to make her feel better. That's tough. It scares me that she could have a short lifespan because she's ill.

Caregiver resources
For a list of caregiver-focused resources, head to the Extra Credit section at the back of the book.

But she's managed to get a good balance. She's still active, she's still able to do a lot of things, and you don't feel like it's impeding her life that much. That makes me feel better because she's leading a full life.

I learned patience with her because I've stood in very odd locations when we were traveling because she needed to use washrooms. You're sort of like, "Okay, we're in a really sketchy bar. I'll just stand over here...twenty minutes later." You understand a bit more that occasionally, it's not all about you.

When we were in Rome, I got sick and so my sister got to experience the other way around, where I'd be like, "I need a bathroom," and she'd be like, "Over there." She'd say, "I walked through the museum when you were in a bathroom, and I get what it is like to stand in random spots."

When someone's gotten sick, you can get wrapped up in that, and sometimes as a caregiver you feel like it's always about you, it's never about me*, and you need to be open about that, because sometimes I think the other person doesn't always realize they're doing that. It can sometimes be an inane thing like, "I just need you to ask how I'm feeling versus always going right into how you're feeling." You feel how you feel, they feel how they feel, but you need to make sure you talk about it.*

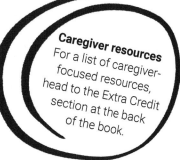

Taking good care of spouse and partner relationships

Your spouse, partner, boyfriend, or girlfriend is likely your primary caregiver. They're the person who sees you at your worst, runs emergency errands, and holds your hair when you're worshiping at the porcelain altar.

They're also the person who gets to see you be strong in the face of adversity, who experiences what it's like to love someone who faces a challenge with style and humor. Right?

You've got to take good care of them, babe.

Give them some time

Is illness talk monopolizing the time you spend with your honey? It's understandable; sometimes urgent circumstances dictate it...but also, sometimes we fall into a rut and don't stop talking about it. And your partner may not feel allowed to change the subject.

Make a commitment to yourself to take a break from illness talk when you can. Get intentional: Ask your partner questions about their work, their friendships, their views on the world. Make dates to spend time hanging out, watching a movie, having a picnic...*anything* besides talking about illness.

Your partner will enjoy some relief, and so will you—this is for both of you.

Give them some space

Does your spouse have any personal space? They may be craving some alone time.

I work from home, and I'm home when I'm sick—so my husband almost never has time alone in the house. When we decided to cohabitate, we talked about creating a personal space for him, but our place is simply too small. So I make an effort to ask him, sometimes: "Would you like me to give you some space?" I can go watch Netflix in the bedroom so he can read quietly in the living room. I can put on my headphones if I want to listen to pop music when he wants to listen to jazz.

Everyone needs time and space to relax. Ask your honey how you can work together to make sure they have the space they need.

Give them some love

Our loved ones carry a heavy weight. While they may not have our illness or pain, they *do* live with many of the same concerns and ramifications: fear of the unknown, anger at the unfairness of it all, fatigue from taking on extra chores, pressure from financial strain.

This is not your fault. Don't mistake my listing these concerns for a reckoning. This illness crud is happening *to* y'all, not *because* of something you did.

While you're not in charge of fixing all this, you can ease the burden a little by showing your partner some love every day. Small things make a big difference. Try:

- Sending a random text midday to say "I love you"
- Writing a love note on a sticky note and sticking it in their briefcase
- Creating a playlist of songs you both love to play during dinner
- Picking some wildflowers from the backyard to put in a vase on their nightstand
- Holding their hand while you're riding the bus together
- Expressing thanks for small kindnesses

Babe, you love this person. They love you. You both want relief, and joy. When things get really tough, remember you're both coming from the same place of love and desire—and take care to try some of these loving gestures. They will cement your bond.

POP QUIZ

The art of the open-ended question

A simple strategy for weaving more meaningful conversations is to ask open-ended questions that elicit more than a *yes* or a *no*. A few examples:

- "Tell me more about the class you've been taking."
- "How have you been feeling since you lost your job?"
- "What kinds of things are you growing in your garden this season?"

The difference between thoughtful dissenters and naysayers

When we're learning to get more courageous and to stand up for ourselves, we start to get stronger when it comes to naysayers. Instead of just quietly listening and staying angry inside for fear of repercussions, we may begin to respond and correct, to tell our side of the story. And that's all good.

But sometimes, we encounter someone who disagrees with us...but isn't a naysayer. Someone who doesn't share our opinion, but doesn't discount our opinion, either.

These conversations provide us with the chance to open ourselves to new perspectives, and you never know what you may learn. These folks can become our allies—even if we never come to a full agreement.

The key is in understanding the difference: A naysayer is purely negative and doesn't give a hoot about us; a thoughtful dissenter listens and tries to appreciate our perspective, even if they don't agree.

Challenging dialogue about anything—including chronic illness—is a great way to create advocates and friends. When we can be strong enough to voice our disagreement and hear the perspectives of others, we can learn.

A few tips for distinguishing naysayers from thoughtful dissenters:

Naysayers:	***Thoughtful Dissenters:***
Tell you you're wrong.	Tell you they feel differently.
Get angry when you disagree.	Stay calm when you disagree.
Don't want to hear your story.	Are open to hearing your story.
Exhibit anger or frustration.	Exhibit patience or compassion.
View your opinion as an affront.	Know your opinion is not about them.
Raise their voice.	Match your tone.
Won't discuss other perspectives.	Will discuss other perspectives.
Prioritize their opinion.	Give equal weight to your opinion.

Both deserve patience and respect. Don't waste energy on a fight.

These guidelines can help you begin to evaluate people when in conversation. I encourage you to stay open to the possibility of meeting someone who presents as a naysayer, but who calms down and opens up once you really get talking. You never know where they're coming from; they may have bad past experiences that shape their initial response.

Can we learn to love naysayers?

Oh, girl...this is some next-level work. To love someone who is a naysayer—who flat-out disagrees with you about your diagnosis or treatment plan—is not easy.

It's usually family members who show up in our lives this way, and we may feel an obligation to spend time with them despite their negative stance. *Resist the temptation.* You're under no obligation to tolerate them—this is *your* life.

But if you're going to see this person on the regular, it's worth doing a little work to make it easier. Consider their experience: Maybe they grew up with a sick parent and experienced feelings of abandonment because of it, and they're mistakenly placing some of that on you today. Maybe they're dealing with feelings of fear about their own health or mortality, for reasons you don't know.

None of this excuses their behavior, but it may help explain some of it. If you get quiet with this understanding, and think about how troubled they must be to react so negatively, it may help you touch a soft spot in your heart—a place of compassion. That may be just enough to help you tolerate some minor exposure to their naysaying.

But if this feels impossible, and spending time with them is hurting you, consider this your hall pass, babe—get outta there and connect with someone who gets you.

Coping with unpredictability is part of the caregiver experience

Dave's wife had undiagnosed chronic pain for about ten years before she received her fibromyalgia diagnosis, and in the fifteen years or so since, they've worked to create a life together that balances each of their needs and deal with the unpredictability of chronic pain and illness.

It's been part of our relationship since the beginning. As we've learned together, we've kind of grown together in that. She's learned better in the last ten years how to ask more for what she needs. We've kind of learned together what she needs.

One of the difficult things for me has been remembering she has chronic pain and that on any given day, she's in pain. She looks fine, you can't tell from her outward appearance, and she's in pain. For the longest time, I kept forgetting that.

She teases me because her parents will call and ask how she's doing and I'll say, "Oh, she's fine." "Fine" becomes such a relative thing that to me, her being fine is she's sitting up and reading a book for the day, or in this case she was lying in bed and resting, but that was "fine." I'll tell someone, "Oh yeah, she's doing fine," and she calls from the other room and says, "I'm not doing fine! I'm wiped out!"

She really loves the Spoon Theory metaphor; that's one thing we use. Some days she'll tell me, "I'm out of spoons today. I used them all up."

I've fallen victim to "Oh, she's been doing great for a couple weeks and therefore everything's going to be great from now on," and then she falls back into getting exhausted and having to take it easy for a couple weeks to recover.

What stands out to me is the unpredictability. One day we could be making plans for the weekend, and the weekend comes and she just can't do it. Or one day she'll be feeling really good and she may overdo it, and the next day she's down. That's a challenge of not knowing where she's going to be on any given day.

Learning to find love in not-so-obvious places

When we are not partnered, it's important to open our minds and hearts to finding love in other ways. And even for those of us who *are* partnered, it's still important; it's not fair to rely on our primary partner as our only source of love.

How do we do that? How do we begin to open our minds and hearts to love?

- One way is to do a small meditation each morning and say to yourself a few times, "I am open to love."
- You may want to journal about it a little bit.
- You may try taking a moment each morning to remind yourself that love exists in *many* places, and that our society's definition of love is often very limited.

I'm not just talking about romantic love. I'm talking about being open to many different kinds of love, affection, and connection.

Start with your morning routine. Do you have a pet? A roommate? Do you live with family members? Plants? Tell them you love them. If you're not comfortable saying the word, say something pleasant and caring to them. "Snuffles, you look super fluffy today, good boy!" or "Jamie, I love being your roommate. Want to hang out tonight?" or "Mom, that breakfast smells awesome. You take really great care of me."

When *you* put out the love feelers, you get some love energy back. Here are a few examples from my life:

Mr. Lovelady has been my postal carrier for five years, and he is awesome. He sings when he delivers the mail. He rings my buzzer if I have a package so it doesn't sit in the foyer. I make an effort to thank him; whenever I see him, I ask how he is, or tell him I love the song he's singing, or wish him a happy day, or thank him for his work. I put that love out there. (And I love that he's named Mr. Lovelady!)

My cleaning woman is adorable. One day, she asked me to get a new mop. I was having the *worst* day—so much stress from a client—so I was happy for a break from the computer. But when I got home with my new mop, she frowned. "This is not worth your money," she said. I burst into tears. It was a breaking point for me—I was so exhausted from work. She hugged me, told me it was okay, and wrote down what kind of mop to get. She hugged me again when she left. The next time she came, she asked after my work situation.

How have I built that loving relationship? Every time I see her, I ask how she is. When she told me the names of her children in Poland, I wrote them down so I could remember to ask after them. I leave her cards at the holidays, offer her a cup of tea when she arrives, and every few months, I call the service that employs her to give a rave review. I put the love out there. She gives me love right back—in the form of support, a graceful attitude, special attention to my needs, and hugs.

If you put love out there, and if you open yourself to the possibility of being loved, it will happen for you. I never planned to be loved by my cleaning person. I never planned to love my mail carrier. But openness and a loving attitude bring all kinds of gifts.

HOMEWORK assignments

1) Can you be quietly generous?

When was the last time you did something nice for someone, without expectation of thanks? Find a way today to treat someone with generosity and kindness. It will feel so good!

2) Use your words

Disclose something to a loved one that you've been keeping to yourself for too long. Write it out for yourself, too.

PEP SQUAD

An Interview with Dr. Val Jones

Building stronger doctor-patient relationships (doctors are people, too!)

Dr. Val Jones is a graduate of Columbia University College of Physicians and Surgeons, board-certified in physical medicine and rehabilitation, and the founder of *Better Health LLC*, one of the most popular medical blogs. With over 130 contributors, *Better Health* is a content partner with the Centers for Disease Control and Prevention, the American College of Surgeons, Harvard Health Publications, Diario Medico, and the Columbia Department of Surgery.

Val is also medical director of admissions, Saint Luke's Rehabilitation Institute. And she's an outspoken advocate for smarter health care solutions.

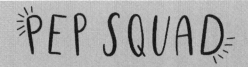

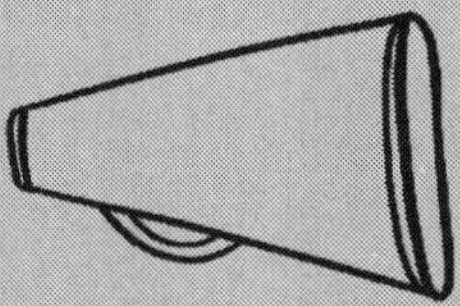

Connect with Val:
Website: GetBetterHealth.com
Twitter: @drval
Email: val.jones@getbetterhealth.com

Jenni: One of the things we all think about as patients is the relationship we have with our health care providers or our doctors. I've been really lucky: I've had the same primary care physician I started with almost fifteen years ago. *(Author's note: Sigh, that recently changed. But it's okay! I'm getting to know my new one.)* I don't think that happens very often any more.

Val: No, it doesn't!

Jenni: I'm very thankful for him and for that opportunity to have continuity with him. But when I first started to find a doctor, when I got sick, it was challenging. A lot of people compare the process of finding a new doctor with diving into the dating pool; do you think this has some accuracy?

Val: I think that's totally accurate! And not only am I a doctor, but I've also needed doctors in my life. When I put my patient hat on, I do think of it not dissimilarly...how you want to find someone you can relate to, that you like, that you think really genuinely cares about you and is going to do a good job because they want to see you succeed and are going to take the time to really notice the details. So I think finding a good doctor is a lot like any kind of long-term relationship.

Jenni: It's the longest relationship I have, besides my sisters and my parents. I have two friends I've been friends with longer. It's kind of incredible. I have a [criterion] too, similar to the dating pool, which is that all my physicians are really good-looking. I joke...but they all are fairly good-looking people. If we put them all on a billboard, they would look like a big awesome fabulous team.

When we go on our first date, we have all kinds of questions. What are some of the questions you counsel people to ask a new doctor for the first time? When you're meeting someone as a prospect, or maybe your insurance has said, "Hey, this is who you get," what are some of those early questions people should be asking?

Val: The overarching principle here is that doctors really are people too. And we're nervous, a little bit, when we meet a new patient and we don't know who they are and what they're about and what they need from us. We want to get to know them.

The first thing out of your mouth when you meet someone at a cocktail party probably is "Where did you go to school?" The tendency with a new doctor is to ask "How many of these procedures have you done?" That's a good question, but I probably wouldn't lead with it. It makes the doctor feel like they're being attacked right away, and being judged. You know, we have feelings.

I prefer a little softer approach. Just giving you some insight into the medical mind, where a doctor is probably coming from, the stresses in their lives and the things they worry about...if you sort of know where they're coming from, you'll naturally be a little bit more patient and understanding toward them, and that'll be reciprocated.

A couple of questions that I thought might be kind of disarming and nice—that doctors don't often hear—were things like "How would you like me to track my progress for you?"

Because then the patient is saying, "I really want to partner with you; I want to get better; I'm not going to just listen to you and then run away and never do anything that you suggest. I'm in it, and I don't want to be in your face or too naggy or clingy or whatever; I just want you to tell me how it's best to contact you and how best to report my progress."

I think that kind of question can be a great disarming one that would really set the tone for a healthy long-term relationship with the patient. Similar questions that follow from that would be things like "What's the best way to contact you if I have questions or updates?"

Maybe you want to ask how frequently the doctor thinks you should meet, just to set expectations: Is this going to be a once-a-month meeting, or is it every six months, or every year? It really depends on the situation, the type of doctor you're seeing, the issue that you have, etc.

Then, maybe ask the doctor who else should be on your medical team, in case you hadn't thought, "Oh, an endocrinologist might be someone who could really help me." Because depending on how long you've had your condition or concern, there's a learning curve, and sometimes patients don't realize there are specialists. Like a diabetes nurse educator, who could be fantastic as a primary liaison for someone with newly diagnosed diabetes. Asking the doctor, "Who else should be on my team? How do you see my team working out?" might be really helpful.

Also: "Which other doctors do you recommend?" If you already know what specialists you need to see and you haven't picked one out, if you like your doctor—well, I can tell you, birds of a feather do seem to flock together—so a nice doctor has probably got nice doctor friends, too.

Jenni: I've found that so much! But I never knew to ask that last question: "Who else should be on my team?" I didn't ask that for the first many years. I had fibromyalgia—I was diagnosed at twenty-five—and then my doctor sent me to a rheumatologist to confirm the diagnosis. I went through a few years of doubting and researching.

Now I know to ask that question. When something pops up—like, I was recently diagnosed with a thyroid condition—I know to ask, "Okay, so do I need to see any kind of specialist?"

"Most of us really, if we had our druthers, would just be like, 'Girl, just call me. Twitter. Let's have an email conversation and **let's make this easy for each other.'** *But in a lot of situations it's not quite that simple."*

—Val

Val: Sometimes, they may say, "Well, right now, I think you've got everybody on the team you need, but if *this* gets worse, or if *this* happens, or if you notice *this*, the next step would be *blank*, then the next step would be to see the endocrinologist," for example. They can give you a sense of what to expect, what to look for, and certain triggers that should encourage you to get back in touch.

That's another question that you could ask: "What would be the reasons why I should call you?" A lot of patients don't know. I've worked with a company called eDocAmerica, and we answer questions for patients via email. They get access to us, we respond usually within three hours—and we don't practice medicine, we don't prescribe or diagnose over the Internet—but I find that a lot of patients are just asking questions like "Is this normal? Is this an emergency? Is this a concern?" Because they're not sure.

There's a lot of wisdom that comes through years of medical practice. You see something that, to you, is obviously an emergency, and to the patient, they're just like, "What? I feel okay right this minute." And you're thinking, *Yeah, but you're going to collapse in an hour, so get in here!*

Jenni: For a while, I obsessed over every little thing, because I had never been really sick before. And then I got sick and suddenly I was examining every freckle and bump and calling my doctor all the time and saying, "Is this okay? Is this okay?" And he finally said, "Look, you've got to calm down. You've got to take it down a notch. You're freaking out."

He gave me some good guidelines on what kinds of things I should be worried about. Because I was overdoing it and going the other way.

Email is becoming such a popular way to communicate with health care providers, but everyone's got different ways to do it, and limits. What's a good way to figure that out with your doctor? Is it good to just say, "Can I email you?" or "How often can I email you?" or things like that?

Val: This is a difficult area, and here's why: Physicians, in many cases, don't get compensated by insurance companies for work they do over email. That is changing; that's been a problem.

If you look at it from the doctor's perspective, when you say, "Can I email you?" you're basically saying, "Can I get you to do some work for free? Would you like to stay after hours at your office and write to me and never get compensated for that?" And that's what they're hearing when you say, "Can you email me?"

But they know it's ridiculous to say, "No, you can't contact me." So they feel obligated, but then they feel like, *Ugh, here's another thing that I won't be able to get compensated for. Here's more of my time that I'm going to be investing in my patients—which I want to do—but I can't get reimbursed for it.* So just understand that doctors are in a difficult place.

The second part that's a little tricky is, with medical liability issues, and HIPAA, and the legal system in this country, doctors are terrified of inadvertently releasing personal information about a patient and then getting in trouble or getting sued. It's so scary; anything we write down can be used in a court of law against us. We just want to do our job and we want to help people, and help our patient, and we want them to have access to our records, but every time a piece of information leaves our hands, we're kind of like, "Oh my gosh, what's gonna happen to us next?"

Just know that, number one, your doctor may not get paid to work with you if you go through certain platforms like email. And number two, your doctor might get sued and lose their medical license, be harassed by lawyers, whatever, if they give you your data in the wrong way.

So we're scared, we're tired, and we just wanna do the right thing and don't know how to do it. But you know what? Most of us, if we had our druthers, would just be like, "Girl, just call me. Twitter. Let's have an email conversation, and let's make this easy for each other." But in a lot of situations it's not quite that simple.

That being said, and knowing the doctor is completely stressed about all of this, what you can say is, "I understand that you may not get compensated for emails, but I wonder, have you found a way we could communicate via email? Because that would be super convenient for me." Then let them know you're aware this could be an issue, that you'd love to email them but you want to make sure they're compensated for the work they do with you. And see what their answer is.

They may say, "Oh yeah, it used to be that way, but there's a code I can use, and it's been working, so yes, I'd be happy to email you." Or you can say, "I also know that keeping medical records is a priority for you; do you have a safe way to transfer information via email?" Some people have encrypted private email processes for that. Feel them out and let them know you're thinking about where they're coming from before you just say, "Hey, can I email you?" And they say, "No!" And you think, "What a bad doctor!"

Jenni: You want them to hear you, you want them to understand you. You're right—we could get into a whole conversation about how the health care system creates these insane boundaries between people, and challenges, and...this isn't the time or place for that.

But so often, we feel separated from our health care providers, like we're on two sides of a river. A certain amount of respect and compassion for each other as human beings can take us far.

Val: When you genuinely like someone, you will definitely go out of your way for them. It's just as true in Starbucks when you get a coffee as it is with your relationship with your doctor. I think it was Maya Angelou who said, "I've learned that people will forget what you said, people will forget what you did, but people will never forget how you made them feel."

It's the same way with doctors and patients. Doctors may not quite remember all the details of the condition a patient has, if they've seen a lot of patients and they've only seen you once before, but they'll remember if you were hostile to them. They won't know what your conditions are or your medical background, but they'll remember, *Oh yeah, that's the one that threatened to sue me already!* Or they remember the anxiety they felt in meeting you.

Or you: When you see the doctor and you're like, *Okay, that was the doctor that, I don't remember what he taught me about my condition, but I know he was short with me, he made me feel anxious, I felt like he didn't know what he was talking about and then he hurried me out the door.* That's why it's so important to set the tone. Both people need to—both the doctor and the patient.

"Doctors may not quite remember all the details of the condition a patient has but they'll remember if you were hostile to them. ***It's so important to set the tone.****"*

—Val

Jenni: I think patients should feel more empowered to do that, and not in a really bossy, bitchy way.

Val: Yeah, no.

Jenni: What kinds of qualities should we be looking for in our health care providers? Is it similar to the qualities you would want in a friend? It's weird, because it's a professional relationship, but it's such an intimate relationship.

Val: The answer to that is complicated. There are some basic things you would want—I can tell you what I would like—but that might be because I have a certain personality and I know what grooves with me.

It's funny, my fiancé is very different than I am. He's this really tough guy, and what he looks for in a doctor is someone who has tough love, who's going to say it to him straight, who's not gonna mess around. Which sounds, to me, kind of nutty because that's not what I want, but I respect [that] there are different people with different personalities who want different things.

One of the qualities I really like is a person who—I don't mean to make light of a serious condition, but in lay terms, we say OCD. Of course, it is a real issue for people who have OCD.

But what we're trying to say is when people are very detail-oriented and they're very compulsive about getting things done, and their day isn't done if they haven't checked that last lab value and they haven't been thorough about following up on patients X, Y, and Z, or calling that family member, or just going the extra mile.

I like physicians who are very thorough about following things up, because so many things can get lost. In this health care system, it's unbelievable what falls through the cracks. I don't know if it's because there are too many cooks in the kitchen, or no one's in charge, or if there are too many experts doing too many things, not knowing what the other guy is doing.

If you have a quarterback, so to speak—a primary care physician, who is really on the ball and kind of compulsive about the details—that is great.

Other than being compulsive about the details and making sure they're following up on all your results and communicating effectively, I think a good sense of humor can go a long way.

Jenni: For me, humor and just a certain kind of compassion are so important. Yes, there are days when I'm freaked out and scared, and I'm really serious, or I'm upset and I'm crying. There have definitely been visits like that but for the most part, when I go in, if I can't laugh about certain things, I'm in trouble.

Let's say we've found the perfect doctor (or not perfect, because nobody's perfect, but you know, Doctor Right) and we want to be as prepared as we can be and show up in the best way. What kinds of things can we do to make sure we're making the best use of our time, and keeping our health care things coordinated?

Val: Three words: *write it down.* When you're preparing to go to your doctor's visit, take some time out of your day or the day before to think it through: *What do I need to tell my doctor? What does he or* *she really need to know since the last time we met? And what are they going to ask me?* You probably know what they're going to ask you; there are things we always ask. What medications are you taking? Has anything changed?

Jenni: I keep a list of all my meds on my phone because I know every appointment they're going to ask me, so I can just hand them the list. I keep it updated, and I hand them my phone and say, "Here's the list, check it against your records." It keeps me from wasting five minutes of writing everything down or listing everything for them.

Val: That's an excellent strategy. It depends on the condition you have, what they're going to ask you. A neurologist is going to ask you certain questions, again and again, that a cardiologist is not.

If you have a chronic disease, you know what those questions are, you become familiar with them. So just know to expect it and have a good sense of humor about it, because you'll feel like you're dealing with a person who has memory loss.

Every time you go in, you're like, "Yes, I know, you're going to ask me this." It's just the way the paperwork and the system is set up, where you have to log certain things in order to be able to submit, to get reimbursed for the time you spent, and there are things you have to document every time.

Even though it feels like a rare form of torture and they're all out to drive you nuts, honestly it's not that; it's just that everybody has to get through it, and if you know in advance it's going to happen, you can take it in stride.

Make sure you write down things like your med list, that you know what your specialist is going to ask you, and [that you] take good notes about anything that's changed. If there's something you've noticed that's a concern, write it down. And try not to be too tangential. That will get you out the door more quickly.

When I say *tangential*, I mean, patients will sometimes tell you the story of what's going on but then they'll say, "So my knee has been hurting more than usual, and when I told my Aunt Sally about my knee hurting, she thought it would be a good idea for me to walk the dog extra far...and then I think the dog found and ate a dead rat when I was on the street, and it really worried me, and I had to take him to the vet, and then the vet said he thought there might have been rat poison on the street, and then..."

Do you see what I'm saying? So you're the knee specialist and you're listening to this and you're like...

Jenni: "I just want to know what it feels like when you get out of bed..."

Val: Yeah, and you feel like such a cad because you don't want to say, "Listen, I can't hear your story about the rat right now, because we really just need to talk about your knee."

As a warm, empathic kind of person, you don't want to interrupt them, but you only have a limited amount of time, and there are other people in the waiting room. You've got someone who just fractured their rib and they're having a hard time with the pain and they can't breathe. You've got all that going in the background and the patient is telling a very tangential story.

As much as the doctor likes you as a person and wants to know what's going on, out of respect for your time and the other patients, think about: what are the critical issues you want to get across? Then, if you guys have extra time and there's no one in the waiting room and you want to shoot the breeze, go for it. Just be aware that tangential stories sometimes are a little hard.

Jenni: Now I'm thinking, *oh no.* I wonder if they're like, "Here comes Jenni, the time waster! Book an extra fifteen minutes, make sure you bill her for the stories."

Val: Well, if they get paid for it, I guess it's okay!

Jenni: What happens when you have a doctor you're just not into, to go with the dating analogy? I tell people all the time that you can fire your doctor—you can make changes. With insurance, that limits our options, but how do you feel about that? Are there things patients should do first? Is it like when you're leaving a job and you want to clear out your desk a little first? Do you want to try and get your medical records before you do that? If you fire them, are they gonna hold your records hostage?

Val: They might! They shouldn't, obviously, but I'm not going to vouch for every doctor. Doctors are people too, and some of them are not very happy when a patient is leaving.

Maybe it won't even be the doctor. Maybe the doctor will be like, "Oh, you win some, you lose some," but then the front-desk person or the admin will be like, "I'll show her, she's gonna ditch Doctor Smith, well, I'm not going to lift a finger to help her get her records." That can happen.

Jenni: How could we ask for our records? I'm not advocating that people go out and fire all their doctors, but I know it does happen.

> *"**Three words: write it down.** Take some time out of your day or the day before to think it through: **What do I need to tell my doctor?** And what are they going to ask me?"*
>
> —Val

Val: The insurance thing is really an issue. I've lived in large metropolitan centers most of my adult life, and in that situation, you have so many options, even with insurance, that switching to another doctor is quite feasible. But imagine if you're in a rural area, and there's really only one rheumatologist or one specialist within three hundred miles of where you live. What are you going to do if you don't like that person?

You should not stay with a doctor who you think is incompetent. If they maybe lack a little social grace, maybe you give them a pass if you don't have any options for changing—you try to work it out. It's like a relationship. It's not always perfect, but you keep with it.

The main thing is you want to make sure they're not incompetent, they're not missing a diagnosis, or treating you improperly. And that, again, can be difficult, because as a layperson, how do you know if your mechanic is doing the right thing on your car? Not to say that doctors are mechanics but in a sense, the complexity level is just as mysterious. I know nothing about my car engine, and a mechanic can be like, "There's a floobidoobydo missing from the flubidub." And I'd be like, "Cool. I'll write you a check."

If you're in an area where you have the luxury of having multiple options, then by all means, feel free to explore other experts, other doctors.

If you aren't in an area where there are options, then I would say, try to stick it out, and be friendly, and have an honest conversation with your doctor to try to heal whatever rift there might have been. But if you think your doctor is incompetent or you're worried about what they're doing, or they're not doing the right thing, then you're going to have to figure out where the next specialist is.

There are services where you can get a second opinion. If you have a complicated issue and you're not sure the doctor is doing the right thing by you, there's a company called BestDoctors.com. It may be difficult to access unless your employer has purchased their service for you, but they do great work. They have experts all over the country in different fields, including oncology, endocrinology, orthopedics.

They'll look at your medical records, and render an opinion about whether or not what's going on with you and what your doctor is doing seem to be within the realm of reasonable, or if there are other options you should think about. I'm a big fan of that. I'm not entirely sure if an individual could go and purchase that for themselves.

Then there's eDocAmerica.com, where I work, and we're primary care–based, so we don't have extensive expertise in oncology and more complex challenging fields that, if you're not a specialist in that field, it's hard for you to really be able to assess. But that's available for purchase on an individual basis, and for a certain fee per month you get unlimited access to primary care physicians who can render opinions.

They can't diagnose or treat you, but they can give you information, give you a sense of, "Well, you should read this..." or "A standard of care in that situation is this..." That's super-helpful.

Jenni: We're talking about relationships—not just transactional relationships, but they're more intimate—with our health care providers. We share really personal stuff, and it's vital for our happiness and wellbeing. I always try to treat my physicians with respect, and I do things—like at Christmas, everybody gets a holiday card from me.

When I've had particularly frightening issues, I've written thank-you notes. When I had a wrist surgery a few years ago after an accident, I wrote a thank-you note to the surgeon, and he expressed to me how awesome that is; he said it's rare for him to get stuff like that.

I think those are optimal behaviors for keeping our patient-doctor relationships really strong. Are there any other things we haven't touched on that you think people should think about in keeping the relationship solid?

Val: I'm thinking, "Wow, if my patients sent me thank-you notes, that would be so great!"

There's a spectrum of behavior. There could be an overdo-it side to it. This hasn't happened to me, but in some cases patients have been a little strange or inappropriately gracious, meaning giving big gifts again and again, and that makes the doctor feel really awkward. Because we're doing our job. We're supposed to do what we're doing. Giving us gifts for it—we know you mean well, but it can get awkward, because there's this professional boundary.

But thank-you notes are, I think, the perfect tone.

And then there are instances of never appreciating everything, just bolting and never giving the doctor the sense that you feel like you're making progress or you're glad that you talked, offering no feedback whatsoever. That might be a little sad.

Jenni: It's like the golden rule. Treat people how you'd want to be treated.

Val: That's right. And I think open and honest communication is really important. The funny thing is, you know what patients always do? They will talk to you for the entire session, and then two minutes before the end, they'll tell you why they're really there. I don't know why everybody does it that way.

I think there's some anxiety about the reason why they're really there. They feel shy or embarrassed or they don't want to say, "The real reason I'm here is because I've got a new ulcer on my butt." And you're like, "Well, let's take a look at that."

Ask any doctor and they'll tell you the real reason why the person came to see them comes out sixty seconds before they leave. And that's not fair to the patient, because then you don't get the chance to explore with them, or let them talk about it and help you figure out the next best step. Because then you're running around thinking, "Oh, I thought this was about knee pain, but it's about something else!"

If you know in your heart that you're really going to go see the doctor about X reason, and it's embarrassing, or you're shy or nervous or scared to say something because it might be serious and you're not ready to deal with it, have an honest conversation with yourself prior to going in. Say to yourself, *Look, this doctor wants to help me, he or she is here to help me, and they won't be able to do a good job if I wait to the end to talk.* Get up your courage and say, "Look, the reason why I'm here today is X."

It's scary to be sick and not know, to be waiting for that determination. There's a lot of fear in medicine. It's hard to put your heart out there and talk about what your issue is. Maybe it's a sexual dysfunction that's been bothering you in your relationship, and it's related to your condition. I would say: Have courage—and you'll get the best help.

This interview has been shortened and edited to fit this book. To read the full transcript or listen to the full recordings of this and all the Pep Squad interviews, head to ChronicBabe101.com.

Lesson 8

ADAPT YOUR *education* AND *career* TO BOOST *success*

A big part of being Chronically Babe-alicious is creating a strategy for education and a career that supports you and your needs. It *is* possible—but you may have to think outside the box (to use a little corporate lingo) to create the career you want.

Don't let go of your dreams

In the twenty years since I've gotten sick, I've been told *countless* times that I would have to give up on my dreams and "get real."

Babe, I'm about as *real* as it gets, and no one is going to tell me I can't achieve my dreams.

But I *have* had to adapt to get the same feelings, qualities, and payoffs I dreamed of. That's what this lesson is all about.

Family, friends, guidance counselors, career coaches—they may tell you to be extra-cautious, or to change course to something that's "safe." It's smart to think about all the possibilities, and prepare in case things change unexpectedly. That's good advice for *anyone*, not just sick folk.

But there's a big difference between learning to adapt—and giving up.

My dream since I was old enough to hold a crayon was to be a writer. As I got older, it evolved into becoming an investigative journalist. As my health became unpredictable, I stuck with writing but shifted to less intense projects. Finally, I started my own company so I could choose every project. I did *not* let go of my dream—but it *does* look very different now from what I had previously imagined.

And who knows what I'll be writing five or ten years from now? The dream is still alive!

Part of hanging on to those dreams includes educating yourself about what's possible and gaining experience in your field. Even if you can't attend a traditional university, there are many online learning opportunities. You could take an internship or apprenticeship, too.

Or: Let go of your dreams (to make space for new ones)

On the other hand, maybe your dream has always been to be a professional dancer, but you have balance issues now that make it impossible. It might be time to practice a little acceptance, like we worked on in lesson 1. It may be time to release that dream; hanging on to it when it's not realistic is unhealthy.

If your first career choice is truly out of your reach, you must release it and make space for a new dream to come true instead.

Emil DeAndreis is a great example of someone who released his original dream, and found a new path he loves. As a boy, he dreamed of becoming a pro baseball player; as a young man, he was on the way to making that happen when rheumatoid disease sidelined him.

Now, he's pursuing another dream: pro writer. His book, *Hard to Grip: A Memoir of Youth, Baseball, and Chronic Illness*, is an inspiring read. Even though he doesn't play ball anymore, he coaches—but his main gig is teaching writing.

Generations ago, it was the norm to choose one career and stick with it for a lifetime. Today, the working world is vastly different; in the U.S., people switch jobs many times throughout their careers.

Does knowing that almost *everyone* will have to change jobs in their lifetime—maybe multiple times—help you stomach the idea of changing your career to better suit your health? I hope so. Making space for new dreams may require you to rethink what "work" means to you; you may need to go back to school or gain experience that makes your *new* dream possible.

Rethinking "work"

When I was preparing to leave my last full-time job and launch my company, I spent time with a coach to get clear about the change. Instead of thinking only about what my new "job" would be, I got clear about the *qualities* I wanted, the *values* I prized.

Writing, for me, has always been about storytelling—specifically, helping people tell stories that might otherwise go untold. I love the feeling of helping people, and I value the connections I make when I'm interviewing my subjects.

Focusing on those two things—helping people and making connections—has helped me choose the best clients and projects. When I forget those values, I goof and say yes to projects that end up being a bummer.

In another example, I have a friend who's an art therapist. In a perfect world, she would work as a full-time artist—but it's tough to make a living that way. As an art therapist, she gets to focus on some values that are essential to her satisfaction, like creativity and community.

What qualities and values are important to you? Now's the time to get clear, babe.

Relationships and boundaries at work and school

Much of what we learned in lesson 3 about boundaries also applies here, with the added twist that there may be truly jerky or bizarre people in your office or class with whom you're forced to spend time. (It's easier to walk away from your uncle at the family picnic than it is to walk out of a work presentation when your colleague is being thoughtless.)

If you've already been at your job for a while and your boundaries have been lax, it may feel awkward to build them up now. The ladies in accounting love your irreverent stories about trying new procedures! Your officemate loves dishing about your dating experiences! But you may be feeling overwhelmed and stretched thin. It's time to preserve your energy.

You can still be friendly, funny, and delightful—but ease into stronger boundaries. *You are not required to share personal stuff to be a valuable part of the team.*

This is not just about managing your energy. It's also about crafting a presence in the workplace or in school. The reality is some people will judge you for having chronic illness, and make assumptions about your abilities. The less ammunition you give them, the harder it is for them to argue later that they should get a promotion instead of you, or that you weren't as strong a team member on your final group project.

POP QUIZ

What are your kickass skills?

Can you braid hair? Are you great at spelling? Can you walk into a room and know immediately which furniture should be moved to create better flow? Is your apple pie the best in the county?

We all have skills we forget to acknowledge, because they might not feel like *job* skills. But they're still valuable!

Take some time today and write down a handful of things you do well; no task is too small. Celebrate! You've got *mad skills*, babe!

The pitfalls and benefits of disclosure

I'm no career expert, so my first piece of advice is to work with a career coach as you navigate the job market—they will know the latest legal requirements, and can advise you on the norms for your field.

But I do know one thing: You are not obligated to tell a potential employer you have chronic illness or disability. Period.

If you're interviewing for a job and some requirements seem like a poor fit for your physical abilities, ask more questions and discuss what accommodations may be made. Or, there might be another position that's better suited to your abilities.

I usually recommend disclosing your chronic illness or disability after you've accepted a job offer, when you're working out details with the human resources representative. But this is a broad generalization; your specifics may necessitate earlier disclosure. Maybe you want to ask for one day a week of remote work or more flex hours, to better manage your doctor appointment schedule. Perhaps the job includes monthly air travel, and you want to ensure they also provide car service because you don't drive.

Sometimes, it benefits you to disclose your status—you're able to negotiate for your needs, showing that you'll be a creative and industrious employee. Some employers *love* people with those qualities.

But some potential employers don't think a sick chick can do the work, and disclosure could close a door on an opportunity to prove them wrong.

These general principles hold true for students, as well. You are not obligated to disclose your disability or chronic illness, but there may come a time when disclosure helps ensure you have the accommodations you need at school. (It may also help you weed out unfit schools; you don't want to move across the country only to find out your new college can't accommodate you.)

In the U.S., your rights are protected by the Americans with Disabilities Act (ADA). This legislation guards you from discrimination on the basis of disability, and spells out what kinds of accommodations you can reasonably expect—both at work and at school. ADA titles II and III protect the rights of college and university students, in public and private schools.

Study up: Your rights

- If you're not current on the ADA, read up: bit.ly/yourADArights.
- Section 504 of the Rehabilitation Act of 1973 protects the rights of younger students. Get the scoop here: bit.ly/section504schools.
- The PACER Center offers a comprehensive breakdown of students' rights and protections, for all ages. Get schooled: bit.ly/PACERschools.

Are you frontin'?

Maybe you should be. If *not* sharing how sick you are means your coworkers take you seriously, it may serve you to put up a front. There's nothing wrong with holding your personal details close; you're not obligated to share that you're trying a new medication or that you're having a flare-up.

But if it's becoming too hard to hide how you're feeling—or if you need more schedule accommodations for doctor visits—you may need to talk with your coworkers about what's going on.

It's best to start with your manager, presumably the person who can help you decide how to explain your situation to the rest of the team.

At my last job, my boss was great at running interference for me. (I had a coworker who complained that I arrived late every Tuesday; my boss explained to HR that I had a weekly checkup, and that I always stayed late on Tuesdays to make up for it.) If you're nervous about your manager, talk to HR about the best way to proceed.

And if you feel like you still can't spill the beans, make sure you have a friend to talk to—someone outside the office. It's difficult to work in an office all day when you're in pain, and having a friend who gets it and cheers you on via text message really helps.

How to make your case for accommodations

When preparing to make your case for workplace or educational accommodations, be ready to explain exactly what you need, and why. Saying you need it isn't enough; offer specifics about how the accommodation gives you necessary access, or which tasks you'll be able to accomplish because of it.

If you're asking for equipment to be changed or installed, be prepared to suggest specific brands or models. You are not *obligated* to do this, but it helps the employer or educator—and shows you're committed to working together on a solution.

Mind your language; you're not asking for a favor. You're requesting a necessity. This is a great time to practice using assertive language; look to lesson 9 for ideas.

Regulations regarding workplace accommodations are different around the globe.

- In the U.S., the Job Accommodation Network (JAN) offers clear explanations of what's "reasonable" according to the government, and you can get assistance through their website or on the phone: bit.ly/JANaccommodations.
- In Canada, the Canadian Human Rights Act prohibits discrimination and spells out an employer's duty to accommodate workers with disability: bit.ly/CANaccommodations.
- In the U.K., the government offers guidance on "reasonable adjustments for disabled workers" under the Equality Act of 2010 (although it does not apply to Northern Ireland): bit.ly/UKaccommodations.

- In Australia, the government offers guidance on creating "disability confident workplaces" through local Disability Employment Service providers: bit.ly/AUSaccommodations.

On being a student with chronic illness

Being a college student with chronic pain or illness is *tough*. You're unlikely to have many peers who understand your experience, and you're in a time of life when people are still forming their ideas about what's "normal"—so you may feel extra-super-duper out of place.

One of my favorite resources on college life with chronic illness is Emily Bradley, who's been blogging about her experience for a few years. She created a collection of articles on coping with illness in higher education: bit.ly/ChronicCollege. She's practical, resourceful, and creative.

Most higher learning institutions offer guidance for students with illness and disability. If your school doesn't, it might be time for you to organize a student group around the topic—it's a chance to make friends, and have your concerns heard.

Schools that accommodate chronically ill students

Some schools are addressing chronic illness head-on, by creating flexible programs for students who can't work at the typical pace, or who need to study from home. The DePaul University School for New Learning is one example; they launched the Chronic Illness Initiative in 2003.

Opportunities for online learning are growing by leaps and bounds, too. Once stereotyped as being of lesser quality, online universities are pushing back—and changing the education field. The Center for Online Education offers extensive guidance on finding a school that can accommodate your needs: bit.ly/OnlineEdCenter.

You used to be able to do X but now you can't...but can you?

When we lose the ability to do certain things—work full-time, create crafts, bathe ourselves—it makes us feel like we're no longer ourselves.

It's important to explore different ways to get our needs met, to find new passions and interests. This means shifting our mindset to become open to new approaches. It can be intimidating, and we may be angry that we even have to try.

This is life. Whether it happens to us when we're young (I was twenty-five) or when we're nearing retirement age (my dad is *just now* slowing down at seventy), eventually we must change our approach. The best thing we can do is to accept that change is inevitable, and get busy finding workarounds and other sources of inspiration and satisfaction. (Maybe a review of lesson 1 will help.)

To begin finding a new way, think of a thing you can't do anymore. Sit with it for a little while. What do you love about that thing? Is it personal connections, a feeling of value, creativity, or independence? What makes the experience?

Then you can begin to think about where else to find those experiences.

For example: I love being a writer, and I used to be able to type all day with no issues. The things I love most about writing are the ability to create, to connect with people, to help people. Now, I can't type more than half an hour before I need a break.

I employ many approaches to make writing doable, and to still get those good feelings:

- I use BreakTime, an app that forces me to take breaks at regular intervals.
- I use a sit-stand desk so I can alter my posture throughout the day.
- I stand on a gel mat so my feet (and back, and neck, and arms) don't hurt as much.
- I schedule work in short bursts.
- I do more audio and video work, which allows me to help people without using my hands.
- I write many more, shorter things, instead of big long projects (mostly).
- I use dictation software, and sometimes farm out transcription of interviews.

It's different, and sometimes it's frustrating. I miss the way I was sometimes. But mostly, I'm proud of myself for finding ways to still write, to still feel of value to the world, to connect, and to create. I think you can find new ways of being, too—it just takes time, and working on ideas with friends and pros, and patience.

POP QUIZ

Do you fear change? Get curious

It's natural. Change brings unknowns into the mix. It can help to get curious. Pretend you're an investigative reporter, digging into a story to figure out what's happening. What kinds of resources can you find? Whom can you talk to for clarification? When you get curious, it eases some of the fear, and your mind is better able to get creative.

What will you get curious about today, babe?

HOMEWORK assignments

1) What do you love about work?

When you think about the work you enjoy doing, what is it that you truly love? Is it the people? The sights? The challenges?

Take some time to think about the qualities you love about your work. Write them down. Getting clear on this can help you reframe opportunities and see them with fresh perspective.

2) What do you love about school?

When you think about the topics you enjoy studying, what is it you truly love? Is it the esoteric? The practical? The variety of topics? Do you love studying solo, or in small group settings?

Take some time to think about the things you love about being a student. Write them down. Clarity can help you consider other fields to study, or focus on the ways in which you learn best.

3) What are your values?

Set aside the idea of work or school for a moment and ask yourself this question: What do you value?

If you could name the handful of things that are of greatest value to you—that make you satisfied, joyful, content—what would they be?

A few of mine: peace, compassion, connection, creativity, friendship, love, respect.

When I'm feeling unclear about a decision that must be made, I pause and ask myself: Does this decision align with my values? This simple question can make the decision instantly easier.

4) Ask a friend: How do they see you?

Need an instant ego boost? Grab a friend to play along. Commit to writing down ten things you love about that friend. Share them. Get a little weepy. Hug. Yay!

PEP SQUAD

An Interview with Rosalind Joffe

Become your own best advocate and craft a unique career

Rosalind Joffe, founder and president of ciCoach, is passionate about coaching people and giving them the tools they need to thrive in their work while living with chronic illness. Rosalind draws on her experience living with chronic illnesses, including multiple sclerosis and ulcerative colitis, for over thirty years. Her unique career coaching firm is dedicated to helping people with chronic illness develop the skills they need to succeed in their working lives.

A recognized and frequently quoted national expert on chronic illness and its impact on career, Rosalind is a seasoned and certified coach, and coauthor of *Women, Work, and Autoimmune Disease: Keep Working, Girlfriend!*

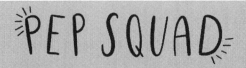

Connect with Rosalind:
Website: ciCoach.com
Facebook: Facebook.com/ciCoach
Twitter: @WorkWithIllness
Email: Rosalind@ciCoach.com

Jenni: Rosalind, so many ChronicBabes have to leave their jobs when they get sick and then they really don't know how to get back into the workforce, whether they are feeling better again or have come to an acceptance of their illness. Do you have a suggestion for a first step for someone who's looking to get back into work?

Rosalind: That's such a big question because everyone's situation is unique to them. In fact, I'd say that's where you should start.

Think about not just your illness and your motivation or where you were before, but think about what your life is about *right now.* Who depends on you? How is this going to impact you and the people around you?

That's where I suggest my clients look first, because it helps to set up a framework for what's going to make the most sense. It's often pretty frightening to take that step and to leave unemployment for employment when you're living with illness, and often what we're most afraid of: disappointing the people around us if we might not be able to hold on.

Jenni: I love that idea! It's not that we want to focus on everybody else before us, but all those factors are a part of the decision-making process.

Rosalind: Exactly. It's not about putting everyone else's needs first, but it's recognizing what impacts you.

Jenni: One of the biggest challenges is that many of us can't do the job we used to be able to do, but we're not sure what we *can* do now, and sometimes we don't know what we *want* to do! It's valuable to take a step back and say *What do I want to do with myself now?* Do you have a favorite exercise that you have people do?

Rosalind: In my workbook, I have a series of exercises, and the first thing is to look at what you used to do and think about it in terms of skills that you've got. The best way of doing that is to go job by job. Take out an old résumé and look at what you did, and look at what you did in that job, so that you're not stuck in this very narrow view of *I was going to medical school* or maybe *I was a cashier;* you're thinking much more like, *These are the things I have done; these are the skills I used and I know how to do.*

The next step might be to look at what I call your needs and wants. You start first with What are your wants? What do you want from a job? And what if you can't do it on your own? It's something I often do with a client, but you can brainstorm it with other people. Take a good friend and talk about the jobs out there. What are the kinds of things that matter to you? Include everything from *short commute* to *working at home* or maybe you want to *make a big move.*

So, what are your wants, and then what are your needs? After that, I suggest to people—if they're really stuck on where to go—I have this whole exercise on networking, but networking just to do this brainstorming exercise.

Jenni: Really?

Rosalind: Yes, I developed it years ago when I first started doing this work, because most of my clients were in the position, at that point, of mostly looking for new careers in new areas. The problem is, they typically were stuck in their box. So, there's this whole script and a way to talk to people you know. It's the first circle in the series of networking steps.

That first circle is talking to people whom you know. Once you have your own list together, you can structure the conversation and start brainstorming with other people, get their ideas.

> *"Think about not just your illness and your motivation or where you were before, but* ***think really about what your life is about right now.****"*
>
> —Rosalind

Jenni: Like maybe the qualities they see in you...

Rosalind: Or jobs they have heard of. I have some who have been working at a job for twenty years, and people have an idea of [them] as that person, and if you want to help them get out of that idea and help [themselves], [they] have to realize *you know what? I can do this, this, and this!* It's taking yourself away from the job description to *What are the opportunities?*

Jenni: That's a challenge. So many people are looking for different kinds of jobs, so thinking very creatively is the way to go.

You mentioned résumés, and that's a question I hear a lot: when we go back into the workforce, and we're interviewing, how do we explain those gaps on our résumé?

Rosalind: The thing to remember is, there's no right answer. I was just talking with a client who has this very diverse background in the law. She finished law school, went into the ministry, and now lives with scleroderma. She stopped working for a couple of years; it is a fairly debilitating illness. It's obvious when you see her, because she needs a walker. She doesn't look "normal and healthy." She decided to be a law professor. In her case, she readily describes the reason she stopped working; she is disclosing illness right off the bat. It really varies.

Most people feel that's really going to hurt them, and it very well can. Especially if what you live with is invisible, there is no way the employer would know. So, how do you explain it?

That gets down to what's most comfortable to you. There are people who are just not comfortable with saying what really happened. And there are people who are not comfortable *not* saying what's going on and why they chose to stop working. So, there is no one piece of advice.

There is always the caveat that, yes, if someone has to choose between someone who has been sick for four years and someone who hasn't been sick for four years, they are probably going to choose the one who hasn't been sick—even though we all know that the healthy person could get sick tomorrow! That's not how people think.

If you're really struggling with this, think of other ways to describe why you might have stopped working. Mothers with children always have that; that's an easy thing to say. Other things people can say include "I moved' or "I took some time off to freelance." It's never going to help you that you were out of the workforce, and that's one of the reasons in my book I say, *keep working*. It will always hurt you; that is the reality, even if you decide to stop working for a home business.

One of my clients found that she was up against people who hadn't decided to have a home business, and what happens then is the employers think maybe you will stop working again. So, you will always have to talk about that. Most employers, recruiting managers, and hiring managers are going to ask you. You definitely want to be sure you are prepared with your answer.

Jenni: It seems like you suggest it's really about comfort level.

Rosalind: Yes, and that's where I do a lot of coaching, because you really have to know what's going to feel comfortable to you to talk about, and what's a way you can explain it so that you are not lying because as soon as you fill out an insurance form and you have to list pre-existing conditions—especially if it's a small company—it could come back and bite you in the ass. There are many factors to think about.

Jenni: We don't want to be dishonest. But you're right: there are times when we want to leave things a little loose, not get so specific.

Rosalind: When you do, the key is to do it in a way that it doesn't seem as if you are avoiding [it].

Jenni: Because I think people can sniff that out.

Rosalind: Absolutely, especially if there is more than one gap period.

In the eighties, I had jumped around a lot and, in fact, I had jumped around because of illness. But it turns out—and I never thought about saying it specifically—each job was a different kind of job. In those days, that was a red flag; people wanted to know why I moved so much from job to job, because it wasn't typical. These days it's very typical to move.

Jenni: Yeah, it's crazy now. Someone who's graduating college right now may have thirty jobs in a lifetime! I have a younger sister who's had three times as many jobs as I have ever had. I've been self-employed for [fifteen] years, and it's really good.

Rosalind: Then you don't have to worry about losing your job.

Jenni: My résumé now looks super steady and mellow, compared to people just five years younger than me. I hear what you are saying and with the way things go, those of us who have those gaps and have moved around a lot, we can almost use that to our advantage.

Rosalind: Most importantly, you should always be very prepared; that's one of the things you should be thinking about.

Jenni: One of the things we think about is the Americans with Disabilities Act (ADA). At the last job I had before I was self-employed, I asked for a couple of accommodations, and it was sometimes challenging to get them because people couldn't see that I needed certain things.

Can we talk about some typical accommodations, or some we may not think of as things we can get if we need them—and things that may not come to mind immediately?

"Take out an old résumé and look at what you did, and look at what you did in that job, so that you're not stuck in this very narrow view of I was going to medical school or maybe I was a cashier; you're thinking much more like, **these are the things I have done, these are the skills I used and I know how to do."**

—Rosalind

Rosalind: In my experience, most people know what they want as far as an accommodation. I have a real thing about that word; what I like to call it is a *workaround*.

Accommodate is someone doing you a favor. What I say is, you want a workaround. That's a word everyone uses in all kinds of ways. Let's see you create the *workaround* for the situation.

First and foremost, the top workaround I've seen people need is flexibility, like flexibility in schedule. Here's where it gets tricky. My suggestion is, if you are interviewing for a job, if you're looking for a job, and you know you have certain differences here—like you are worth nothing in the morning, your brain doesn't work and you're going to have to work longer days, or you're never sure when it's going to hit you so you're going to need to work at home some days, or whatever it is—figure that part out.

That's the process I go through with people, is figuring out: what are their needs? Your best bet, of course, is try to find a job, an industry, a career, that's going to offer you that—so that you don't have to ask for something that they are not already doing.

Going back to the ADA: There have been revisions, and it supposedly includes people with chronic illness, but not every illness is recognized as a real illness, like fibromyalgia. Although the Centers for Disease Control has said it is, it's still not [considered one] among most people.

The other part about the ADA is that it only applies to organizations at a certain level, certain size. And furthermore, it's still written for the employer, so when you ask for something, it has to be something that is not going to hurt the employer. In the long run, if you are going to ask the employer for something that's really not going to be in their best interest or going to be harmful to them or the way they get work done, it's not going to be a very good fit and, especially these days, they are not going to have to look very hard for a way to let you go.

> ***"The top workaround people need is flexibility.*** *If you're looking for a job, and you know you have certain differences here, figure that part out."*
>
> —Rosalind

Look for a place where they are already doing those kinds of things, the flexibility or whatever it is that you need—and a job you can really see will work for you in terms of what your needs might be. Some people need to be near a bathroom, [so] if you are going to be out working in the fields all day, that's not going to work.

I have one client who had been working in a garden center, but she needed air conditioning and they didn't air condition the garden center. Well, they weren't going to start air conditioning for her—they weren't going to put it in. So, you have to think long and hard about *what's the fit*? And certainly before you ever invoke the ADA, most employers, definitely of a certain size—especially if they have anyone who is a human resources specialist—are fully aware and afraid of the ADA. It also makes them more uptight about you.

Your best bet is to approach this as gingerly as possible, from the point of view that *this is what I need,* and also, you want to document everything in case you ever do need to go back on disability. Any words around "what you do" you want to have documented.

Jenni: I advocate mega-documentation!

These days, a lot of people get told that they need to give up on their dream job. They might have been doing something, and then they got sick and they can't do it anymore, and now they just need to give up on ever being able to do something that they are super-passionate about and settle for whatever they can take.

I think that's crap; I feel really strongly about that. Can you tell me what you think about that?

Rosalind: What makes you say that you think it's crap?

Jenni: The idea that people should give up on a dream, give up on doing something they are really passionate about—I think saying that outright is an energy killer. It's really negative.

My dream, when I was younger, was to be an investigative reporter and travel the world, cover big stories. Now, do I know that is a lifestyle my body can't maintain? Yes. That was my dream job, but I didn't give up on the dream of doing something that I love and am passionate about and that helps people, which were the ultimate goals of that work.

Now, I've figured out a way to take those writing skills and do something I'm passionate about and that helps people. I still get to travel some when I do speaking engagements, and I do it on my terms, so it's like I get to achieve those goals and get that great feeling of satisfaction that I feel I also would have had from being a worldwide investigative reporter.

But I feel like I didn't give up on my dream; my dream just looks a little different. Instead of thinking about it as a job title, I tried to change how I thought of it as *what I wanted to get from that type of work* and get that somewhere else.

Rosalind: Jenni, you just basically said what I would have said.

And what you might not realize is that what you just talked about was not being resigned, that's the word I often use. Resignation is not acceptance.

Accepting what is, is what we have to do. But often, that transforms into resignation. *I'm resigned to this*, and with that is a defeatist attitude, a victim's attitude, powerlessness.

Acceptance, certainly in the Buddhist sense, is becoming much more of a term we are hearing these days. And acceptance, I propose, is much more about coming to terms with *being at peace with what is*, and from that place you can then say *This is what gave me joy in the past. I can't do that anymore—maybe I can't run a mile or swim six miles a day, or maybe I can't stand and sling hamburgers all day or maybe I can't be in the courtroom like I used to—but what did I get that was joyful from that? What skills did I bring? What did it do for me?*

Then think about *Okay, I'm looking at who I am now, what other opportunities are there?*

Then, as you said very well, it isn't about thinking about the job title. As I said to my kids, it didn't matter what college they went to in the end, if they were going to be happy—they would be happy wherever they went because we have the ability to find what's good. Some people are better at that than others, but knowing what makes you happy, knowing what fulfills you, and being able to accept life limitations, helps you realize that *Yeah, a dream job, that's what it was, it was a dream, not necessarily a reality.*

Often, as we think about the past, it can look either better than it was or worse, so what we need to do is look to the future without fear and just think in terms of *What makes me happy?*

This interview has been shortened and edited to fit this book. To read the full transcript or listen to the full recordings of this and all the Pep Squad interviews, head to ChronicBabe101.com.

Lesson 9

become a talented communicator

It's easy to decide people are against us if they don't understand us. But that would be a mistake; often, they just need more information. ChronicBabes know it's up to us to walk into a room, conversation, or dinner party with an open heart. This lesson will help you be at ease in any situation and take control of the conversation—and get the outcome you want (and deserve).

The challenge of invisible illness and communicating our experience...without seeming like a whiner

Most of us crave connection and understanding. We live with so much challenge—and it's natural that we want people to understand us.

How do we describe what it's like to live with chronic illness or pain, without seeming like we seek sympathy? This is a difficult task.

Here's what happens to me sometimes:

Me: I have fibromyalgia.
Them: I'm so sorry!
Me: It's okay!

They jump to sympathy, and I jump to soothe their discomfort.

What the hell? That's not a helpful dialogue. It's being operated by our *habits*, not our *hearts*.

Lately I've been trying a new approach. Let's see if you can apply it to your conversations.

> **Me:** I have fibromyalgia.
> **Them:** I'm so sorry!
> **Me (smiling):** Thank you, but that's not necessary. The thing is, I do well in spite of it because I'm committed to kicking ass.

Talk about setting the tone—for the other person, and for *me*.

We never owe others an explanation of what we're going through, but it can help to describe it sometimes. Take our friends, for example. They probably want to understand our experience, and we can help them. Set the tone:

> **You:** Remember how I was flaring up last week, and had to cancel our dinner plans? I was hoping we could talk about it—I want to be sure you understood what happened, because I could tell you were disappointed.

Lead with a connection; you were *both* disappointed, right?

From there, you can describe what a flare-up is like—not just the sensations you experience, but how it impacts you emotionally.

Emphasize that you're sharing this because you want to create understanding, not because you're looking for sympathy.

Ask if your friend has more questions, and answer them as best you can.

End with something like:

> **You:** Thank you for listening, and talking about how this impacts me. I don't want to seem like a flake or a whiner, but sometimes I need to talk about this crud—it helps to know you care and want to understand.

Do you suffer? The words we choose matter

I can't stand the word *sufferer*. When people say I "suffer from fibromyalgia," I flinch. When we casually use the word *suffer* over and over, we drive home the idea that to have our condition is to truly suffer...and that's simply not always true.

Instead, I choose to say I "live with" or "experience the effects of" fibromyalgia.

Distinctions matter, and we get to choose how we describe our lives. Making thoughtful choices about the words we use helps us craft the story of our lives, both for others and for ourselves.

When you speak to others about your experience, do you use words like *suffer*? When you talk about your pain, do you use highly charged words like *agonizing, searing,* or *crippling*? The choices you make create a resonance that can deeply impact the other person.

Sometimes this is useful—you want your doctor to know you're in agony, for example—but maybe you don't need to use that word with your eight-year-old niece, who may then worry unnecessarily. It's a good practice to choose your words wisely.

The words you choose also deeply impact *you*. It may be true that you're in agony, that you're in so much pain you can barely stand it. But also: If you keep saying that to yourself over and over, you leave no room for improvement. You make it impossible to distract yourself with something else that could ease your pain.

Practice mindfulness when it comes to the words you use to describe your situation. I think you'll find you can steer your experience a little by using a more positive vocabulary.

POP QUIZ

What noises do you make?

When you're not feeling well, do you moan and groan? Are you like a grape stepped on by an elephant...do you let out a little *whine*?

Consider making new noises. On big pain days, I've started making silly noises instead of groans as I stretch my sore muscles—and the laughter it generates for me (and sometimes, my husband) is liberating.

For more ideas, watch my video: bit.ly/WeirdSounds. BRAAAAPPPP!

I am not a mind reader

...and neither are you. Neither is your spouse, your sister, or your best friend.

Yet *so many* women have asked me how to subtly convey their needs to people because they don't want to sound *needy*.

Forget subtlety. Use your words. Asking for what you need is not needy.

"My hands are really sore today; could you please unload the dishwasher so they don't get worse?"

"I'm having fibro fog today and can't remember what we needed at the grocery. Can you text me the list, please?"

"It's usually cold in your apartment. Do you mind turning up the heat when I come over tomorrow?"

I've said those three things in the last month. Do any of them sound *needy* to you? Or do they sound reasonable?

If you ask your wife to text you once an hour to check on you because you're lonely, that's a bit needy. And a lot of pressure on her.

If you ask your boyfriend to grab you a soda from the fridge because you don't feel like getting up—blaming it on fatigue—that's selfish.

If you're secretly wishing your friend would invite you over to watch movies this weekend, but you don't say anything, and then feel angry if she doesn't, that's unfair.

Most of the time, using our words nets us the result we want. We get into trouble when we don't speak up, or when we speak disingenuously.

Speaking in code

Poop alert! People freak about poop, butts, and other bodily functions. But if you live with chronic illness, you sometimes find yourself having to discuss these less-than-pretty topics.

I'm going to contradict myself; I said earlier that you should use your words. But sometimes, it's better to speak in code.

The trick: Establish the code upfront. Don't spring code words on someone and expect them to understand!

Let's go back to the poop stuff.

Occasionally, I poop myself. It's part of having irritable bowel syndrome, and it's *so* not sexy. When it happens, I may want to tell my husband, but I may use humor and code words to ease my momentary embarrassment: "Fire in the hole!"

Maybe you're simply tired of repeating your flare-up list when a friend asks how you're doing. A mutually understood code word for texting could replace the list: "I'm having a 💩 kind of day."

Not only do code words save you from having to relate all the gory details, they also give you some relief from retelling the same tale. Everyone wins.

The all-important "I" statements

When we're all fired up, we can become accusatory. We start listing all the things the other person is doing to annoy us or make us feel crummy. Even if the things we're saying are true, the delivery puts the other person on the defensive.

A calmer way to have this conversation is to start with "I" statements—sharing how you feel about something and how you viewed the situation, instead of how wrong the other person is. Let's try it:

> **Instead of:** You always leave the sink full of dishes, and it's not fair that I have to clean up, especially on flare-up days!
>
> **Try:** I feel overwhelmed when I see a sink full of dirty dishes, especially on flare-up days. I could handle flare-up days better if I didn't have to tackle last night's dishes.

> **Instead of:** You're always planning get-togethers that are impossible for me to attend; it's like you don't even want me there.
>
> **Try:** I want to hang out, but I have a hard time attending events the way they're usually planned. Sometimes I feel isolated, and I want to see more of you. Can we think of some ideas for hang times I can manage?

> **Instead of:** You haven't made any accommodations in this office, so it's hard for me to get work done. When will the changes be made?
>
> **Try:** I'm having a hard time meeting deadlines because we haven't made my workspace changes. I want to do my best work, and those changes will make all the difference. Is there something I can do to help facilitate getting them done soon?

Do you see the difference? When you lead with how you're feeling—how you're impacted—instead of blaming the other person, you open the door for a more productive conversation.

PEP SQUAD

Jackie Sloane, MCC

For greater success, speak your mind with compassion

Jackie Sloane, MCC, has been my coach and friend for many years. She's based in my city of Chicago, and she works with people to transform their situations—to clarify what they want to achieve and what approaches will help them achieve it. She is all about action and results, so I wanted to share some of a recent conversation we had.

"There's more and more research about compassion," Jackie says. "The most powerful thing is to cultivate some compassion for yourself and the other person, because...when you experience compassion for yourself and you express compassion, and when doctors express compassion for you, we actually release the brain hormone oxytocin—and that produces bonding."

Jackie advises from the start that when there's a communication breakdown, take a moment to first cultivate some compassion for yourself, and then for the other person. It creates an opportunity for connection even in a difficult conversation.

Clarify: What do you want to achieve?

It's important to understand what you really want to achieve. "What do you want in this situation? Oftentimes, people have not clarified *What do I want here?*" That lack of clarity, she says, leads people to simply vent frustration without any goal in sight, which doesn't help anyone. Instead, she counsels, "when you know what you want, you can look to see *How can I be more compassionate toward this other person that's not doing what I want? And how can I be compassionate toward myself?*"

That moment of connection, she says, makes space for things to cool down. You can balance your needs with the needs of the other person, without sacrificing your needs.

Jackie says this is crucial when considering interactions with health care providers, who go into their field with only the greatest hope of helping people, but who also face innumerable roadblocks and time-sucks every day—so they're imperfect.

"Perhaps they misunderstood something, perhaps they are tired, or perhaps they missed something important," says Jackie. "But that doesn't mean you shouldn't also be honored." She says when there are difficult conversations to be had with health care providers, remembering to be compassionate and connect authentically can lead to a de-escalation and greater understanding.

In any challenging conversation, Jackie advises taking time beforehand, if possible, to draft out what you would say if there were NO consequences. Write it out, or type it, and review: Take out highly charged words, swear words, and any words that are blaming or critical.

Strategy: Make a personal connection

You can shape what you would say in a difficult conversation by starting out with something you might share as a connection with the other person. Maybe acknowledge that you've been friends a long time, or that you share the same passion for justice, or whatever feels most authentic.

Then, once you've made that connection, you can speak your truth. "This idea of coming from a space of compassion for yourself and other people, and then clarifying what it is that you want here...you're giving yourself a little bit of a process to organize what it is you're looking to accomplish and say in this situation," Jackie says.

If we don't do this, if we're just intent on venting our frustration, we can get into a ping-pong match and it turns into a "frustration fest," which serves no one, warns Jackie. "Start out with acknowledging this other person for who they are—to create this connection with the person first before you make your request—so that you have their attention."

Jackie also emphasizes the value of "I" statements. "If we speak from 'I,' like 'I'm feeling uncomfortable' or 'I'd really prefer that we do this' or 'I want something different for dinner'...that's legitimate," she explains. "Nobody can argue with you that that's not true because you're expressing what's so for you."

"Where we get blaming is we can say things like, 'Well, you always do this' and 'You never do this' and 'You cut me off all the time.' All those phrases are blaming. The other person can feel attacked and blamed, and it quickly gets into a negative exchange," says Jackie. If you cultivate some compassion and then speak in "I" sentences, she says, the conversation can go from negative to neutral. "When you don't blame, it gives people more space to honor what you're asking for."

Jackie emphasizes that it's on us, babes, to pay attention to how we talk to people, and to learn how our body language, tone, and words are having an impact on others. "But I would also say there are doctors that are abrupt; there are caregivers that need a lot of learning themselves. You deserve to be treated by somebody you feel comfortable with. It's very important that you feel safe talking to your doctor, to your caregiver."

"This whole idea of compassion and the release of oxytocin is good for your wellbeing, and it's good for your immune system to feel comfortable around the people who are taking care of you," Jackie says. "So if you think the doctor is not serving you, then find a different doctor that will serve you better. I've totally done that myself." (Refer to lesson 6 for help on this.)

Learn more about Jackie and her incredible work at SloaneCommunications.com.

For a more detailed conversation about communication techniques for ChronicBabes, head to ChronicBabe101.com and listen to the full recording of my conversation with Jackie, or download the transcript.

How to start difficult conversations about sex with partners (or potential lovers)

Whether it's the first conversation you have with a new partner about chronic illness and its impact on your sex life, or a challenging negotiation with your spouse because you want to reignite your sex life, conversations about sex can be tough.

Start with "I" statements, like we talked about earlier. Sentences like "I feel unattractive when we go for a few weeks without touching" are much less threatening than "You never touch me anymore and it makes me feel bad."

Don't start a conversation:

- if you're exhausted
- if you're naked
- if you've been drinking
- if you're angry

Pick a time when things are chill: after Sunday morning brunch, while you're taking a walk together, or after you've spent a great day hanging out. Why add additional stressors to what's already challenging?

Be prepared for baby steps. If you're trying to reignite a fizzled sex life, don't expect one conversation to change things back to where they were before—you may need to try (you may even enjoy!) pretending like you're on a first date again, and slowly work up to more. If you want to try something new, the first time might not work—be ready to take it in small steps.

Don't make a date for a "big conversation." Seriously—this never works. It only stresses out everyone in advance, so emotions are already strong before you've said one word. Weave it into your conversations, starting small—and be ready for a series of smaller conversations, which may be more productive than trying to work it all out at once.

Be prepared for some give and take. You may have wants and needs the other person has a hard time with. You may want more or less than they want. Sex is best when it's a mutually beneficial experience, so be prepared to give as much as you get. Maybe more. You never know what you'll learn to love!

Enlisting support when you're making a big change

Sometimes, people who've known us for a long time have a hard time believing we can truly change. We may be unsure how to explain *why* we're making a change.

Here are some sentences focusing on positivity, collaboration, and inclusivity—which you can use when talking with folks about change:

- "I've wanted to try something new for a while, so I'm exploring a new approach. Would you like to hear about it?"
- "It's time for me to change X and I could really use your help, since we're in this together. I have some ideas, but would love to discuss this more with you—can we dedicate time to this tonight?"
- "Even though I've struggled to make this change in the past, I recognize it's important—so I'm trying again, extra-hard this time, and I could use your encouragement. This time will be the one that sticks."
- "It's true, I tried to make this change before and wasn't successful—but now I know some things that will help me approach it differently."
- "I know this change may take you by surprise, but I've been doing my homework and I think this is going to make a positive impact on my life. Can I tell you more about it?"
- "It may be hard for you to get used to this change—it will be hard for me, too. But I think the payoff will be worth it."
- "Change is hard—you know this, too, because you made X change in your own life, which was difficult. I know you understand when I say I need to do this, and I need your support."
- "I acknowledge that by making this change, I'll be impacting you in X way. Let's talk about how it will affect you and address any concerns you may have."

POP QUIZ **Words that trigger and words that bond**

Are there words that trigger horrible feelings and bad memories for you? Are there words that help solidify connections with friends and family?

Make a list. Consider how you can weave in more of the positive and less of the negative in day-to-day conversation.

Assert yourself

While I love to cuss and shout as much as the next sailor, I think we can all agree communicating like that won't get you far in most situations. Learning how to use assertive—instead of aggressive—language is quite helpful. Here are some examples of assertiveness and aggressiveness:

Assertive:	***Aggressive:***
Reminding someone of their commitment	Telling someone they're a jerk for letting you down
Using language that is strong and firm	Using language that is pushy and forceful
Maintaining a physical stance that's welcoming	Getting in someone's face or using a mean physical stance
Using proper, professional language	Using profanity or slang
Showing up with progress toward a productivity goal	Emailing a ton of web research and then getting angry in a meeting
Asking someone for more help around the house	Shouting about how you're the only one who gets anything done around here
Suggesting that together, we find a solution to an issue	Saying the other person better figure this out or we're gonna be real mad

Assertive language builds stronger conversations

When I'm thinking about how I can be more assertive, I can refer to a list of words that are strong, collaborative, and forward-thinking. It helps me come up with emails and conversation starters that set the tone for a productive conversation—one that serves me well. Some of the words I like most:

- focused
- goal-oriented
- fundamental
- powerful
- respect
- science-backed
- professional
- instructive
- compromise
- opportunity
- amenable
- collaborative
- promising
- committed
- strong
- flexible
- open-hearted
- willing
- tenacious
- creative

For example, I have noisy upstairs neighbors. Some nights, I want to go up there and pound on their door and shout about how disrespectful they are. But that would *not* get me the results I want, and it would raise my blood pressure and anxiety level even further. Instead, I thought about how to phrase my request. Here's one that's worked well so far:

> **Me:** Hi, guys, could you please turn your TV down a bit? I'm trying to go to sleep. I hate coming up here over and over—I'm sure it's a hassle for you, too. How can we put our heads together to reduce these noise issues?

The words *collaborative*, *committed*, and *creative* inspired that conversation starter. I knew approaching it like a collaboration (let's put our heads together) would feel less accusatory. I'm committed to finding a solution (cuz I'm sick of going up there!), so I make it clear I want to reduce the noise issues long-term (not just tonight). We might have to get creative to work it out (by which I really mean, *they* might need to get creative about putting down a rug or using headphones for late-night gaming), but I phrase it as collaborative to set the tone.

Is all this effort to craft an assertive conversation starter worth it? Yes! If I went up there and shouted every time they got noisy, they would *hate* me. Instead, we're amiable when we see each other around the building, and they're responsive when I ask them to turn down the TV. (Do I still flip them the bird from the comfort of my own couch sometimes? Sure, I'm human. But big picture: We're all better off.)

It's essential for caregivers to find the joy in every day

Patrick's girlfriend has fibromyalgia and several other chronic pain conditions. They put a lot of effort into building strong communication habits so they are clear about their individual needs, and he works hard to find joy in every day.

Support has to be front and center at all times, whether mental or emotional support on a bad day, [or] more of a physical support for when my ChronicBabe isn't moving very well. It's important in the little things, too. It could be a flower, it could be a card, it could even be a nice text. I think those things help keep it alive.

When I feel particularly frustrated, exhausted, I try as much as I can to do things that help give me fulfillment. In a lot of cases that relates to cooking, because I really enjoy cooking and it's kind of a nice outlet for me. It's something I can use, it's very tactile, where so much of what may happen day-to-day isn't tactile and [it's] really hard to put your hands on some of those feelings and some of those ways that pain is being expressed.

Caregiver resources
For a list of caregiver-focused resources, head to the Extra Credit section at the back of the book.

I also have a few people I can reach out to, say, "Hey, things are a little tough or a little challenging."

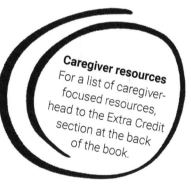

People automatically associate everything with the negativity and don't have the foresight to realize, Hey, the good is still there. *Even in the midst of that sort of down-turning spiral, there are positives. There is support from one another, there are things we can laugh and joke about, there is music we can listen to, there are things like*

food or art or some kind of entertainment that can help us find our way through.

I think one of the most important but overlooked things that can really help as a caregiver is to still find joy, to still find happiness because it's so, so easy to lose that. If you lose that, then I think you don't even have the strength to fight the battle for that day. But that joy, that happiness, it can keep you grounded, and I think it also allows for you [to] fully live in the moment. Finding that joy allows you to be fully open to the entire experience rather than being shut down and only getting into that dark side of frustration and disappointment, or anything else that may be happening.

One hundred ways to answer the question "How are you?"

"How are you?" It's a simple question, just three little words and a question mark.

But for us ChronicBabes, the question may give us pause. It's not always the easiest to answer. We may not want to talk about what's going wrong. We may yearn for support but not be sure how someone will respond to a blunt response. We may wish we could tell the whole truth but hope we can get away with a little white lie. We may not feel safe enough to be completely authentic.

I came up with one hundred potential answers. I can't fit them all in this book, but here are a few options:

- "Staying grounded. How 'bout you?"
- "Not so hot, but nothing a stiff drink and some girl talk can't fix."
- "Get back to me on that, okay?"
- "Currently under construction."

For the rest, head to bit.ly/CBhowRU for the full download.

HOMEWORK assignments

1) Make a request

Is there something you've wanted from another person, but have been afraid to ask? Now is the time to push yourself outside your usual approach.

Use what you've learned in this lesson and make a request. Make it reasonable, simple, and clear.

2) Write some code

Earlier in the lesson, we talked about speaking in code. What words could you use to replace scary, triggering, or gross words? Write them down and share them with loved ones.

3) Can you flip the script?

When someone asks about your illness and you don't want to discuss it, can you flip the script? In lesson 4, we talk about deflecting; flipping the script uses that skill. Write down a few phrases (and then practice them out loud) that will be useful the next time you want to flip the script.

PEP SQUAD

An Interview with Jennette Fulda

Better communication strategies ensure you'll get your needs met

Jennette Fulda is a writer, web designer, chronic headache sufferer, weight-loss inspiration, blogger, and former governor of the fourth grade. She lives in Chapel Hill, North Carolina.

In 2008 Jennette got a headache that still hasn't gone away. She wrote about her ordeal in a humorous headache memoir called *Chocolate and Vicodin: My Quest for Relief from the Headache that Wouldn't Go Away.*

She tells the Internet stories about her life on her blog, develops WordPress websites, and inspires me to find more joy whenever I feel cruddy.

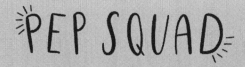

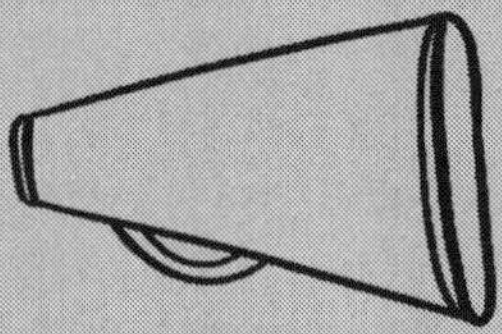

Connect with Jennette:
Website: JennetteFulda.com and MakeworthyMedia.com
Facebook: Facebook.com/JennetteFulda
Twitter: @jennettefulda

Jenni: Today we're going to talk about communication techniques. Can you name all the ways you communicate with people about your health? All the mediums you use?

Jennette: One of the first things I used was my blog, because at the time I was running a blog and I got this headache. I remember the exact day, it was February 17, 2008. I got this headache and it wouldn't go away. I tried to avoid writing this for the first few months because I didn't know what was going on, but then it became such a huge part of my life. I felt like I needed to write about it or else I was keeping this huge secret.

Then, it really felt good pouring my soul out and telling people what was going on. The good thing is, I got a lot of support and a lot of good comments. The bad thing, though, is people start to send you lots and lots of cures, and you get this list of, literally, over a hundred things—I've collected a list over the years and it's just like *How could I possibly do all these things? I'd still be working my way through everything*—so you kind of have to pick and choose the ones you really think might work for you.

The blog is one way. I also visited a lot of online forums. I didn't necessarily post a lot, though; I tended to just read what was there and use that as leads to investigate other things or to figure out what headache clinics might be good for me.

I also have actually met a few people on Twitter, where we sometimes have Twitter chats, or we'll hashtag things, or maybe someone who has read my book contacts me. I have also shared a lot of emails between people who have read my blog, who perhaps have chronic headaches themselves and have been doing web searches and [have] said, "I have had this condition," and [been] asking me, "What have you tried?" and "What has worked for you?" We'll have a back-and-forth talking about our own problems.

(Author's note: Hashtags like #spoonie, #HospitalGlam, and #ChronicBabe are a fun way to find community online.)

That's actually really great, because those people really understand what you are going through, and some of them are farther down the line than where I am, and they have come to more of a point of acceptance and coping. Some of them have just started. They are at "What should I do?" and "What can I try?" and "How can I get rid of this thing?"

Then I also talk to some people in person—either because I had a book signing or something like that, or when I was doing promotions for my book I got to meet a couple of bloggers—and they, too, can really relate to what you go through, even if they don't have chronic headaches. You have to learn a lot of the same techniques, like how to communicate with people and how to deal with your condition.

Jenni: I'm guessing you also use the phone?

Jennette: Yes, I think most of the conversations I have are in person at appointments, with health care providers. I have used the phone for refilling my prescriptions or phoning the nurse, that you can contact or leave a voicemail message with if you have a question, something that is non-urgent, not something that needs to be taken care of right away; they usually call you back.

I haven't ever emailed any health care providers, even though I would like to. Usually the problem is they have to comply with HIPAA to maintain privacy—your doctor can't just set up an email account and have you send stuff to them. They have to be sure that the emails can't be intercepted and that only the person that is authorized to read it, reads it.

(Author's note: See lesson 7 for a conversation with a doctor about the challenges involved in emailing health care providers.)

I have a friend who is a radiologist, and I've emailed her informally about some of my scans. I was able to get my MRIs and CT scans on CD. She took a look at them for me and she said, "This is where you have the weird veins and all that stuff," but she never interpreted. She's not my doctor; she's my friend who's a radiologist. She's not telling me in a professional capacity.

One nice thing with this technology is my neurologist is able to prescribe medications through the computer. He is able to send the prescription through to my pharmacy, so I don't have to bring in a slip or anything, which is convenient.

Jenni: My doctor has been doing that too, and he can even send them to the mail-order prescription pharmacy that my insurance company requires me to use. It saves so much time and hassle, and then everything is really well documented.

Jennette: Some of my doctors use laptops for everything, and my most recent neurologist has everything on a laptop, and he's able to scroll through and look at previous medications we've tried and find out how I've rated my pain at different appointments and run through all the information right in front of him. Sometimes, maybe some of my older doctors who are not necessarily adapting, are not taking on the new technology, so it will be interesting to see how long it takes [those] doctors to really get the digital formats.

Jenni: It does seem like it would improve the way we communicate with them; if they have all that stuff they can show us so quickly, and do statistical analysis, too. Do you see your neurologist more often? Is that kind of your main one?

*"The most common way you give up power is when **you believe you don't have any**."*
—Jennette

Jennette: Yes. The first year or two I had the headaches, I saw a lot of different doctors. I started with my primary care physician and got referred to a lot of other people, and I also tried Eastern medicines, like acupuncture, deep-muscle massage, and that kind of stuff. Now my pain is lower than it was, is maintained at that level. It would be good just to get rid of the headache before a hard day's work wears it out, but I'm coping and doing okay.

I'm still seeing doctors, but not as actively as I did at first. I see the neurologist every three months or so. At this point, we are just altering the dosages of my medications, and [we've tried] things like some steroid injections around my head and neck to see if that would help, but I didn't get any results from that. I see him pretty regularly—I see him more than my regular doctor.

Jenni: When you are communicating with him, what kind of techniques do you use? What's your primary mode of communication, and what has wound up working well for you?

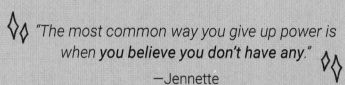

Jennette: They actually have a standard questionnaire I fill out every time I go there and it asks: "How much better/worse do you feel since you first came here? Since the last appointment? How often has your headache prevented you from doing things like work or activities like that? How many times has your headache made you frustrated?"

That helps him track things over time to see if they are getting better or worse. That's one of the best ways to communicate with him.

Sometimes, it's hard to bring things up if you are embarrassed—I needed to talk to him about birth control because I wanted to know how going on birth control [would] affect my headaches, since it affects your hormonal levels, but I was a little bit embarrassed. But you do it because you need to. You just kind of get over it.

Jenni: You've got to figure they hear every kind of weird thing all the time. Every year I go to the gynecologist. I've had the same doctor for a few years, and he comes in and spends a lot of time with me. He asks me how I am, he asks how my [husband] is, *how's your work, how's your family*, all that kind of stuff.

Jennette: It's good to have a good rapport with your doctor, someone who knows who you are—literally. Someone who would notice if there's something off or if you are more stressed out than normal, [if you] don't look as healthy, or if you gained weight or lost weight, that might be related to some sort of medical condition.

I moved recently. I lived in Indianapolis for about ten years, and had a really good relationship with my doctor there. So the bad thing about moving is I had to get a whole new set of doctors.

I got a recommendation from my old headache clinic for the new place and I've been really happy there, but it's hard—you have to start from scratch, you have to go and form a relationship. My doctor, the neurologist in the office, is less talkative than my old one, but I think I have had better results with the latest one, which is strange. I don't know what accounts for that, other than maybe he just lucked out and got the right medications or what?

That's one of the things with moving; it was kind of a big thing—something I really had to consider.

Jenni: Thinking more on the personal side, when you're not feeling well, how do you communicate that to people you know personally? Like your friends? I don't know if you have family in town.

Jennette: I have a brother and sister-in-law in town.

One of the headache clinics that I went to did a scale of one-to-five for your headache, and a lot of places make you keep a headache diary and you have to record it either when you have a headache—or with me, I had to record it in the morning, afternoon and evening, what number I was, and look for patterns. Sometimes right before your period, your headache will be worse because of the hormone changes; sometimes it can be weather or something you've eaten, so you keep track of it on that one-to-five scale.

I've educated my family and my friends on the scale, so when they ask me "How are you doing?" I say, "I'm on a number three right now." They understand where I am pain-wise. Having that language really helps. I prefer the one-to-five [scale], although the one-to-ten is actually more common, but I like the one-to-five because there is definitely a distinct difference between each number. Whereas if you do the one-to-ten, you're like a seven, but there isn't much difference [between] an eight [and] a six.

Jenni: My pain clinic, where I get treatment and see my pain psychologist, they use the one-to-ten scale, and sometimes I'm like, "Well, last night I was at a six, but maybe it was a seven, I don't know, but for a few minutes there I think I was at an eight; I really wanted to throw something through the window."

How do you know? I remember one day I went in for PT and he was so funny. He said, "You look like you are going to kill someone!" and I said, "Yeah, my pain is so insane today, it's not a ten, it's more than a ten!"

We are both fans of *Spinal Tap*, and he said, "You turned that pain up to eleven!" and I started laughing so hard. I was like "Yes, it's an eleven! Not on the scale, dude! The scale is meaningless to me right now, all I can tell you is I can't function." It's cool when you can find someone you like and relate to.

Jennette: And there's a difference between pain and suffering. Pain is an irreversible level of whatever is going on in your head, that kind of static state. Suffering is more the way you perceive it.

Some people at circuses can lie down on a bed of nails, and they will say they're not in pain. I think somehow you are able to access parts of your brain where you are able to turn it off or not pay attention to it; I think they are like Zen monks. They have this way to do something that, even though they are in pain, they are not suffering from it.

One of my coping techniques is to try to not think about the pain, and actually it helps me.

And that's kind of counter to the idea of communication when you communicate about your pain, your headaches—sometimes you don't want to communicate it, you don't want to think about it, but you have to go into it and be there with it.

"I get a lot of emails from people who are going through the same thing, and ***you can kind of support each other, and really can understand what they are going through."***

—Jennette

Jenni: I've learned there are times when I can be in a lot of pain and, for example, a friend would say to me "How are you doing?" and I may say "You know what? I'm in a lot of pain, but let's just not think about it."

People who are close to me get that. If I say that to them, they know I'm really struggling, but I want to be distracted and think about and do other things and that helps me. But I think over the years I've needed to learn how to say to people, "Hey, if I say this to you, this is what I mean." I've been explicit with people; I think that's one thing I've learned.

Jennette: In the beginning, you are just holding on to your old reality. You don't want this thing to stop you from doing all the stuff you used to, but when you accept the new normal, you are able to say, "I really can't go out to a club until three in the morning anymore." I just need to tell people that.

Jenni: I hear a lot of people talk about not feeling well and they really come off as whiners; I might catch a lot of flak for saying that, but heck, I've been a whiner myself. I'm wondering if you have a favorite thing to say to people that lets them know? It sounds like you've got the pain-scale thing worked out, but do you have anything else you ever say to people so they know you're in pain, but not like, *"Owwee, I'm reeaaallyyy hurrtinng..."*

Jennette: It really is a challenge. It's easier with people who really know you, because they understand more what you go through. I probably don't complain about my pain as much as I should in other situations, because I don't want to be a whiner. I don't know that I've really found a way to say things without looking like I'm weak; you don't want to be the weak person at work, the person that can't keep up with things.

Jenni: Some people, you could say the mildest thing and people would perceive you as being a huge whiner, and that's on them, because you can't change the baggage they bring to the situation.

Jennette: Yeah, I think it's more other people's problem. If you say it calmly and don't use that *"Aaaaaa..."* tone of voice, I think there's only so much you can do so people can understand what you are going through.

Jenni: When I ask for what I need and I'm clear with my communication, I almost always get it. I think part of that is the relationships I've built with people in my life.

You are a freelancer like I am, so you probably have lots of different clients, and maybe you don't have to meet some of them in person ever. But maybe you have work situations, and you must have to sometimes communicate about your health—don't you?

Jennette: Yeah, if there's been a week where I haven't been able to get things done because I have to go lie down, or working in front of the computer really isn't the best thing for a headache. You need to make sure you are in an ergonomic position; you are not putting a strain on your neck, because if you aggravate nerves in your neck, it can cause your headache to be worse. You also have to make sure you don't have glare on your computer. I also need to get up regularly for breaks, which I do not do as much as I should.

Basically, there are times when I really can't work. Usually my clients are okay. It's kind of good to know who has deadlines that are very firm and they have to get done, while other people are more flexible. You have to reorder your priorities, so it's less likely you have to let someone down.

There have been times I've emailed people and said, "I'm sorry, I will probably get this done this week, but my headaches have been kind of bad and..." Or I'll not even say that; I'll just say I'm not feeling well, because they may not necessarily know about my headache story and I don't feel the need to go into my long tale of woe, you know what I mean? I'll just be like, "I'm not feeling well."

Jenni: With my clients and different work situations, the vast majority know I have chronic illness. Some of them get it, some of them don't, and I agree with you: Keep track of priorities and be really clear. What I've found is that, it's an extremely rare, very rare client that's fussy about it; I just can't work with them again.

Jennette: Yes, you can fire your clients. That's important to remember—fire them.

Jenni: Some people in an office job may not have that option, but can choose to not talk about health stuff to a certain coworker who is really thoughtless. Hopefully they have a supervisor who understands it, or someone in HR who can get their needs met.

Also: using good boundaries to shield yourself from those coworkers. Maybe you don't really want it to be about that, you don't want to be "headache girl." I don't want to be "fibromyalgia girl." We want to be professional.

Jennette: I was working full-time for a media company when I got my headache, and had only been there for about a month; I really did become "headache girl." It was kind of strange for me to have that be so much of my identity. Actually, it was pretty good. My boss there got migraines a few times a year, so he was really sympathetic to my condition. They did everything to make my workstation ergonomic.

As for socializing with people, I usually go to coffee shops to do my work, just so I'm out among the people. This type of getting out is really good. Even if you aren't talking about your headache, it's good to be out among people and doing regular things. You're not just sitting in the bed in the dark, even though that can be hard.

Jenni: Sometimes when I have my worst kind of flare-up, and I really feel like I'm stuck in the house, I will text my sisters or friends just to say, "Hey, I am a mess over here," and they'll text me a joke, or they'll call me and we'll chat for a few minutes. On the rare occasion, I've had people bring me food or come hang out with me.

Maybe I can't get out, but I can sit on the couch with a friend and watch a movie, and I don't feel I am alone with illness. But I have to reach out to make that connection because we're all really busy. My best friend has a son who is in preschool, and people are busy and have big lives, so I know they're not just going to be checking on me all the time and going, "Hey are you okay? How are you doing?" It's up to me to say to people, "Hey, I'm a mess; I need a little TLC over here."

"You don't want this thing to stop you from doing all the stuff you used to, *but when you kind of accept the new normal, you are able to say, 'I really can't go out to a club until three in the morning anymore."*

—Jennette

Jennette: I find that Twitter and Facebook are good for me because those are the places people go to check in on their friends. So if you put out a message saying, "I really feel like crap today," someone will comment or ask, "How are you doing?" It's those little things that really do help.

Jenni: Twitter has been great for me with that. I try not to do too much because I really don't want to be that person who's tweeting every day about their health.

Jennette: You don't want to wallow in it.

Jenni: You can really wallow in it, and then you are kind of being a whiner.

I'm certainly not saying everyone who talks about their pain is a whiner. But I think there are ways to communicate that you need support that are really healthy and are going to result in more support.

Jennette: I get sick of feeling bad all the time, and they can get to a point where they get sick of hearing how you feel bad all the time.

Jenni: I've actually had moments when I've tweeted things like "Argh…I feel like crap!" I will actually apologize to my followers: "I'm sorry, I kind of dumped on you. Here's a picture of a kitten" or "Here's a dirty joke," just to say, "I'm sorry, I totally polluted your Twitter feed with whining, here is my recipe for bacon chocolate chip cookies," or whatever.

I was wondering if you have any favorite communication tips for sick folks that we haven't touched on?

Jennette: The most common way you give up power is when you believe you don't have any, and you have to remember that you have the power to ask for what you need to make things happen, to help you. So remember: you have the power to communicate, and you can reach out to people for what you need to take care of yourself.

This interview has been shortened and edited to fit this book. To read the full transcript or listen to the full recordings of this and all the Pep Squad interviews, head to ChronicBabe101.com.

Lesson 10

GET ORGANIZED:
tips, tricks, tools, and systems

It's time to organize your paperwork, kitchen, bathroom, meds, nightstand, clothes. Simplify. Get it together, babe. No one is going to do it for you. You got this.

Get educated: Your chronic illness

If you don't understand your condition(s) forwards and backwards, now's the time to get schooled. And if you're an old-timer like me (twenty years of fibromyalgia!) it may be time to get *re-educated.*

- What's the latest research say?
- Which organizations are leading the fight for patients' rights?
- What clinical trials are going on?

You may feel tired of researching, and that's fair. Take a little break and then get back to it, though—you can't afford to miss an opportunity to feel better.

Old school: The Eisenhower Decision Matrix

The Eisenhower Decision Matrix, developed by U.S. President Dwight D. Eisenhower and popularized by time-management expert Steven Covey, is popular in the corporate world.

The matrix can help us determine how important a thing is—and how urgent a thing is—and make decisions based on our findings.

There are lots of decision-making apps and tools online, but I find the matrix most useful in problem solving. With it, we can examine a problem, or a component of a problem, and quickly figure out how vital it is. Sometimes we can abandon a problem, or a component of it, and focus on the most urgent task.

"What is important is seldom urgent, and what is urgent is seldom important," Eisenhower said. We can apply that to day-to-day decisions as ChronicBabes and simplify our lives.

Try this: Examine a problem you're facing using the matrix below. Get real with what is urgent or not, important or not. Try breaking your problem into chunks and test each one with the matrix.

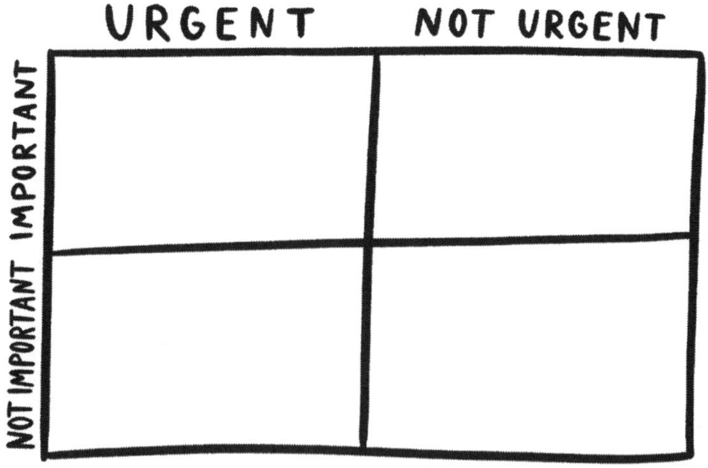

New school: Make friends with technology

There are hundreds of links in the Extra Credit section of *ChronicBabe 101*—all thoroughly vetted by me and a trusted assistant—and it's a sure thing that a handful will be outdated by the time you're holding this book. That's how fast technology moves today. While I'm confident in the resources I'm sharing, be prepared to expand on them in your own homework.

Smart ChronicBabes know there's much to be gained from staying up to speed with current technology. You don't need disposable income to benefit from free file-sharing apps like Evernote, Google Docs, and Dropbox, for example. Play around with your health care provider's patient portal or your insurer's website, and you just might find helpful tools. Smartphones offer the chance to connect with hundreds of apps and websites to help you track your symptoms, exercise, medications, and more.

If you feel like technology is passing you by, pause. Ask yourself: *Who can get me up to speed?* My mom frowned on computers for almost forty years—but with help from her cell phone provider, Apple, me, and my siblings, she's now a pro with her smartphone, and she *loves* it. It is *never* too late to learn.

POP QUIZ **What can you declutter in five minutes?**

Is there a quick fix you can perform to provide visual relief? Maybe you can swipe all the makeup off your bathroom counter and into a drawer, or clear all the old magazines off your coffee table into a recycling bin. Decluttering creates visual peace.

Organize your medical records

We sick chicks generate a *lot* of paperwork. I've kept a file folder for every year since I first got sick—that's twenty years of material—and while some folders are skinny, others are inches thick.

Here's how my system works

After many years of trial and error, I feel comfortable with the system I'm about to describe. It's simple and straightforward. If you're struggling to get paperwork organized, try this on for size:

Starting with this calendar year (you can go back and reorganize previous years' paperwork later), make these piles of paperwork, in chronological order when applicable:

- Insurance company documentation, including your plan and benefits
- Public health benefits paperwork (Medicare, Medicaid, Veterans Administration, etc.)
- Explanations of Benefits (EOBs)
- Prescription paperwork (flyers from the pharmacist, directions from your doctor, prescription drug benefit cards)
- Paperwork from doctor visits
- Paperwork from hospitalizations, collated in one pile per hospitalization
- Dental paperwork
- Vision paperwork

Take each pile and clip it together. Use a bigger clip to combine the stacks of hospitalization stacks. Use a sticky note or other colorful method and label each stack. Put all this in a folder or binder marked with the year. Boom! You're organized.

The next trick is to *stay* organized. There's no use putting a system in place if you're not going to stick with it. Make this commitment to yourself:

From now on, every time I receive paperwork related to my health, I will file it.

Lovely. Here's how I implement my system: the *moment* I receive paperwork, I file it; if I don't do it immediately, it will get lost in the shuffle. When I walk in the front door from a doctor's appointment, I go right to the file cabinet and stash that stuff. Then I take my coat off.

To make this system work for you, *make it your own*. You may not need to be as vigilant as I am about filing, but don't let it slide.

Let's get digital

If you don't want to deal with piles of paperwork, or don't have room for a file cabinet, try something I'm implementing now: scan your documents.

My insurance company says they keep a file of all my documents, but I trust them about as far as I can throw them...so I keep my own copies. And now I'm going digital.

Grab a scanner or borrow one from a friend. Make sure it scans double-sided documents. Recruit someone to help you remove staples and paperclips, and host a little scan-in.

File your digital files the same way I described for physical paperwork: in folders. Make sure you can keep filing this way, especially if you're borrowing a scanner...maybe keep a pile and scan it in once a month. Then shred your physical paperwork (don't just throw it away).

You can apply this method to other paperwork, too

The key points:

- Consistency of filing
- Subdivision of paperwork into folders that make sense to you
- Flexibility dependent on your preferences, the storage space you have, your favorite color
- Consistency

Did I mention consistency? It is your friend...especially come tax time, when you're prepping for a surgery, or if you need to review your situation with an expert advisor of any kind.

Mind your meds

It's essential to know exactly what medications you take. This may seem obvious, but some folks—even those with serious illness—are casual when it comes to details. Let's change that STAT.

A couple years ago, I took someone to the emergency room. When the doctor asked about her meds, she couldn't name them. She referred him to a slip of paper in her wallet—but it was outdated.

Frustrated, I headed to her house to gather the details. *This is basic ChronicBabe behavior,* I thought—*girlfriend's gotta know her meds!*

Here's a list of actions to ensure you know everything you're taking, and your whole health care team knows, too:

Make a list of every pill, inhaler, eye drop, vitamin, and supplement you take:

- Full name (brand and generic)
- Dosage and directions (once a day? before or after breakfast? only as needed?)
- Prescribing doctor name and phone number
- Pharmacy name and phone number
- Bonus points for tracking when you're due for refills

Put this list in your smartphone.

Print out a copy of the list and put it in your wallet.

Update your list with your medical alert jewelry company.

Add the list in an Evernote file, in Dropbox, in Google docs—or whatever you use for file sharing—and share it with your significant other, family, and other caregivers. You may feel like you know your meds by heart, but in an emergency, you may not be able to articulate details.

Contact each of your health care providers using their preferred method (phone, email, portal) to share your updated list. Confirm they have received it. On your next in-office visit, double-check your list against their records. This may feel redundant but mistakes happen.

Don't blow off this essential task, babe. And don't make assumptions. The U.S. Food and Drug Administration says medication mistakes injure or kill more than 1.3 million people each year...and that's in just *one country.*

Pricing: Do your homework

In the Extra Credit section, I've included a handful of sites for price-checking and prescription assistance programs. It may seem like a pain in the tush to call around, but it's worth the work if you can score some savings.

Some grocery and big-box stores offer one-time deals for transferring prescriptions, but they may not make financial sense in the long run...and as my friend Kevin Rynn, Pharm.D., shared in lesson 6, it's likely better for your health to find one pharmacy and stick with it.

If you're still having trouble affording your meds, ask your health care providers for ideas. They may have samples to tide you over during a lean month; they may be able to help you appeal to pharmaceutical companies or your insurance company for special consideration.

POP QUIZ

Can you schedule self-care?

We make appointments for the doctor, dentist, and dermatologist. We should make appointments for self-care, too!

I have a weekly repeating appointment in my calendar on Sunday nights to do a home facial and mask. It's a calm, beautifying ritual that I would otherwise blow off.

What self-care items can you schedule?

Research: Become a curator

Feel like you're experiencing information overload? Me too! And so much of it is *bad*.

In my training as a journalist, I learned to be a curator of good info—someone who collects reliable sources. It's more work, but it pays off.

Curating starts with knowing where *not* to look. If you're getting most of your health news via Facebook groups, you may be misled. Fake news stories and sites are so prevalent now, Facebook has created tools to combat them (more at bit.ly/FakeNewsTool).

Before clicking "Share" on a "news" story, read it through and ask yourself: Does this cite credible sources, or is it mostly conjecture? Is it clearly written, or is it full of typos and unnecessary punctuation? Is the focus on information, or is every paragraph followed by sketchy-looking ads? If you see bogus health "news," report it to Facebook and ask the friend who shared it with you to be more cautious, for all our sakes.

Curating gets fun when you start collecting sources you *can* rely on. I use Feedly.com to catalog my links; there are many other options. When I read a story I like and trust, I save the source to my list. I spend about half an hour each day catching up on what's new at those links.

Ask your health care providers what sites they read regularly, and include some in your list. Check out recommendations by reputable patient advocacy groups, research organizations, and health care nonprofits. Keep curating!

Think like MacGyver

When faced with an obstacle, we have two choices: quit, or figure out a workaround. I *know* you are not a quitter, babe—so, workarounds it is. Here are a few tricks I use:

Think like MacGyver: Use every single tool you have. Need to go somewhere but can't drive yourself? Ask a friend, fellow churchgoer, family member, neighbor, or someone in your book club. How about a bicycle? Can you find a discount coupon for a car-sharing service? Reschedule the appointment when you have car access? Is there a shuttle for people with disabilities in your area? A senior shuttle? Public transit? Can you barter with someone?

The Internet is your friend: Do your homework. Google it. Search YouTube for a how-to video. Ask a question in a forum, in a Facebook group, or in your Facebook feed. Ask your friends to ask *their* friends. Research on LinkedIn, Twitter, Instagram, and Pinterest. Crowdsource an answer.

Keep an open mind: Don't say no. You may be tempted to let previous experiences dictate your behavior today. You asked your neighbor for a ride a few weeks ago, and she wasn't available; that doesn't mean she can't do it today. You failed to get a discount on medication through the manufacturer last year; that doesn't mean they haven't launched a new discount program. Check their website, call their HQ, write an impassioned letter to their president (and copy their public relations department). Ask your pharmacist, your docs, and friends in support groups for ideas. Imagine a "yes."

Be persistent. Be a pest. Be relentless. Do not give up. If you feel like there's no way around this mess, take a moment to let yourself whine about it...and then put on your thinking cap. Successful workarounds come from a diligent and creative mind.

POP QUIZ

Are you a planner?

Some babes love using a planner. You can find lots of how-tos by searching online for "bullet journal" or "personal planner." Creating your own planner can be a fun way to organize and beautify a schedule that's packed with un-fun tasks.

Create your sanctuary

For fifteen years, I've worked from home, and I love it. But some days, my home feels like a prison because I'd rather be out having fun, doing something other than work, or *anything* other than feeling like crud.

But home is where I am, so I make it a sanctuary—a place that brings me peace. There are two components to this practice:

Physical preparation and acceptance of your home

If you follow me on Instagram (@ChronicBabe) or YouTube (@ChronicBabeJenni), you'll see occasional pics of my home...filled with decoration. Each room contains an eclectic mix of art, photos, and inspirational artifacts. Having lots of beautiful things to look at and think about is a terrific way to feel at home.

Photos of people you love remind you you're not alone, even if they're not by your side.

The more blankets, quilts, and fluffy pillows, the better. Make it cozy.

Little "comfort stations" all over the house keep necessities at hand. I always have a basket of lip balm, nail files, hand lotion, essential oils, notepads, and writing implements in reach, so I don't have to go hunting.

Don't worry about what a decorator would think. Focus on what makes *you* smile.

Clutter is a bummer. Some of it can't be helped when we're sick, but if we let it get out of control, it's depressing. Use a cute clothes hamper so you can clear the floor. Use decorative boxes or bins to store your craft materials so you can easily find what you need.

Recruit help. My friend Amy, a personal organizer, has helped me a couple of times; she's ruthless when it comes to decluttering (I need a firm hand!). I bet you can find a friend or two to help you.

Get your space as clean, organized, and cozy as possible. This helps you gain acceptance of the place you stay all the time.

Internal preparation and acceptance of your home

Here's where meditation matters. I have one corner of the house that's all mine, where I can get quiet and meditate. Creating a spiritual connection with your home is powerful—I want you to *love* your space so even when you're stuck there, you won't resent it.

This comes back to good old acceptance. In lesson 5, we learned to make friends with illness as part of our acceptance practice. Now, I'll ask you to do the same practice with your home.

You might look at the old bathtub and say something like, "Hello, funky old bathtub. Looks like we're in it for the long haul. What would make our friendship lovely?" Maybe it's a candle on the windowsill, a collection of bath oils, a new loofa, an inflatable bath pillow, a cute shower curtain—or a rubber ducky.

You might look at your couch and say, "Oh friend, are you sick of me? I'm a little sick of you, too. How can we take better care of each other?" Consider restuffing your couch cushions (find materials at most large craft stores) to revive your couch. Add some cute throw pillows or a pretty quilt. Make a "comfort station" to keep nearby. Ask a friend to help vacuum it thoroughly. Or buy a slipcover for your old couch, to make it feel like new without breaking the bank.

In this way, you can make friends with your old, funky house. You can help it be the most supportive environment it can be—and boost your acceptance.

Try these suggestions one at a time. Even if it's just a tiny amount each day, a string of days adds up, and suddenly, your house feels like *home*—not prison.

Clean up your life, ChronicBabe-style

Laundry is piled everywhere. Your sink's fully of dirty dishes. You're avoiding a friend's texts because you need to have a difficult conversation.

Girl, life gets messy. Let's get you cleaned up. Try these approaches to handling mess:

- Too tired to do all the laundry? Sort out what you need for the next three days and do one small load.
- Try a service like TaskRabbit.com to hire folks for small projects—for a small fee.
- Use the timer on your phone to block out ten-minute bursts of cleaning.
- Explore the KonMari method of organizing. (Her book, *The Life-Changing Magic of Tidying Up: The Japanese Art of Decluttering and Organizing,* is full of great advice.)
- Label everything. When you know what's in each drawer, box, and cabinet, you waste less time hunting.
- Work toward Inbox Zero (these tips help: bit.ly/ZapInbox).
- Purge your pantry, one cabinet or shelf at a time. Trash outdated boxes and cans, and donate unwanted food to a local pantry.
- Hire someone to scrub your bathroom and kitchen once a month, or perform a quarterly mega-clean.
- Make a rule: Nothing enters your house unless something else leaves. If you buy a book, donate an old one to the local library. If you buy a new blouse, donate an old one to a women's shelter.
- Pick one room each day to clean for ten minutes. Set a timer, and stop when it goes off—no cheating! *Do not overdo it, babe.*
- Use baggies and containers to organize your bathroom stuff: hair products, skin care, and makeup all get their own containers. Give them cute labels (my box of tampons is labeled "Lady Business").
- Take ten minutes to clean the junk out of your car.
- Speed up your work by using keyboard shortcuts (Apple: bit.ly/ShortMac; Windows: bit.ly/ShortWindows).
- Once your kitchen sink is clear, commit to washing dishes as you use them. It's easier to wash one plate at a time than three days' worth at once.
- Try 1Password.com to save your passwords.

- Ask your family for gift certificates to a local cleaning service when the next holiday comes around.
- Set up a Calendly.com account to organize your calendar, sync it with your computer and phone, and allow people to book appointments with you.
- Spend ten minutes today throwing out (or donating) clothes that don't fit. Or plan a swap, where everyone brings unwanted clothes and accessories. (Many charities will pick up of all the stuff no one claims.)
- Use a service like CatalogChoice.org to cancel the catalogs that clog your mailbox.
- While you're at it, don't renew the magazines that pile up; instead, use Texture.com to read individual issues of hundreds of magazines.
- When you're well enough, cook a few pots of food and save them in meal-size containers. (And throw out all the freezer-burned stuff to make room for tasty chow.)
- Enlist help from friends to clean. Use Doodle.com to create an event (or series of get-togethers). Thank your friends with pizza and flowers.
- Start a garbage bag in the messiest room of the house, and commit to throwing away *at least* one item every day.
- Pill organizers: Get them. Decorate them. Keep them stocked for many days in advance.
- Barter with a friend—she dusts your place and you copyedit the latest chapter of her book.
- Create a place for everything, and stick with it. Your inhaler is always in your medicine cabinet; your keys are always on a hook by your front door.
- Commit to spending ten minutes a day answering email. Or if your inbox is truly disastrous, search with keywords for things you *must* save, then commit email bankruptcy—I give you permission. (How to: bit.ly/EmailBankrupt.)
- Put this year's medical paperwork in one box. Tomorrow: do the same for the previous year. This is how to start taming the beast.

- Consider hiring a personal organizer for a consultation.
- Spend ten minutes deleting unused apps from your phone.

Finally: Lower your standards.

Yes, you heard me right. Before you were sick, maybe your place was immaculate—but that may not be possible now. Can you get cool with things being a little cluttered but clean? Can you get cool with making the bed with just a sheet and pillows, instead of dressing it up like a magazine spread? Can you get cool with vacuuming twice a month instead of every other day? Think about small tweaks you can make that preserve a few minutes a day...they add up.

1) What are your tools?

Are you using all the tools in your tool chest? I'm talking about people who can provide support and help; items in your home that can make tasks easier; online tools and resources that inform or streamline your process.

Throughout *ChronicBabe 101*, I've shared many of my favorite tools. Try listing *your* favorite tools now. Keep adding to the list over time—it's empowering!

FINAL EXAM:

putting all the pieces together

Each lesson in *ChronicBabe 101* is packed with resources and ideas; they all add up to a more successful, fulfilling life—even if you're a total sicko.

But they're just the tip of the iceberg. There is so much more out there, if you go looking for it...I hope I've shown you the way.

Like any good teacher, I can only introduce you to knowledge and tools. It's up to you to implement what you've learned here, in ways as unique as you.

How will you craft a more incredible life? I want to know! Share your experiences at ChronicBabe101.com, and be sure to tag your social media posts with #ChronicBabe and #ChronicBabe101 so I (and our whole community) can see how you implement your newfound skills.

My pledge to you: To continue to create more tools, resources, and inspiration every day, for women like us—badass babes who won't let chronic pain and illness squash our spirits. If you've got ideas for new things I can create, don't be shy!

Get in touch at ChronicBabe.com/contact.

You're a ChronicBabe now, my friend. Get out there and rock this life!

XO,

Jenni

EXTRA CREDIT:

my favorite resources for CHRONICBABES

Eager to earn a few extra points before you finish *ChronicBabe 101*? This Extra Credit section is packed with resources! It's just the tip of the iceberg, so don't stop with these. Let them be your starting point down a path of further research. (At the time of publication, all links were active, but you know how the Internet is...if a link is broken, keep searching!)

ChronicBabe101.com

Start here, where you can watch ten videos about my personal journey as a ChronicBabe; listen to full audio recordings of all our Pep Squad interviews (or read transcripts if you prefer); download a handful of PDFs, including a study guide for book clubs; and more.

Addiction

Alcoholics Anonymous: aa.org
Narcotics Anonymous: naws.org
Al-Anon/Alateen: al-anon.alateen.org
Nar-Anon: nar-anon.org
Overeaters Anonymous: oa.org
Gamblers Anonymous: gamblersanonymous.org
Co-Dependents Anonymous: coda.org

Advocacy organizations and events

Invisible Illness Awareness Week: invisibleillnessweek.com
Self Advocacy Resource and Technical Assistance Center: selfadvocacyinfo.org

PBS's WHO CARES: Chronic Illness in America: bit.ly/WhoCaresPBS
Improving Chronic Illness Care: improvingchroniccare.org
Patient Advocate Foundation: patientadvocate.org
State Pain Policy Advocacy Network: sppan.aapainmanage.org
The Assertive Patient: assertivepatient.org
The Alliance of Professional Health Advocates: aphadvocates.org
The Empowered Patient Coalition: empoweredpatientcoalition.org

Art therapy

American Art Therapy Association: arttherapy.org
Art Therapy Credentials Board: atcb.org
The British Association of Art Therapists: baat.org
Art Therapy Alliance: arttherapyalliance.org

Assistive technologies

Apple's resources on accessibility: apple.com/accessibility
iPhone's Live Listen app for connecting with hearing aids: bit.ly/iPhoneHearingAids
Microsoft's resources on accessibility: bit.ly/microaccess
My preferred ergonomic software: break-reminder.en.softonic.com
Software for ergonomic reminders: publicspace.net/MacBreakZ
Information on U.S. law governing accessibility: section508.gov
Assistive Technology Industry Association: atia.org
World Health Organization guide to assistive technologies and devices: who.int/disabilities/technology/en/
Rehabilitation Engineering and Assistive Technology Society of North America: resna.org

Beautiful things

Adaptive clothing for people with disabilities and illness: accessiblewear.com
Cabana Life sun-protective beachwear: cabanalife.com
Mott50 sun-protective beachwear: mott50.com
Adaptive clothing for kids with disabilities: bit.ly/adaptivekidsclothes

One of many designers partnering with nonprofits to create beautiful adaptive clothing (Google your fave designers!): usa.tommy.com/en/runway-of-dreams-spring-2017
Designer color crutches: castcoverz.com/designer-color-crutches
Chic Alert medical IDs: chicalertmedid.com
Beautiful and funky medical IDs: laurenshope.com
Beautiful panties and other covers for ostomy bags: ostomysecrets.com
My favorite heating pads of all shapes and sizes: bit.ly/FerrisHeat
Use a cuter cane: fashionablecanes.com
Beautiful, custom bras for mastectomy patients, and postsurgical panties and camisoles: secondactchicago.com
Reviews of over a thousand shoes for babes with foot pain and other issues: barkingdogshoes.com
StepIn2Now swimsuit: stepin2now.com/the-swimsuit

Budgeting

The Simple Dollar: thesimpledollar.com
Daily Worth: dailyworth.com
Get Rich Slowly: getrichslowly.org
Suze Orman: suzeorman.com
Dave Ramsey: daveramsey.com

Caregivers, friends, and loved ones

Lotsa Helping Hands: lotsahelpinghands.com
National Eating Disorders Association guide to creating a support network: bit.ly/NEDAnetwork
Caregiver Action Network: caregiveraction.org
American Caregiver Association: americancaregiverassociation.org
National Alliance for Caregiving: caregiving.org
Caregivers Support Network: caregiverssupportnetwork.com
Caring Bridge: caringbridge.org
Caring from a Distance: cfad.org
National Caregivers' Library: caregiverslibrary.org

Disability

U.S. Department of Labor Disability Resources: dol.gov/odep/topics/disability.htm
Resources for the disability community: abilities.com
National Center on Health, Physical Activity, and Disability: nchpad.org
National Organization on Disability: nod.org
Never Walked in Heels: neverwalkedinhighheels.com
Disability Visibility Project: disabilityvisibilityproject.com
Invisible Disability Project: invisibledisabilityproject.org
INvisible Project: stories in words and pictures: invisibleproject.org
National Disability Rights Network: ndrn.org
Disability Rights Advocates: dralegal.org
Invisible Disabilities Association: invisibledisabilities.org

Education

Free college courses: bit.ly/yousosmart
Universities with the best free online courses: bit.ly/bestonlineclasses
Forty-nine free educational websites and apps to learn: bit.ly/morefreeschool
One hundred thirty-five completely free distance education courses: bit.ly/distanceschool
Education and creative cultivation: brainpickings.org
How Stuff Works: Howstuffworks.com
Duolingo: Learn a foreign language: duolingo.com

Exercise and fitness

PopSugar: popsugar.com/fitness
Mayo Clinic on exercise: bit.ly/MayoExercise
Babes who want to quit smoking: quitnet.meyouhealth.com
Women's Sports Foundation: womenssportsfoundation.org
The Disabled Hiker: thedisabledhiker.blogspot.com
Sports for anyone with a disability: disabledsportsusa.org
New workouts daily: dailyburn.com/365

Fashion

Fashionably Ill: JessicaGimeno.com
ChronicBabe Shop: zazzle.com/chronicbabe
Online thrift store: thredup.com
Online thrift store: swap.com
Disabled fashion: instagram.com/disabled_fashion
Sixteen fashion bloggers with disability: bit.ly/disabilityfashion

Finance

Financial Planning for Chronic Illness: bit.ly/illnessmoney
Penny Hoarder: pennyhoarder.com
One Hundred Dollars a Month: onehundreddollarsamonth.com
Entrepreneurship help: score.org
Online discounts: retailmenot.com
Grants for creative people: bit.ly/creativegrants
Groupon: groupon.com
Ebates: ebates.com

General health

Our Bodies, Our Selves: ourbodiesourselves.org
Mayo Clinic Symptom Checker: bit.ly/mayosymptom
Med Nauseam: mednauseam.com
MedLinePlus: nlm.nih.gov/medlineplus
Medscape: medscape.com
WebMD: webmd.com
World Health Organization: who.int/topics/chronic_diseases/en
Science Daily: bit.ly/SDchronic
FDA: fda.gov
Health Canada: hc-sc.gc.ca
European medicines: ema.europa.eu/ema
Iceland Health: ima.is/ima/links
National Pain Report: nationalpainreport.com
Library of medical journals: doaj.org
TED Talks Health: bit.ly/TEDhealth
HealingWell: healingwell.com

Buzzfeed: buzzfeed.com/health
MindBodyGreen: mindbodygreen.com
Giant list of chronic illness blogs: chronicillnessbloggers.com/sites

Health care system issues

Health care provider perspectives: Insureblog.blogspot.com
Bypass voicemail systems: gethuman.com
Kaiser Family Foundation (KFF): kff.org
KFF global health issues: kff.org/global-health-policy
Partnership to Fight Chronic Disease: fightchronicdisease.org
The Collaborative on Health and Environment: healthandenvironment.org
U.S.: healthcare.gov

Housecleaning/personal organization

UFYH: unfuckyourhabitat.com
FlyLady: flylady.net
Unclutterer: unclutterer.com
A Beautiful Mess: abeautifulmess.com
I Heart Organizing: Iheartorganizing.com
Container Store blog: containerstore.com/blog
GTD: Gettingthingsdone.com
Kitchen organizing: bit.ly/HGTVcleankitchen
Closet organizing: bit.ly/wwwcloset
Bathroom organizing: bit.ly/RealSimpleBath
Marie Kondo: tidyingup.com
Cleaning apps: bit.ly/GlitterClean

Legal issues

Patient Advocacy Foundation (formerly Advocacy for Patients with Chronic Illness, Inc., and the Jennifer Jaff Center): patientadvocate.org
ADA complaint form: ada.gov/complaint
The Legal Aid Society: legal-aid.org

LGBTQIA

It Gets Better Project: itgetsbetter.org
CenterLink: The Community of LGBT Centers: bit.ly/CenterLink
LGBTQIA Health Care Guild: healthcareguild.com
CDC: cdc.gov/lgbthealth
Poz: Health, Life, and HIV: poz.com
BGD, for queer and trans people of color: bgdblog.org/category/wellness
Gaylesta: The Psychotherapist Association for Gender and Sexual Diversity: gaylesta.org/community-resources
Chronic Sex: massive list of resources: bit.ly/ChronicLGBTQIA
Howard Brown Health: howardbrown.org
Trans Bodies, Trans Selves: bit.ly/TransBodies
Gender Services at Lurie Children's Hospital of Chicago: bit.ly/LurieGender
The Asexual Visibility and Education Network forum on intersectionality: asexuality.org/en/forum/127-intersectionality
The Pride Study: A decades-long research project: pridestudy.org
ChronicBabe LGBTQIA reading list: bit.ly/CBlgbtqia
The Savage Lovecast: savagelovecast.com

Medication assistance

RxCut: rxcut.com/chronicbabe
NeedyMeds: needymeds.org
DrugBank (Canada): drugbank.ca
RxAssist: rxassist.org
RxHope: rxhope.com
Partnership for Prescription Assistance: pparx.org
Patient Advocate Foundation Co-Pay Relief: copays.org

Mental health

Resources in your area: 211.org
National Alliance on Mental Illness: nami.org
Centre for Global Mental Health: bit.ly/CGMHealth
American Psychiatry Association: psychiatry.org

American Psychological Association: apa.org
Crisis Call Center: crisiscallcenter.org or 1-800-273-8255
International Help Lines: togetherweare-strong.tumblr.com/helpline
Talk through your secrets: postsecret.com
PsychCentral: psychcentral.com

Pregnancy, childbirth, and parenting

LactMed Drugs and Lactation Database: bit.ly/drugslactate
Sidelines High-Risk Pregnancy Support: sidelines.org
American Association for Marriage and Family Therapy: bit.ly/AAMFTchronic
American Academy of Pediatrics: healthychildren.org
La Leche League on illness and disability: bit.ly/LLLchronic

Recipes and nutrition

Academy of Nutrition and Dietetics: eatright.org
Delicious Decisions: recipes.heart.org/categories/31/delicious-decisions
Fit Day Diet and Weight Loss Journal: fitday.com
National Institutes of Health on herbs: bit.ly/NIHHerbs
Organic Consumers Association: organicconsumers.org
Slow Food: slowfood.com
Tea: tching.com
Amazon Subscribe & Save for delivery of special foods: bit.ly/sub2save
I Quit Sugar: iquitsugar.com
101 Cookbooks: 101cookbooks.com
Friendsgiving: bit.ly/cheapdindin

Service animals and emotional support animals

Dogs for the Deaf: dogsforthedeaf.org
Seeing Eye Dogs: seeingeye.org
Active Dogs gear: activedogs.com
Right to Emotional Support Animals in "No Pet" Housing: bit.ly/housingpets
HOUSING Best Friends for Life—Doris Day Animal League: bit.ly/DDALbusiness

Commonly asked questions about service animals in places of business: ada.gov/archive/qasrvc.htm
CDC Guidelines for Service Animals in Health Care: bit.ly/CDCserviceanimals
ADA Business Brief: Service Animals: ada.gov/archive/svcanimb.htm
2015 Service Animal DOJ update (most recent): bit.ly/DOJserviceanimals
Traveling with a Service Dog, a Complete Step-by-Step Guide: bit.ly/ServiceDogTravel
Assistance Dogs: Access to Public Places: bit.ly/ServiceDogAccess

Sexuality

Hedonish: hedonish.com
Chronic Sex: chronicsex.org
Good Vibrations: goodvibes.com
For moms: goodvibessexymama.com
Sexual Health Network: sexualhealth.com
The Well-Timed Period: thewelltimedperiod.blogspot.com
Holistic Help for Chronic Illness: holistichelp.net/sex.html
Kinkly, for exploring new things: kinkly.com
Disability-friendly tips and toys: bit.ly/DisabilitySexToys
My fave woman-owned and woman-operated sex shop/toy store: early2bedshop.com
Disability dating website: outsiders.org.uk/outsidersclub

Spirituality and inspiration

Danielle LaPorte: daniellelaporte.com
Marie Forleo: marieforleo.com
Thich Nhat Hanh: plumvillage.org/about/thich-nhat-hanh
Pema Chödrön: pemachodronfoundation.org
Oriah Mountain Dreamer: oriahsinvitation.blogspot.com
Anne Lamott: facebook.com/AnneLamott
Lisa Copen: *Illness Oasis*: restministries.com

Suicide awareness and prevention

To Write Love on Her Arms: twloha.com
National Suicide Prevention Hotline: suicidepreventionlifeline.org
Suicide hotlines organized by state: suicide.org/suicide-hotlines.html
The United Way: 211.org
Veterans Crisis Line: veteranscrisisline.net
I Am Alive: imalive.org
Thinking...About Suicide: thinkingaboutsuicide.com
Kevin Briggs (Golden Gate guardian)—TED Talk: bit.ly/suicidebridge
Suicide Awareness Voices of Education: save.org
PsychCentral: psychcentral.com/resources/Suicide_and_Crisis
American Foundation for Suicide Prevention: bit.ly/LostSomeone
Survivors of Suicide: survivorsofsuicide.com
Alliance of Hope for Suicide Survivors: allianceofhope.org
Live Through This: livethroughthis.org
American Association of Suicidology: suicidology.org

Tech resources

Make the most of Evernote: blog.evernote.com
Create healthy, fun, and free memes: makeameme.org
Perspectives on being a digitally educated patient: e-patients.net
Free photo-editing software: picmonkey.com
Google Drive: drive.google.com
Free music streaming: spotify.com
Manage your inbox: unrollme.com
Create multi-choice stories to problem solve: twinery.org
For just about everything: lifehacker.com
File sharing: dropbox.com
Video calls: skype.com
Adorable hilarious gifs: giphy.com
Escape into TV: hulu.com
Inspiration: pinterest.com
Meditation apps: bit.ly/MeditateApps

Travel

Accessible Travel Center: accesstravelcenter.com
Accessible Journeys: Disabilitytravel.com
Equal access to transportation: transportation.gov/accessibility
Disabled Travelers: disabledtravelers.com
Eco-Adventure International: eaiadventure.com
Emerging Horizons: emerginghorizons.com
Gimp on the Go: gimponthego.com
Society for Accessible Travel and Hospitality: sath.org
Traveling with exhausting illness: bit.ly/FibroTravel

Women's organizations

Feminist.com: bit.ly/bestfeminists
Media Report to Women: bit.ly/MediaReportWomen
National Organization of Women: now.org
National Women's Studies Association: nwsa.org
HealthyWomen: healthywomen.org
Women's Law Project: womenslawproject.org
Working with Chronic Illness: ciCoach.com
Catalyst: organization for women and work: catalyst.org
Geek Feminism: geekfeminism.org
The F Bomb: thefbomb.org
Bitch magazine: bitchmedia.org
Bust magazine: bust.com

Women of color

NIH: Women of Color: bit.ly/NIHWomenOfColor
Perspective on being black and looking good while ill: bit.ly/BlackGoodIll
Devri Velazquez on being pretty and sick: devrivelazquez.com
Jessica Gimeno on Asian mental health issues: bit.ly/JessicaMentalHealth
Heart and Soul: heartandsoul.com
For Harriet on black women's bodies: bit.ly/HarrietBodies
Black Women's Health Initiative: bwhi.org

Ebony magazine resources on mental health: bit.ly/EbonyMentalHealth
Black News health focus: bit.ly/BlackNewsHealth
Center for Black Women's Wellness: cbww.org/who-we-are
Psychology Today on black women's health and happiness: bit.ly/BlackWomenHealthyHappy
National Alliance for Hispanic Health: healthyamericas.org
Latino Health Resources: latinohealthresources.com
National Resources Center for Hispanic Mental Health: nrchmh.org
National Alliance on Mental Illness—Latino focus: bit.ly/NAMILatino
National Alliance on Mental Illness—African American focus: bit.ly/NAMIAAHealth
National Indigenous Women's Resource Center: niwrc.org
Tewa Women United: tewawomenunited.org
Native American Women's Health Resource Center: nativeshop.org
American College of Obstetricians and Gynecologists (ACOG) American Indian and Alaskan Native Women's Health Programs: bit.ly/ACOGAIAN
Women of Color Sexual Health Network: wocshn.org
Elyse Fox's @SadGirlsClub, social media for women of color and mental health: bit.ly/SadGirlsClub

about the author

Jenni Grover is founder of ChronicBabe.com, where she draws on her experience with fibromyalgia and a handful of other conditions to teach women how to craft incredible lives beyond illness. Since 2005, Jenni has helped countless women through her website, magazine articles, videos, and speeches around the world.

For more than twenty-five years, Jenni has consulted with hundreds of organizations worldwide, helping them craft and share their messages. She focuses on working with health care organizations—sharing stories of strength, wellness, and inspiration in the face of adversity.

Jenni was raised in Texas, but she calls Chicago home. She lives there with her husband, Joe, along with an army of house plants. When she's not writing, she's in the garden, sewing a quilt, dancing to techno music in her living room, or watching sci-fi. She's never met a taco she didn't like.

Want to hire Jenni to speak at your support group or other event? Reach out: ChronicBabe.com/contact.

Materials to support book clubs that study *ChronicBabe 101* are available at ChronicBabe101.com.

Interested in a bulk order of this book, and/or accompanying study guides? Direct inquiries to ChronicBabeAssistant@gmail.com.

Made in the USA
Columbia, SC
15 September 2020

20879611R00159